KU-386-335

Applying
E-Commerce
in Business

RANA TASSABEHJI

SAGE Publications
London • Thousand Oaks • New Delhi

© Rana Tassabehji 2003

First published 2003

Apart from any fair dealing for the purposes of research
or private study, or criticism or review, as permitted
under the Copyright Designs and Patents Act, 1988, this
publication may be reproduced, stored or transmitted in
any form, or by any means, only with the prior
permission in writing of the publishers, or in the case of
reprographic reproduction, in accordance with the terms
of licences issued by the Copyright Licensing Agency.
Inquiries concerning reproduction outside those terms
should be sent to the publishers.

SAGE Publications Ltd
6 Bonhill Street
London EC2A 4PU

SAGE Publications Inc.
2455 Teller Road
Thousand Oaks, California 91320

SAGE Publications India Pvt Ltd
B-42, Panchsheel Enclave
Post Box 4109
New Delhi - 100 017

British Library Cataloguing in Publication data
A catalogue record for this book is available
from the British Library

ISBN 0–7619–4874–0
ISBN 0–7619–4875–9 (pbk)

Library of Congress Control Number available

Typeset by Photoprint, Torquay, Devon
Printed in Great Britain by The Cromwell Press Ltd,
Trowbridge, Wiltshire

125044

BCFTCS

£24.99

Applying
E-Commerce
in Business

BIRMINGHAM COLLEGE OF FOOD, TOURISM & CREATIVE STUDIES
COLLEGE LIBRARY, SUMMER ROW
BIRMINGHAM B3 1JB
Tel: (0121) 243 0055

DATE OF RETURN		
	2 7 NOV 2008	
2 1 MAY 2007		
1 1 OCT 2007	0 8 JAN 2009	
3 0 NOV 2007		
1 1 DEC 2007		
_ 6 FEB 2008		
30/4/08		

Books <u>must</u> be returned by the last date stamped
or further loans may not be permitted

Contents

B.C.F.T.C.S.

125044

Preface

This book is about e-commerce. As a consultant and lecturer on e-commerce I have come across a variety of businesses and students with a wide range of (often pre-conceived and strongly held) views about the subject. Many views are shared but even more are contradictory. Some feel that because they have surfed the Web and are familiar with the jargon, then they have all the knowledge and expertise necessary to understand and manage e-commerce for business.

The objective of this book is to put the subject of e-commerce into a framework that can be used by both business managers and students. It will introduce some consistency and bring together different academic and management theories and frameworks into a coherent whole.

INTRODUCTION

Chapter 1 explores the different definitions and meanings of e-commerce and related terminology. It makes a clear distinction between e-commerce, which takes a macro-environmental view, and e-business, which takes the view at the level of the firm, of the new technology and business. A framework for classifying e-commerce is introduced and is the basis on which this book is structured.

PART I – THE TECHNOLOGY OF E-COMMERCE

Chapters 2–4 deal with the issues of technology – the foundations on which e-commerce and e-business are built. It is crucial for every manager and decision-maker to understand these foundations and it is no longer acceptable or good business practice for technology to be the sole responsibility of the IT departments.

All managers must understand how the telecommunications infrastructures work, how these applications can be used for the benefit of business, and that all business processes and technology are inextricably linked. Technology is an essential part of business in the twenty-first century and will continue to be so in the future.

PART II – BUSINESS AND E-COMMERCE

Chapters 5–7 examine businesses that have been built on the technology foundations. It explains the concept of the business model and explores the different kinds of business models and frameworks that have emerged as a result.

This section also explores the phenomenon of the 'dot com' bubble, drawing on examples of businesses that have failed and succeeded to sum up lessons learnt. It identifies legal and regulatory elements that impact on businesses operating in the e-commerce world, drawing attention to issues that organisations must address to protect themselves, their employees, their customers and other stakeholders from a whole range of potential liabilities that they might face.

PART III – ECONOMICS, MANAGEMENT THEORY AND E-COMMERCE

Chapter 8 explores the impact of e-commerce on economics and management thinking. It introduces the 'laws' of technology that have emerged by observing the rapid progress and advancement of innovation in computing, networking and telecommunications. This section presents two different views of the impact of these 'laws' on the laws of economics and management theory. Porter's Five Forces Theory is put under stringent examination as the impact of e-commerce is discussed from different perspectives.

CONCLUSION

Chapter 9 brings together all the strands that have been expounded in the book. It identifies the different stages of e-business development and summarises the importance of technology, business, management and economics. It concludes with a glance to the future, briefly examining the potential of m-commerce as the new wave of technology.

This book can be used either as a core text for a Foundations Course in e-commerce or e-business by third year undergraduates or by postgraduate and MBA students.

Alternatively the different parts of the book can be used to support core modules in Marketing, Economics, General Business Management, Strategy, Operations Management and any other subject area which requires an understanding of e-commerce or e-business.

Appendices, presentation slides, case studies, updates and exercises for teachers and students that are mentioned in this book are available from the accompanying website: *www.tassabehji.co.uk*

LEGAL DISCLAIMER

Information in this book (especially Chapter 7) is intended as a guide to the legal and ethical areas relevant to e-commerce and the application of technology. The author, editors and publishers in no way advocate that this information be used without prior consultation with legal or other advisors. Readers are advised to consult with their lawyers or legal consultants concerning applicable national and international laws and regulations whether mentioned here or not. The author, editors and publishers assume no liability or responsibility for any claim for injury and/or damage to persons, property or business incurred as a direct or indirect consequence of the use and application of any of the contents of this book.

Introduction

Introduction to e-commerce

LEARNING OBJECTIVES

- To understand the complexity of e-commerce and its many facets.
- To explore how e-business and e-commerce fit together.
- To identify the impact of e-commerce.
- To recognise the benefits and limitations of e-commerce.
- To use classification frameworks for analysing e-commerce.
- To identify the main barriers to the growth and development of e-commerce in organisations.

WHAT IS ELECTRONIC COMMERCE?

Even today, some considerable time after the so called 'dot com/Internet revolution', electronic commerce (e-commerce) remains a relatively new, emerging and constantly changing area of business management and information technology. There has been and continues to be much publicity and discussion about e-commerce. Library catalogues and shelves are filled with books and articles on the subject. However, there remains a sense of confusion, suspicion and misunderstanding surrounding the area, which has been exacerbated by the different contexts in which electronic commerce is used, coupled with the myriad related buzzwords and acronyms. This book aims to consolidate the major themes that have arisen from the new area of electronic commerce and to provide an understanding of its application and importance to management.

In order to understand electronic commerce it is important to identify the different terms that are used, and to assess their origin and usage.

According to the editor-in-chief of *International Journal of Electronic Commerce*, Vladimir Zwass, 'Electronic commerce is sharing business information, maintaining business relationships and conducting business transactions by means of telecommunications networks'.[1] He maintains that in its purest form, electronic commerce has existed for over 40 years, originating from the electronic transmission of messages during the Berlin airlift in 1948.[2] From this, electronic data interchange (EDI) was the next stage of e-commerce development. In the 1960s a cooperative effort between industry groups produced a first attempt at common electronic data formats. The formats, however, were only for purchasing, transportation and finance data, and were used primarily for intra-industry transactions. It was not until the late 1970s that work began for national Electronic Data Interchange (EDI) standards, which developed well into the early 1990s.

EDI is the electronic transfer of a standardised business transaction between a sender and receiver computer, over some kind of private network or value added network (VAN). Both sides would have to have the same application software and the data would be exchanged in an extremely rigorous format. In sectors such as retail, automotive, defence and heavy manufacturing, EDI was developed to integrate information across larger parts of an organisation's value chain from design to maintenance so that manufacturers could share information with designers, maintenance and other partners and stakeholders. Before the widespread uptake and commercial use of the Internet, the EDI system was very expensive to run mainly because of the high cost of the private networks. Thus, uptake was limited largely to cash-rich multinational corporations using their financial strength to pressure and persuade (with subsidies) smaller suppliers to implement EDI systems, often at a very high cost. By 1996 no more than 50,000 companies in Europe and 44,000 in the USA were using EDI, representing less than 1 per cent of the total number of companies in each of the respective continents. According to Zwass, electronic commerce has been re-defined by the dynamics of the Internet and traditional e-commerce is rapidly moving to the Internet.

With the advent of the Internet, the term e-commerce began to include:

- Electronic trading of physical goods and of intangibles such as information.
- All the steps involved in trade, such as on-line marketing, ordering payment and support for delivery.
- The electronic provision of services such as after sales support or on-line legal advice.

- Electronic support for collaboration between companies such as collab-orative on-line design and engineering or virtual business consultancy teams.

Some of the definitions of e-commerce often heard and found in publications and the media are:

Electronic Commerce (EC) is where business transactions take place via telecommunications networks, especially the Internet.[3]

Electronic commerce describes the buying and selling of products, services, and information via computer networks including the Internet.[4]

Electronic commerce is about doing business electronically.[5]

E-commerce, ecommerce, or electronic commerce is defined as the conduct of a financial transaction by electronic means.[6]

The wide range of business activities related to e-commerce brought about a range of other new terms and phrases to describe the Internet phenomenon in other business sectors. Some of these focus on purchasing from on-line stores on the Internet. Since transactions go through the Internet and the Web, the terms *I-commerce* (Internet commerce), *icommerce* and even *Web-commerce* have been suggested but are now very rarely used.

Other terms that are used for on-line retail selling include *e-tailing*, *virtual-stores* or *cyber stores*. A collection of these virtual stores is sometimes gathered into a *'virtual mall'* or *'cybermall'*.

WHAT ABOUT E-BUSINESS?

As with e-commerce, *e-business* (electronic business) also has a number of different definitions and is used in a number of different contexts. One of the first to use the term was IBM, in October 1997, when it launched a campaign built around e-business. Today, major corporations are rethinking their businesses in terms of the Internet and its new culture and capabilities and this is what some see as e-business.

E-business is the conduct of business on the Internet, not only buying and selling but also servicing customers and collaborating with business partners.

E-business includes customer service (e-service) and intra-business tasks.

E-business is the transformation of key business processes through the use of Internet technologies. An e-business is a company that can adapt to constant and continual change.[7]

The development of *intranet* and *extranet* is part of e-business.

E-business is everything to do with back-end systems in an organisation.

In practice, e-commerce and e-business are often used interchangeably.

E-COMMERCE, E-BUSINESS, WHO E-CARES?[8]

Some analysts and on-line business people have decided that e-business is infinitely superior as a moniker to e-commerce. That's misleading and distracts us from the business goals at hand. The effort to separate the E-commerce and E-business concepts appears to have been driven by marketing motives and is dreadfully thin in substance.

Here's the important thing: E-commerce, E-business or whatever else you may want to call it is a means to an end.[9]

The different names, definitions and words referred to in the previous sections are merely a sample of the glossary that has originated from marketing departments to sell a concept, the media to describe a sensational 'new' phenomenon, consultants to justify their fees and recommendations, and business to validate and implement the new technology. In fact there is no one definitive meaning of e-commerce or e-business that is universally established. The different terms are used to illustrate different perspectives and emphases of different people in different organisations and business sectors. Some argue that it makes little sense to have a restrictive definition for the term e-commerce since it is unlikely that there will be agreement on a single unique definition. 'Attempting to define E-commerce or E-business is guaranteed to generate Byzantine debates with meaningless origins. It reminds me of trying to answer the following question: "If one synchronized swimmer drowns, would the others follow?" '[10]

Because of this trend, it is necessary when undertaking any electronic commerce, electronic business or any other e-related project or assignment, to clearly define any term in the context and environment in which it is being used.

AN E-DISTINCTION

For the purpose of clarity, the distinction between e-commerce and e-business in this book is based on the respective terms commerce and business. Commerce is defined as embracing the concept of trade, 'exchange of merchandise on a large scale between different countries'.[11] By association, e-commerce can be seen to include the electronic medium for this exchange. Thus electronic commerce can be broadly defined as the exchange of merchandise (whether tangible or intangible) on a large scale between different countries using an electronic medium – namely the Internet. The implications of this are that e-commerce incorporates a whole socio-economic, telecommunications technology and commercial infrastructure at the macro-environmental level. All these elements interact together to provide the fundamentals of e-commerce.

Business, on the other hand, is defined as 'a commercial enterprise as a going concern'.[12] E-business can broadly be defined as the processes or areas involved in the running and operation of an organisation that are electronic or digital in nature. These include direct business activities such as marketing, sales and human resource management but also indirect activities such as business process re-engineering and change management, which impact on the improvement in efficiency and integration of business processes and activities.

Figure 1.1 illustrates the major differences in e-commerce and e-business, where e-commerce has a broader definition referring more to the macro-environment, e-business relates more to the micro-level of the firm.

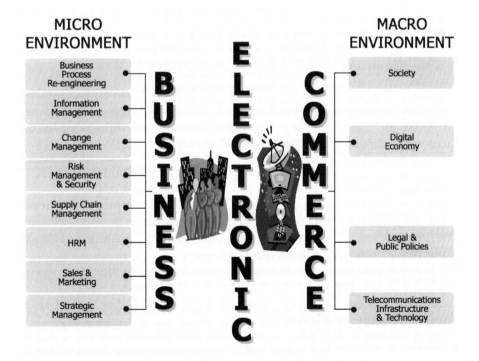

Figure 1.1   Electronic commerce and electronic business

Although different, both e-commerce and e-business are also highly integrated and reliant upon each other.

WHAT ARE THE KEY DRIVERS?

It is important to identify the key drivers of e-commerce to allow a comparison between different countries. It is often claimed that e-commerce is more advanced in the USA than in Europe. These key drivers can be measured by a number of criteria that can highlight the stages of advancement of e-commerce in each of the respective countries. The criteria that can determine the level of advancement of e-commerce are summarised in Table 1.1 and can be categorised as:

1 *Technological factors* – The degree of advancement of the telecommunications infrastructure which provides access to the new technology for business and consumers.
2 *Political factors* – including the role of government in creating government legislation, initiatives and funding to support the use and development of e-commerce and information technology.
3 *Social factors* – incorporating the level and advancement in IT education and training which will enable both potential buyers and the workforce to understand and use the new technology.
4 *Economic factors* – including the general wealth and commercial health of the nation and the elements that contribute to it.

Since a distinction has been made in this book between e-commerce and e-business for consistency, the key drivers of e-business are also identified. These are mainly at the level of the firm and are influenced by the macro-environment and e-commerce, which include:

- *Organisational culture* – attitudes to research and development (R&D); its willingness to innovate and use technology to achieve objectives.
- *Commercial benefits* – in terms of cost savings and improved efficiency that impact on the financial performance of the firm.
- *Skilled and committed workforce* – that understands, is willing and able to implement new technologies and processes.
- *Requirements of customers and suppliers* – in terms of product and service demand and supply.
- *Competition* – ensuring the organisation stays ahead of or at least keeps up with competitors and industry leaders.

These key drivers for the implementation of e-business can be put into the context of the classic economic equation of supply and demand illustrated in Figure 1.2.

TABLE 1.1 Key drivers of E-commerce

Key drivers	Measurement criteria

Technological factors	• Telecommunications infrastructure
	  Backbone infrastructure and architecture
	  Industry players and competition
	  Pricing
	  Internet service providers
	  Range of services available (e.g. ADSL, ISDN)
	  Ownership (private or public sector)
	• Access to new technology developments
	• Bandwidth
	• Speed of development and implementation of new technology by industry sector

Political factors	• Number and type of government incentives and programmes to support the use and development of new technology • Legislation – number and type of supportive or restrictive laws and policies that govern electronic data, contacts and financial transactions. For example, laws that recognise and enforce the validity of electronic documentation, contracts and transactions in a court of law; the validation of digital signatures; the legal usage of electronic security measures such as encryption • Public policies – whether government supports the growth of electronic transactions and processes. For example, filing tax returns to the Inland Revenue electronically, the national education curriculum and training
Social factors	• Skills of workforce • Number of users on-line • Penetration rate of PCs • Level of education; computer literacy and IT skills • Culture of technophilia – a willingness and ability to adopt new technology and the speed at which technology achieves critical mass as in Japan
Economic factors	• Economic growth – GDP • Average income • Cost of technology (hardware and software) • Cost of access to telecommunications infrastructure – pricing structures and rates • Commercial infrastructure – advancement of banking sector; payment systems • Innovative business models

Thus, e-commerce provides the infrastructure and environment that enables and facilitates e-business. Within this, the implementation of e-business is solely dependent on whether there is a demand by the organisation and whether it can be supplied within the organisation. Demand is created largely by the need to cut costs, improve efficiency, maintain

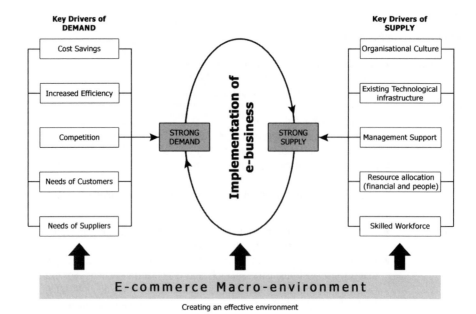

Figure 1.2 Key drivers of e-business

competitive advantage and meet stakeholder requirements. These business objectives can be met through the supply of a technological infrastructure to improve organisational processes, a willingness, ability and commitment to integrate new technology and improve working practice within the organisation, and crucial to all this is the allocation of resources.

WHAT IS THE IMPACT OF ELECTRONIC COMMERCE?

E-commerce and e-business are not solely the Internet, websites or dot com companies. It is about a new business concept that incorporates all previous business management and economic concepts. As such, e-business and e-commerce impact on many areas of business and disciplines of business management studies. For example:

- *Marketing* – issues of on-line advertising, marketing strategies and consumer behaviour and cultures. One of the areas in which it impacts particularly is direct marketing. In the past this was mainly door-to-door, home parties (like the Tupperware parties) and mail order using catalogues or leaflets. This moved to telemarketing and TV selling with the advances in telephone and television technology and finally developed into e-marketing spawning 'eCRM' (customer relationship management) data mining and the like by creating new channels for direct sales and promotion.

- *Computer sciences* – development of different network and computing technologies and languages to support e-commerce and e-business, for example linking front and back office legacy systems with the 'web-based' technology.
- *Finance and accounting* – on-line banking; issues of transaction costs; accounting and auditing implications where 'intangible' assets and human capital must be tangibly valued in an increasingly knowledge based economy.
- *Economics* – the impact of e-commerce on local and global economies; understanding the concepts of a digital and knowledge-based economy and how this fits into economic theory.
- *Production and operations management* – the impact of on-line processing has led to reduced cycle times. It takes seconds to deliver digitized products and services electronically; similarly the time for processing orders can be reduced by more than 90 per cent from days to minutes. Production systems are integrated with finance marketing and other functional systems as well as with business partners and customers (see Intel mini-case).

CASE STUDY

Intel launched their on-line business in summer 1998 when their sales shot from zero to $1 billion per month in the first month of operation. The reason for this is that they totally re-engineered their processes to include small and medium-sized businesses. Previously only Intel's larger customers were connected to them by expensive EDI networks, leaving the small and medium-sized companies sending faxes or phoning in orders or requirements. Intel concentrated on procurement and customer support for a range of their products (including computer chips and microprocessors), developing an extranet (which is the linking of a number of intranets using Internet technology with added security creating virtually private networks). By using the extranet, authorised small and medium-sized business partners could place orders, track the orders and look at product documentation on the site. The savings for Intel and their customers were large – they eliminated 45,000 faxes in a quarter to Taiwan alone – saving on time, telephone charges and fax paper. Eleven of the larger Intel companies were connected to another system which let Intel link to customer plants across the Internet to track part consumption.

- *Production and operations management (manufacturing)* – moving from mass production to demand-driven, mass customisation customer pull rather than the manufacturer push of the past. Web-based Enterprise Resource Planning systems (ERP) can also be used to forward orders directly to designers and/or production floor within seconds, thus cutting production cycle times by up to 50 per cent, especially when manufacturing plants, engineers and designers are located in different countries. In sub-assembler companies, where a product is assembled from a number of different components sourced from a number of manufacturers, communication, collaboration and coordination are critical – so electronic bidding can yield cheaper components and having flexible and adaptable procurement systems allows fast changes at a minimum cost so inventories can be minimised and money saved.

- *Management information systems* – analysis, design and implementation of e-business systems within an organisation; issues of integration of front-end and back-end systems.
- *Human resource management* – issues of on-line recruiting, home working and 'intrapreneurs' working on a project by project basis replacing permanent employees.
- *Business law and ethics* – the different legal and ethical issues that have arisen as a result of a global 'virtual' market. Issues such as copyright laws, privacy of customer information, legality of electronic contracts, etc.

These issues will be discussed in more detail throughout the remainder of this book.

WHAT ARE THE BENEFITS OF E-COMMERCE?

The previous sections have included discussions about what e-commerce is and its impact, but what are the benefits of e-commerce? What does it offer and why do it? The benefits of e-commerce can be seen to affect three major stakeholders: organisations, consumers and society.

Benefits of e-commerce to organisations

International marketplace. What used to be a single physical marketplace located in a geographical area has now become a borderless marketplace including national and international markets. By becoming e-commerce enabled, businesses now have access to people all around the world. In effect all e-commerce businesses have become virtual multinational corporations.

Operational cost savings. The cost of creating, processing, distributing, storing and retrieving paper-based information has decreased (see Intel mini-case).

Mass customisation. E-commerce has revolutionised the way consumers buy good and services. The pull-type processing allows for products and services to be customised to the customer's requirements. In the past when Ford first started making motor cars, customers could have any colour so long as it was black. Now customers can configure a car according to their specifications within minutes on-line via the www.ford.com website.

Enables reduced inventories and overheads by facilitating 'pull'-type supply chain management – this is based on collecting the customer order and then delivering through JIT (just-in-time) manufacturing. This is particularly beneficial for companies in the high technology sector, where stocks of components held could quickly become obsolete within months. For example, companies like Motorola (mobile phones), and Dell (computers) gather customer orders for a product, transmit them electronically to the manufacturing plant where they are manufactured according to the customer's specifications (like colour and features) and then sent to the customer within a few days.

Lower telecommunications cost. The Internet is much cheaper than value added networks (VANs) which were based on leasing telephone lines for the sole use of the organisation and its authorised partners. It is also cheaper to send a fax or e-mail via the Internet than direct dialling.

Digitisation of products and processes. Particularly in the case of software and music/video products, which can be downloaded or e-mailed directly to customers via the Internet in digital or electronic format.

No more 24-hour-time constraints. Businesses can be contacted by or contact customers or suppliers at any time.

Benefits of e-commerce to consumers

24/7 access. Enables customers to shop or conduct other transactions 24 hours a day, all year round from almost any location. For example, checking balances, making payments, obtaining travel and other information. In one case a pop star set up web cameras in every room in his house, so that he could check the status of his home by logging onto the Internet when he was away from home on tour.

More choices. Customers not only have a whole range of products that they can choose from and customise, but also an international selection of suppliers.

Price comparisons. Customers can 'shop' around the world and conduct comparisons either directly by visiting different sites, or by visiting a single site where prices are aggregated from a number of providers and compared (for example www.moneyextra.co.uk for financial products and services).

Improved delivery processes. This can range from the immediate delivery of digitised or electronic goods such as software or audio-visual files by downloading via the Internet, to the on-line tracking of the progress of packages being delivered by mail or courier.

An environment of competition where substantial discounts can be found or value added, as different retailers vie for customers. It also allows many individual customers to aggregate their orders together into a single order presented to wholesalers or manufacturers and obtain a more competitive price (aggregate buying), for example www.letsbuyit.com.

Benefits of e-commerce to society

Enables more flexible working practices, which enhances the quality of life for a whole host of people in society, enabling them to work from home. Not only is this more convenient and provides happier and less stressful working environments, it also potentially reduces environmental pollution as fewer people have to travel to work regularly.

Connects people. Enables people in developing countries and rural areas to enjoy and access products, services, information and other people which otherwise would not be so easily available to them.

Facilitates delivery of public services. For example, health services available over the Internet (on-line consultation with doctors or nurses), filing taxes over the Internet through the Inland Revenue website.

WHAT ABOUT THE LIMITATIONS OF E-COMMERCE?

There was much hype surrounding the Internet and e-commerce over the last few years of the twentieth century. Much of it promoted the Internet and e-commerce as the panacea for all ills, which raises the question, are there any limitations of e-commerce and the Internet?

Isaac Newton's 3rd Law of Motion, 'For every action there is an equal and opposite reaction' suggests that for all the benefits there are limitations to e-commerce. These again will be dealt with according to the three major stakeholders – organisations, consumers and society.

Limitations of e-commerce to organisations

Lack of sufficient system security, reliability, standards and communication protocols. There are numerous reports of websites and databases being hacked into, and security holes in software. For example, Microsoft has over the years issued many security notices and 'patches' for their software. Several banking and other business websites, including Barclays Bank, Powergen and even the Consumers' Association in the UK, have experienced breaches in security where 'a technical oversight' or 'a fault in its systems' led to confidential client information becoming available to all.

Rapidly evolving and changing technology, so there is always a feeling of trying to 'catch up' and not be left behind.

Under pressure to innovate and develop business models to exploit the new opportunities which sometimes leads to strategies detrimental to the organisation. The ease with which business models can be copied and emulated over the Internet increase that pressure and curtail longer-term competitive advantage.

Facing increased competition from both national and international competitors often leads to price wars and subsequent unsustainable losses for the organisation.

Problems with compatibility of older and 'newer' technology. There are problems where older business systems cannot communicate with web-based and Internet infrastructures, leading to some organisations running almost two independent systems where data cannot be shared. This often leads to having to invest in new systems or an infrastructure, which bridges the different systems. In both cases this is both financially costly as well as disruptive to the efficient running of organisations.

Limitations of e-commerce to consumers

Computing equipment is needed for individuals to participate in the new 'digital' economy, which means an initial capital cost to customers.

A basic technical knowledge is required of both computing equipment and navigation of the Internet and the World Wide Web.

Cost of access to the Internet, whether dial-up or broadband tariffs.

Cost of computing equipment. Not just the initial cost of buying equipment but making sure that the technology is updated regularly to be compatible with the changing requirement of the Internet, websites and applications.

Lack of security and privacy of personal data. There is no real control of data that is collected over the Web or Internet. Data protection laws are not universal and so websites hosted in different countries may or may not have laws which protect privacy of personal data.

Physical contact and relationships are replaced by electronic processes. Customers are unable to touch and feel goods being sold on-line or gauge voices and reactions of human beings.

A lack of trust because they are interacting with faceless computers.

Limitations of e-commerce to society

Breakdown in human interaction. As people become more used to interacting electronically there could be an erosion of personal and social skills which might eventually be detrimental to the world we live in where people are more comfortable interacting with a screen than face to face.

Social division. There is a potential danger that there will be an increase in the social divide between technical haves and have-nots – so people who do not have technical skills become unable to secure better-paid jobs and could form an underclass with potentially dangerous implications for social stability.

Reliance on telecommunications infrastructure, power and IT skills, which in developing countries nullifies the benefits when power, advanced telecommunications infrastructures and IT skills are unavailable or scarce or underdeveloped.

Wasted resources. As new technology dates quickly how do you dispose of all the old computers, keyboards, monitors, speakers and other hardware or software?

Facilitates Just-In-Time manufacturing. This could potentially cripple an economy in times of crisis as stocks are kept to a minimum and delivery patterns are based on pre-set levels of stock which last for days rather than weeks (see Case Study).

> **CASE STUDY**
>
> In September 2000 in the UK, protestors demonstrating over the high price of petrol blocked petrol depots, preventing the delivery of petrol to petrol stations. Within *days* this led to petrol shortages throughout the UK. The knock-on effects were disruption in public transport, hospital services (with cancellation of non-emergency operations), school closures, shortages in food as supermarkets reported panic buying and some warned supplies could run out 'in days rather than weeks'. Petrol and other essential supplies such as bread and milk were rationed.[13] Even after the blockade was lifted, it took two to three weeks for supplies to get back to normal.

Difficulty in policing the Internet, which means that numerous crimes can be perpetrated and often go undetected. There is also an unpleasant rise in the availability and access of obscene material and ease with which paedophiles and others can entrap children by masquerading in chat rooms.

The benefits and limitations discussed here are by no means definitive or exhaustive. This chapter is setting the scene and introducing ideas, which will be explored in more detail in the rest of this book.

CLASSIFYING E-COMMERCE

Why classify e-commerce? What does it tell us? Why is there more than one way of classifying e-commerce?

Earlier in the chapter, it was pointed out that there is no one definition of e-commerce or e-business. Different associations of the terms come from people with different perspectives and it is similar with frameworks for classifying e-commerce and e-business. Academics have already drawn up a number of frameworks for classifying e-commerce but each one tends to explain it from a particular perspective. Some of these frameworks are discussed in more detail below.

A macro-environmental perspective

This framework, first developed by Kalakota and Whinston,[14] Professors of Information Systems and prolific authors on the subject, takes a holistic view and identifies the different components of business and technology that make up e-commerce. Using the analogy of the architecture of a building illustrated in Figure 1.3, they explain how the different components fit and interact together, emphasising the relative importance of each component.

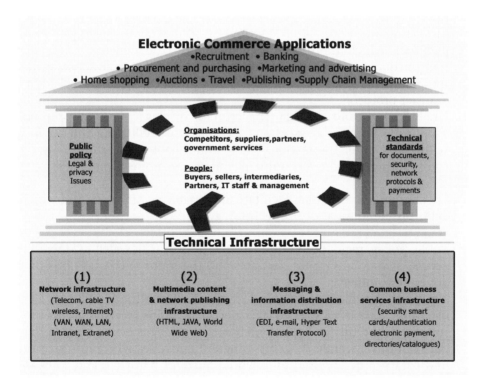

Figure 1.3 A framework for electronic commerce

The technological foundations of e-commerce are largely hidden, but they are the base on which electronic commerce is built. Kalakota and Whinston use the analogy of a traditional transportation company to describe the complexity of the network and how the different components that make up the technology infrastructure are interlinked. (The terms and technology mentioned here are described in full in Chapter 2.)

- The network infrastructure is like the network of roads that are interconnected and are of different widths, lengths and quality – for example, the Internet, local area networks, intranets. Network infrastructures also take different forms such as telephone wires, cables, wireless technology (such as satellite or cellular technology).
- The publishing infrastructure (including the World Wide Web, Web servers) can be seen as the infrastructure of vehicles and warehouses, which store and transport electronic data and multimedia content along the network. Multimedia content is created using myriad tools such as HTML and JAVA. This content can be very different with varying degrees of complexity similar to different vehicles travelling on the roads. For example, text only, or more complex is an application, such as a computer game, containing audio, video, graphics and a programme.
- Messaging and information distribution infrastructure are the engines and fuel, which transport the data around the network. Once the multimedia content is created, there has to be a means of sending and retrieving this information, for example by EDI, e-mail, Hyper Text Transfer Protocol.
- Once content and data can be created, displayed and transmitted, supporting business services are necessary for facilitating the buying, selling and other transactions safely and reliably. For example, smart cards, authentication, electronic payment, directories/catalogues.

The next components which facilitate and enable e-commerce and which are built on the foundations of technology are:

- Public policy, regulations and laws that govern issues such as universal access, privacy, electronic contracts and the terms and conditions that govern e-commerce.
- Universal agreement of technical standards dictate the format in which electronic data is transferred over networks and is received across user interfaces, and the format in which it is stored. This is necessary so that data can travel seamlessly across different networks, where information and data can be accessed by a whole range of hardware and software such as computers, palmtops, and different kinds of browsers and document readers.

- The interaction of people and organisations to manage and coordinate the applications, infrastructures and businesses are all necessary to make e-commerce work.

All these elements interact together to produce the most visible manifestation of e-commerce. These applications include on-line banking and financial trading; recruitment; procurement and purchasing; marketing and advertising; auctions; shopping are just a few examples.

This is a particularly useful framework for managers to understand the importance of technology and business, both within the organisation and external to it, in the planning and development of any e-commerce or e-business solution.

Identifying transacting partners

Another method for classifying e-commerce is by identifying the partners directly involved in the transaction. An informal version of this framework is being loosely applied in the use of the terms business-to-business (B-to-B), business-to-consumer (B-to-C) and consumer-to-consumer (C-to-C). But what exactly does this mean?

The framework that is summarised in Figure 1.4 identifies a range of relationships based on the party that initiates the transaction and the party that accepts the transaction. The party originating the e-commerce transaction also includes the facilities for initiating and fulfilling it. For example in the case of B-to-C, a business sets up a website that invites and enables consumers to buy their products and then fulfils the purchase. But the

TRANSACTION ORIGINATING FROM AND BEING FULFILLED BY

TRANSACTION INITIATED & ACCEPTED BY		Business	Consumer	Government	Peer
	Business	B-to-B	B-to-C	B-to-G	B-to-P
	Consumer	C-to-B	C-to-C	C-to-G	C-to-P
	Government	G-to-B	G-to-C	G-to-G	G-to-P
	Peer	P-to-B	P-to-C	P-to-G	P-to-P

Figure 1.4 Classification of e-commerce by transaction partners

consumer actually initiates the transaction by requesting and then accepting the purchase. So there are a number of exchanges that take place between the parties before the transaction is completed and fulfilled.

Each of the categories identified in Figure 1.4 are described as:

Business-to-Business (B-to-B)   The exchange of products, services or information between business entities. According to market research studies published in early 2000, the money volume of B-to-B exceeds that of B-to-C by 10 to 1. The Gartner Group estimates B-to-B revenue worldwide will be $7.29 trillion by 2004, a compound annual growth of about 41 per cent. Web-based B-to-B includes:

- *Direct selling and support to business* (as in the case of Cisco where customers can buy and also get technical support, downloads, patches online).
- *E-procurement* (also known as industry portals) where a purchasing agent can shop for supplies from vendors, request proposals, and, in some cases, bid to make a purchase at a desired price. For example the auto-parts wholesaler (reliableautomotive.com); and the chemical B-to-B exchange (chemconnect.com).
- *Information sites* provide information about a particular industry for its companies and their employees. These include specialised search sites and trade and industry standards organisation sites. E.g. newmarket makers.com is a leading portal for B-to-B news.

Many B-to-B sites may also fall into none or more than one of these groups. Models for B-to-B sites are still evolving and are discussed in more detail in Chapter 5.

Business-to-consumer (B-to-C)   The exchange of products, information or services between business and consumers in a retailing relationship. Some of the first examples of B-to-C e-commerce were amazon.com and dell.com in the USA and lastminute.com in the UK. In this case, the 'c' represents either consumer or customer.

Business-to-Government (B-to-G)   The exchange of information, services and products between business organisations and government agencies on-line. This may include,
- *E-procurement services*, in which businesses learn about the purchasing needs of agencies and provide services.
- *A virtual workplace* in which a business and a government agency could coordinate the work on a contracted project by collaborating on-line to coordinate on-line meetings, review plans and manage progress.

- *Rental of on-line applications and databases* designed especially for use by government agencies.

In the UK, the Department of Trade and Industry's target was that by March 2001, 90 per cent of routine procurement of goods would be conducted electronically. In the government's expenditure plans for 2001–02[15] (published in March 2001) the report gave an update of this target:

> Keeping closely in touch with the Office of Government Commerce (OGC), DTI is working towards the 90% target through increased usage of the Government Procurement Card. Two studies by ICL Unitas highlighted that the market for electronic purchasing was not fully developed. A scoping study for the delivery of electronic procurement in DTI is underway.[16]

According to the Gartner Group, B-to-G revenue is expected to grow from $1.5 billion in 2000 to $6.2 billion in 2005.

Business-to-Peer Networks (B-to-P)   This would be the provision of hardware, software or other services to the peer networks. An example here would be Napster who provided the software and facilities to enable peer networking (discussed in more detail in Chapter 5).

Consumer-to-Business (C-to-B)   This is the exchange of products, information or services from individuals to business. A classic example of this would be individuals selling their services to businesses.

Consumer-to-Consumer (C-to-C)   In this category consumers interact directly with other consumers. They exchange information such as:

- *Expert knowledge* where one person asks a question about anything and gets an e-mail reply from the community of other individuals, as in the case of the *New York Times*-affiliated abuzz.com website.
- *Opinions* about companies and products, for example epinions.com.

There is also an exchange of goods between people both with consumer auction sites such as e-bay and with more novel bartering sites such as swapitshop.com, where individuals swap goods with each other without the exchange of money.

Consumer-to-Government (C-to-G)   Examples where consumers provide services to government have yet to be implemented. See Government-to-Business.

Consumer-to-Peer Networks (C-to-P)   This is exactly part of what peer-to-peer networking is and so is a slightly redundant distinction since consumers offer their computing facilities once they are on the peer network.

Government-to-Business (G-to-B)   (Also known as e-government, discussed in detail in Chapter 5.) The exchange of information, services and products between government agencies and business organisations. Government sites now enable the exchange between government and business of:

- Information, guidance and advice for business on international trading, sources of funding and support (ukishelp), facilities (e.g. www.dti. org.uk).
- A database of laws, regulations and government policy for industry sectors.
- On-line application and submission of official forms (such as company and value added tax).
- On-line payment facilities.

This improves accuracy, increases speed and reduces costs, so businesses are given financial incentives to use electronic-form submission and payment facilities.

Government-to-Consumer (G-to-B)   (Also known as e-government). Government sites offering information, forms and facilities to conduct transactions for individuals, including paying bills and submitting official forms on-line such as tax returns.

Government-to-Government (G-to-G)   (Also known as e-government). Government-to-government transactions within countries linking local governments together and also international governments, especially within the European Union, which is in the early stages of developing coordinated strategies to link up different national systems.

Government-to-Peer Network (G-to-P)   As yet there is no real example of this type of e-commerce.

Peer–to-Peer Network (P-to-P)   (Peer-to-peer networking is discussed in more detail in Chapter 5). This is the communications model in which each party has the same capabilities and either party can initiate a communication session. In recent usage, peer-to-peer has come to describe applications in which users can use the Internet to exchange files with each other directly or through a mediating server.[17]

Peer Network-to-Consumer (P-to-C)   This is in effect peer-to-peer networking, offering services to consumers who are an integral part of the peer network.

Peer Network-to-Government (P-to-G)   This has not yet been used, but if it was, it would be used in a similar capacity to the P-to-B model (see below), only with the government as the party accepting the transaction.

Peer Network-to-Business (P-to-B) Peer-to-peer networking provides resources to business. For example, using peer network resources such as the spare processing capacity of individual machines on the network to solve mathematical problems or intensive and repetitive DNA analyses which requires very high capacity processing power.

This framework can be used by organisations to segment their customers and distinguish the different needs, requirements, business processes, products and services that are needed for each.

Degree of digitisation

Choi et al.[18] created a framework for the categorisation of e-commerce into different configurations based on the degree of digitisation of the product or service sold, the process of the transaction and the delivery agent. From the model in Figure 1.5, three main dimensions can be isolated as:

● *Traditional e-commerce*, where products or services are physical, the process of the transaction is physical and the delivery agent is physical. For

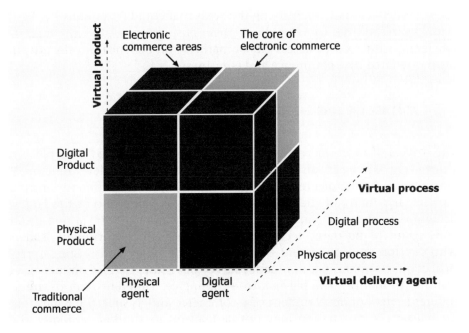

Figure 1.5 A framework for assessing the degree of digitisation

Source: Choi *et al.*

example a corner shop stocks newspapers that are bought with cash over the counter and are taken away by the customer out of the shop. However, in reality in today's world, it is very rare that a business is truly traditional because of the use of EPOS systems for payment (electronic point of sale systems).

- *Pure e-commerce*, where products or services are digital, the process of the transaction is digital and the delivery agent is digital. For example, software update services of companies like Microsoft, Cisco, Symantec; downloading of electronic books; peer-to-peer file sharing like Napster would also be considered pure e-commerce.
- *Partial e-commerce*, where either one or two of the dimensions are physical. For example in the case of booksellers Amazon, the products (books) are physical, the process is digital and the delivery agent is physical.

A study by Forrester Research[19] predicted that by 2003, most Web-based retailers will deliver products electronically and that almost a quarter of retailers will obtain 16–50 per cent of their revenue from these digital downloads.

Classifying e-commerce by degree of digitisation is a useful way for managers to analyse the range of products/services they sell, the processes of carrying out and finalising the transaction and the way the product/service is delivered. By identifying the areas that could potentially be digitised, organisations can re-engineer their business processes to improve efficiency, reduce costs, access global markets and benefit from the advantages presented by e-commerce and e-business.

WHAT ARE THE BARRIERS TO E-COMMERCE?

The drivers of e-commerce were identified and summarised in Table 1.1. Conversely, there are also barriers to the growth and development of e-commerce. Numerous reports and surveys identify the different kinds of barriers, and many of them focus on security as being one of the largest inhibitors to and problems for e-commerce. CommerceNet[20] (a non-profit consortium of business, technology, academic and government leaders who develop and implement e-commerce technology and business practice) conducts an annual time series survey of visitors to the CommerceNet website, to identify the barriers to e-commerce. Different nations are at different stages of development of e-commerce and as such the issues that are relevant to one nation may not be relevant to another. Similarly, the issues that are relevant to the type of organisation also differ. For example, large organisations have different needs and infrastructures to SMEs. The study of 1,000 visitors divides the findings into the perspectives of three different types of organisation: large B-to-B organisations; SME B-to-B enterprises; and B-to-C retailers. The study also divides the results into US and non-US based. This is particularly useful because the USA is at a more advanced stage in the e-commerce adoption lifecycle than the majority of other nations and so can be used as a predictor of things to come or as a warning to prevent followers experiencing similar pitfalls and problems.

The findings summarised in Figure 1.6 show that barriers to e-commerce can be seen as being relevant both to the macro-environment and the micro-environment level of the firm itself. Overall, all three kinds of organisations have similar barriers but with different emphases.

Internet infrastructure deals with issues such as availability and quality of the Internet in terms of speed and reliability. This barrier is of particular concern to SMEs and B-to-C organisations, since their business relies more on general consumers, and so the ease with which the general public can connect to the Internet has a direct impact on their Web-based business.

Technology infrastructure deals with issues of standardisation of systems and applications, which is a particular concern for larger organisations who want to implement solutions such as value chain integration and e-supply chain management.

Security in its broadest term is one of the most significant barriers to e-commerce both within the organisation and external to it. Identified as *Security and Encryption*; *Trust and Risk*; *User Authentication and Lack of Public Key Infrastructure*; *Fraud and Risk of Loss* it relates to the development of a broader security infrastructure and it also relates to the kinds of measures

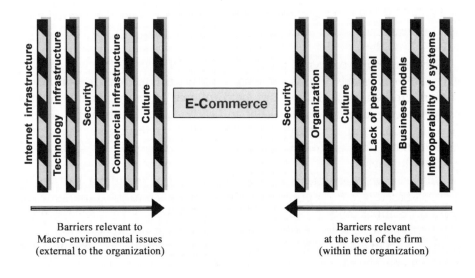

Figure 1.6 Barriers to e-commerce

organisations can take to improve security. Although security is a major concern for all types of organisations, it is a dominant concern for companies in the B-to-C e-commerce retail sector, since it reflects the concerns and perceptions of users and potential customers that are conducting financial transactions on-line.

The *commercial infrastructure* relates to issues such as international trade agreements, taxation laws and other legal agreements that facilitate all kinds of on-line trading and so is a barrier relevant to all types of organisations.

At the level of the organisation itself, there are many barriers to e-commerce that relate to issues of *organisational structure* and *culture*. These are most significant for large organisations that have to deal with change management issues. For example, there is a sense that much work still needs to be done to design the right organisational structure and corporate culture that will promote and be able to maximise the benefits of widespread e-commerce applications. Additionally, there is a perception that business partners face similar organisational and technological problems, which raises the barrier further.

Another significant issue was found to be the *lack of qualified personnel* to implement in-house and third-party e-commerce systems. For SMEs, this is a particularly strong concern because internally they do not have sufficient resources to attract and maintain their own support staff to develop a sophisticated technology infrastructure. With regards to third parties, the qualified personnel tended to work for larger organisations, which were more concerned about serving the more lucrative larger clients than SMEs. One respondent noted that, 'small firms get lots of vague and general exhortations to go "online" but find it very difficult to get reliable, well informed advice and also to get honest, effective support from a Web services provider'.[21]

Another major barrier to the development of e-commerce was a *lack of proven business models*. This is a reflection of the instability of the whole dot com phenomenon, and the poor performance of the dot coms on the world's stock exchanges in late 1999 and early 2000 after the dizzy heights to which dot com companies rose in 1998–9. A financially successful business model has yet to emerge into the business world's limelight as the model to follow.

Interoperability of systems is identified as one of the major barriers for large US-based B-to-B corporations. This refers specifically to implementation and compatibility problems of integrating new e-commerce applications with existing legacy systems and resources within organisations. This problem also extends to interacting with systems of business partners and stakeholders. The fact that the USA is ahead in the adoption lifecycle of e-commerce suggests that these issues will become more prevalent in other nations that are further behind in the lifecycle. Thus there is a need for standards to be introduced to overcome issue of incompatibility and interoperability. For SMEs that have fewer legacy systems, the issues are more a matter of interoperability with partner systems.

Many of the top barriers recognised by respondents in 2000 were also top concerns in 1999, especially security. This illustrates a consistency and reliability of the measures being taken by the survey and also underlines the fact that they are not being addressed adequately. The two major changes were increased concern over lack of business models and lack of qualified personnel. This reflects the downturn in the fortunes of the dot coms and also illustrates the increasing skills shortages problems to deal with the increasing IT implementation and maintenance problems. These issues will be dealt with in the remaining chapters of this book.

SUMMARY

There is no one commonly agreed definition of e-commerce or e-business. Thus, there is a need to clarify terms being used and explain the context in which they are being applied. E-commerce has an impact on three major stakeholders, namely society, organisations and customers (or consumers). There are a number of advantages, which include cost savings, increased efficiency, customisation and global marketplaces. There are also limitations arising from e-commerce which apply to each of the stakeholders. These include information overload, reliability and security issues, cost of access, social divisions and difficulties in policing the Internet. Successful e-commerce involves understanding the limitations and minimising the negative impact while at the same time maximising the benefits.

In order to aid general understanding of e-commerce a number of frameworks have been introduced to explore it from different perspectives: the macro-environment, which identifies the interaction of technology, people, organisations, policy and technical standards working together to enable e-commerce; the different participants and the kind of e-commerce transactions that occur between them; and the degree of digitisation that analyses product, processes and delivery agents in an organisation. These frameworks help identify the elements of e-commerce and how businesses can better understand e-commerce and its practical applicability.

The issues raised in this chapter will be dealt with in more detail in the remainder of this book.

1 To which definition of e-commerce and e-business do you subscribe and why?

2 Identify one country in Europe and one in Asia. Using the measures for the key drivers of e-commerce, compare the degree of advancement of e-commerce in each of the two countries.

3 Select a pure e-commerce company and analyse its product/service, process and delivery agent, explaining the implications of having digitised each aspect. Can this company continue to exist in the long term?

4 Which industry stands to benefit most from e-commerce?

5 Which activities are least likely to be affected by e-commerce?

REFERENCES

1 V. Zwass, 'Structure and macro-level impacts of electronic commerce: from technological infrastructure to electronic marketplaces', http://www.mhhe.com/business/mis/zwass/ecpaper.html (accessed May 2001).

2 T. Seideman, 'What Sam Walton learned from the Berlin airlift', *Audacity: The Magazine of Business Experience*, Spring 1996, 52–61.

3 E. Turban, J. Lee, D. King and H.M. Chung, *Electronic Commerce: A Managerial Perspective*. Prentice Hall, 1999.

4 www.whatis.com/ecommerce (accessed September 2000).

5 P. Timmers, *Electronic Commerce – Strategies and Models for Business-to-Business Trading*. John Wiley & Sons, 2000.

6 http://www.straight-on.com/ecommerce_definition.htm (accessed September 2000).

7 www.ibm.com/e-business (accessed September 2000).

8 Walid Mougayar, Chairman of CommerceNet Canada.

9 Walid Mougayar 'E-commerce? E-business? Who E-cares?', *COMPUTERWORLD*, 2 November 1998; http://www.cybermanagement.com/cw7.htm (accessed September 2001).

10 Walid Mougayar 'E-commerce? E-business? Who E-cares?' *COMPUTERWORLD*, 2 November 1998; http://www.cybermanagement.com/cw7.htm (accessed September 2001).

11 *The Shorter Oxford English Dictionary*, Vol. I, p. 376. Book Club Associates, 1983.

12 *The Shorter Oxford English Dictionary*, Vol. I, p. 256. Book Club Associates, 1983.

13 'Crisis continues as fuel blockades lift Thursday', http://news.bbc.co.uk/hi/english/uk/newsid_924000/924478.stm (accessed 14 September, 2000).

14 R. Kalakota and A.B. Whinston, *Frontiers of Electronic Commerce*, Addison-Wesley, 1996.

15 *DTI Report – Government's Expenditure Plans for 2001–2002* (March 2001): http:// www.dti.gov.uk/expenditureplan/expenditure2001 (accessed December 2001).

16 *DTI Report – Government's Expenditure Plans for 2001–2002* (March 2001), Chapter 1 – 'Delivering Better Public Services' (Figure 1.2): http://www.

dti.gov.uk/expenditureplan/expenditure2001/intro_chap1/chap1/section3.htm (accessed December 2001).

17 Definition of peer-to-peer networking: www.whatis.com (accessed December 2001).

18 Choi *et al.*, *The Economics of Electronic Commerce*. Macmillan Technical Publications, 1997, p. 18.

19 'A study of on-line retailing 2000 – Forrester Research': www.forrester.com (accessed March 2000).

20 'CommerceNet – barriers to e-commerce, Study 2000': http://www.commerce. net/research/barriers-inhibitors/2000/Barriers2000study.html (accessed December 2001). Over 1,000 respondents (members of and website visitors to CommerceNet) from six countries completed the year 2000 survey and although not a random sample, the respondents represented a broad spectrum of interests, backgrounds, experiences and expertise on electronic commerce.

Top 10 U.S.	Rank	Top 10 Non-U.S.
Interoperability with complementary companies	1	Security and encryption
Interoperability between eCommerce applications and with legacy systems	2	Trust and risk
Lack of qualified personnel	3	Lack of qualified personnel
International trade barriers	4	Lack of business models
Customers can't find me	5	User authentication and lack of public key infrastructure
Culture	6	Culture
Security and encryption	7	Organisation
Organisation	8	Fraud and risk of loss
User authentication and lack of public key infrastructure	9	Legal issues such as contracts and liabilities
Lack of standards	10	Ability to make and receive payments

CommerceNet 2000 Survey: Barriers to Electronic Commerce

21 'CommerceNet – Barriers to E-commerce, Study 2000': http://www.commerce. net/research/barriers-inhibitors/2000/Barriers2000study.html (accessed December 2001).

The technology of e-commerce

The technology

LEARNING OBJECTIVES

- To understand the importance of technology.
- To be able to explain the basics of networking and related technical jargon.
- To identify the different kinds of networks architectures and their uses.
- To understand the origins of the Internet and its strengths and weaknesses as an infrastructure.
- To understand the structure of the Internet access provider industry.
- To be able to identify the different ways of connecting to the Internet and their respective advantages and disadvantages.

WHY BOTHER WITH THE TECHNOLOGY?

The IT community seems to have developed a language of its own, full of buzzwords and jargon, which often obscures understanding for the non-technical. The aims of this chapter are to explain the technology and language of e-commerce and its relevance to business.

In the UK, the Commons Public Accounts Committee published a report[1] examining over 25 cases of government IT projects from 1990–9. The report identified why the implementation of public sector IT systems resulted in delay, confusion and inconvenience to the citizen and led to taxpayers' money being wasted or providing 'poor value for money'.[2] Some of the projects included:

- *The Home Office* – a £77 million computer system designed to stream-line asylum applications had to be abandoned by the government after it failed to meet a growing backlog of applications.

- *The Ministry of Defence* – an investment in project 'Trawlerman' started in 1991 was delayed and had to be written off at a cost of £41 million after it was found that the system being built to handle classified documents across the different departments was incompatible with different systems – it was replaced with a system costing £6 million.
- *Passport Agency* – the failure of management to check a new computing system properly before it was introduced and the failure to make contingency plans cost taxpayers an estimated £12 million.[3]
- *Inland Revenue* – the failure of a new computer system for recording national insurance payment led to 17 million contribution payments not being registered on claimants' records. Over 170,000 pensioners were underpaid their pensions. The final compensation bill was estimated at £40 million by the National Audit Office.

Such failures not only happen in the public sector, but also in the private sector. The London Stock Exchange (LSE) experienced similar problems in the mid–1990s, when the £400m Taurus project to implement a new back office system in-house collapsed because of numerous problems and delays. In April 2000, a time of unusual turbulence in international stock markets and also the end of the English tax year, the LSE, whose computer programs were managed by Andersen Consulting (now Accenture), experienced a fault that caused its share trading system to collapse for eight hours, losing millions of pounds worth of business and damaging its reputation. It was discovered that an error between two computer programs had resulted in the system transmitting share prices before they had been updated.[4]

These are just a few high-profile examples of the kinds of problems that are experienced by IT systems and projects and the consequences that can arise because of them. One of the key recommendations from the report states that, 'Key decisions on IT systems are, therefore, business decisions, not technical ones, and should involve senior management. And the commitment of senior management can be a critical factor in securing a successful outcome.'[5] It is often the case, though, that senior management and other business managers distance themselves from anything to do with IT and seem to pass the responsibility to technical managers. This is not just a UK phenomenon, as these experiences are duplicated in the rest of Europe and America.

A study by Professors Bensaou (INSEAD) and Earl (London Business School) compared Western and Japanese IT-management practices.[6] It found that Japanese companies rarely experience the IT problems so common in the USA and Europe mainly because of how Japanese and Western managers think about technology. The Japanese see IT as just one competitive lever amongst many. Its purpose is to help the organisation achieve its operational goals, so the Japanese bias is to adopt appropriate technology rather than adopting technology for technology's sake. Japanese managers were found to spend two to three years in the IT department, often against their will – so sometimes the director of finance and the director of IT planning is the same person. While acknowledging that Japan has its own weaknesses with technology, particularly in white-collar office settings, the study nevertheless urges senior managers in the West to consider the solid foundation on which Japanese IT management rests: 'Abandon the dangerous idea that IT requires special technocratic means of management.'[7] Too many managers in the West are intimidated by the task of managing technology and feel that they can comfortably pass on the responsibility to the IT department.

It is therefore crucial that business managers understand the technology and are confident in that knowledge to be able to ask critical questions and make critical decisions. The remainder of this chapter will introduce and explain the technology that is particularly relevant to e-business and e-commerce.

WHAT IS A NETWORK?

In IT, a network is a series of points or nodes interconnected by communication paths. In a network, a node is a connection point for transmitting data, where it either recognises and processes transmissions or it forwards them to other nodes. Networks can interconnect with other networks to form large global networks.

Mainframes

An industry term for large computers. Mainframes are mainly used for handling very large amounts of data or many complicated processes, typically for the commercial applications of very large businesses, scientific or military applications or other large-scale computing purposes. The main advantage of mainframes is their reliability. The chief difference between a supercomputer and a mainframe is that a mainframe uses its power to execute many programs simultaneously, but supercomputers can execute a single program faster.

Historically, mainframes used to occupy several rooms full of equipment. Some of the first mainframes were the UNIVAC (Universal Automatic Computer) and the Electronic Numerical Integrator and Computer (ENIAC), illustrated in Figures 2.1 and 2.2. They were inflexible and costly machines often requiring special climate-controlled rooms

CASE STUDY

Figure 2.1   The UNIVAC (Universal Automatic Computer)

Figure 2.2   The ENIAC – the first digital computer

Source: http://icarus.brainerd.net/~kuck/history/mainfram/html

and were not easy to use. The operating system on a mainframe was cryptic, requiring a specialized skill set, and it was difficult for ordinary users to get information from the computer. Today, this is no longer the case. Mainframes, although still relatively expensive, can occupy the size of a laptop with relatively easy to use operating systems.

Midrange computers

These are medium-sized computers that are less expensive and smaller than mainframes, but are capable of supporting the processing needs of smaller organisations or managing networks. These include mini-computers and servers. In the past decade, the distinction between large minicomputers[8] and small mainframes has blurred. But, in general, a minicomputer is a multiprocessing system capable of supporting between 4 and 200 users simultaneously.

A server is a computer or device on a network that manages network resources and provides software and other resources (such as sharing files, printers, software applications, database facilities, e-mail) to other computers over a network. Sometimes, servers are dedicated, meaning that they perform no other tasks besides their server tasks. For example, a *file server* is a computer and storage device dedicated to storing files. Any user on the network can store files on the server. A *print server* is a computer that manages one or more printers, and a *network server* is a computer that manages network traffic. A database *server* is a computer system that processes database queries.

Micro-computers

These are even less expensive than mid-ranged computers and vary widely in terms of processing power and price. Micro-computers include work-stations (which are supposed to have more processing power and are part of a network) and personal computers (PCs) (which are supposed to be largely for home users). However, in reality, there is little distinction between workstations and PCs because of the ease with which PCs can be configured. The principal characteristic is that they are single-user systems but it is common to link them together to form a network.

Historically, a mainframe was associated with centralised rather than distributed computing. Today, with the advent of e-commerce, improved

technology and increased networking, centralised processing where all processing is accomplished by one large central computer has largely been
replaced by distributed processing. This is where processing is distributed
to a range of micro, midrange and/or mainframe computers linked
together on a network. This means that when a command is typed in by
the user, the operating system allocates jobs to processors, locates, trans-
ports and stores the appropriate files to and from the processor, and deals
with all other system functions to ensure there is an optimum usage of all
the resources available automatically without the user being aware of it.

CASE
STUDY

Distributed computing case study

BASF, based in Germany, is one of the world's leading chemical companies whose
chemicals can be found in everything from snowboards, textiles and shoes, to cars,
building materials and carpets. It has a large polymer physics department which studies
problems in chemistry – two teams are devoted to molecular modelling and quantum
physics. One of the key areas of study is in accelerated chemical reactions by catalysts –
a task that requires highly complex and computationally intensive numerical simulations
that can take days to run. Each team uses different cluster and departmental computer
systems for their applications depending on the degree of criticality. BASF found that too
much of their researchers' time was being taken up with manually scheduling and
processing tasks – for example researchers had to meet face-to-face with colleagues to
select appropriate computers to schedule their jobs for submission. They also had to
manually copy and retrieve files to and from the different machines. BASF did not want
to spend money on hardware since they already had adequate resources, including the
300 office PCs and cluster of 10PCs with 2 processors each, but felt these were not
being used as effectively as they could be.

The solution was distributed computing software that views the different computing platforms as one system and automatically selects the strategy for processing the
required tasks. The software reads the actual load of the different host computers,
defines the resource requirements and the number of processors needed, and the
appropriate architecture for the job. It then decides the optimal computer for the job,
places it in the queue and transmits it to the existing machine when it is available. When
different hosts are available, the distributed computing software sends the job to the
system with a free load. Files are now automatically copied from the workstation to the
computing engine and the results are returned to the users' workstations without the
need of manual intervention. BASF estimates that distributed computing has saved 20
per cent of employee time for scientific research work and processor utilisation has
grown from 70 per cent to 95 per cent. They also estimate that they can now process ten
times more structure because of the reduced demand for interactive work and a more
robust, faster and automated workflow.

Source: BASF (www.basf.com)

WHAT ARE THE BENEFITS OF NETWORKS?

There are a number of benefits that can be achieved by a computer net-work. Different types of network deliver different benefits; however, in general the following benefits are common to all networks:

- *Facilitating resource sharing* – where all programs, data and equipment are available to anyone on the network without regard to the physical location of the resource and user.
- *Providing reliability* – by having back-up resources. For example, all files can be replicated and so there may be more than one copy of the same file; if a computer or printer is unavailable then another on the network can be used instead.
- *Cost effectiveness* – a small computer has a much better price/perform-ance ratio than a large one. Mainframes are 10 times faster than a microprocessor but 1000 times more expensive and cumbersome; now a single file server machine can be used to service a number of personal computers on a network. Also, using networks is cheaper than one computer directly contacting another.
- *Provides a powerful communication medium among geographically separated people* – exchange of text, graphics, video, audio and real time inter-action can take place easily across networks.

WHY ARE THERE DIFFERENT KINDS OF NETWORKS?

A network can be characterised by a number of different features, which describe its architecture and the kinds of facilities it enables. It is useful for non-technical managers to understand the different categories of networks and whether the functionality of those networks meets the organisation's business criteria. Some of the different network characteristics are described below:

1 *Whether it carries voice, data or both* kinds of signals and thus the potential of using data networks for telephony purposes.
2 *The nature of its connections*[9] – dial-up,[10] dedicated,[11] or virtual connec-tions.[12] This has implications for the organisation's security, network scalability and cost structure.
3 *The types of physical links* – for example, *optical fibre*[13] is faster, lighter and more durable but is expensive and difficult to install; *coaxial cable*[14] is faster than copper wire with reduced interference from external 'noise'; unshielded *twisted pair*[15] is less expensive but with more inter-ference. Physical links have cost, performance and 'future-proofing' implications for the organisation.

Distance	Location of Nodes In Same	Network Type
10 m 100 m	Room Building	Local Area Networks (LAN)
1 km 10 km 100 km	Campus City Country	Metropolitan Area Networks (MAN) Long Haul Networks (WAN)
1,000 km 10,000 km	Continent Planet	Interconnection of Long Haul Networks (Internet)

Figure 2.3 Classification of networks by geographical distance

4 *Geographical distance* – there are four major distinctions of networks by geographic distance (summarised in Figure 2.3):

- A *local area network (LAN)* is a group of computers and associated devices that share a common communications line and typically share the resources of a single processor or server within a small geographic area (for example, within an office building). A local area network may serve as few as two or as many as thousands of users.
- A *metropolitan area network (MAN)* is a network that interconnects users with computer resources in a geographic area or region larger than that covered by a large local area network but smaller than the area covered by a wide area network. The term is applied to the interconnection of networks in a city into a single larger network (which may then also offer efficient connection to a wide area network). It is also used to mean the interconnection of several local area networks by bridging them with backbone lines sometimes referred to as a *campus network*. Large universities also use the term to describe their networks.
- A *wide area network (WAN)* is a geographically dispersed telecommunications network, the term distinguishing a broader telecommunications structure from a local area network. A wide area network may be privately owned or rented, but the term usually connotes the inclusion of public (shared user) networks.
- *The Internet* is a network of networks that geographically covers the whole globe.

5 *Topology* – In the context of communication networks, a topology describes pictorially the configuration or arrangement of a (usually conceptual) network, including its nodes and connecting lines. The topology of a network illustrates the way data is transmitted and outlines the important nodes in the network. Common topologies include:

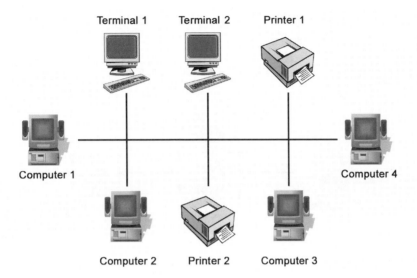

Figure 2.4 Bus network topology

- *A bus network* or circuit arrangement where all devices (for example printers, computers, terminals) are attached to a central cable directly and all signals pass through each of the devices in both directions (illustrated in Figure 2.4). Each device has a unique identity and can recognise those signals intended for it. Only devices addressed by the signals pay attention to them; the others discard the signals. One of the main advantages is that since there is no host computer to control the network, if one of the nodes in the network fails, none of the other components will be affected. The main disadvantage is that the bus channel can only handle one message at a time, so performance can degrade if there is a high volume of network traffic. The bus network is most predominantly used in local area networks.
- *A star network* consists of a backbone (main circuit) to which a number of outgoing lines can be attached, each providing one or more connection ports for devices to be attached. All devices (printers, computers, terminals, etc.) on the network are connected to a central hub where data comes together and is then forwarded to the necessary device (as illustrated in Figure 2.5). The main advantage of this topology is that it is more efficient because traffic is centrally controlled and applications can be processed centrally or locally. One of the disadvantages is that all communication between points in the network must pass through the central hub or host computer. Because this is the traffic controller for all other devices on the

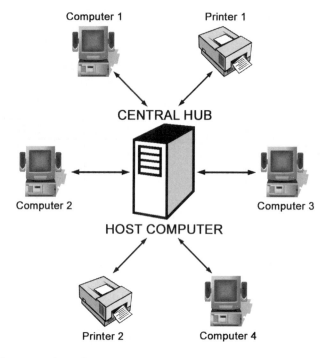

Computer 1   Printer 1

CENTRAL HUB

Computer 2   Computer 3

HOST COMPUTER

Printer 2   Computer 4

Figure 2.5   Star network topology

network, the network will cease to function if the hub stops working. This is the kind of topology common to Internet access
providers.
- *A ring network* is where each device is attached along the same signal
  path to two other devices, where the connecting wire or cable is in
  the shape of a ring or closed loop (as illustrated in Figure 2.6). Each
  device in the ring has a unique address. Information flows in one
  direction, and a controlling device intercepts and manages the flow
  to and from the ring. The advantage of this is that each computer
  operates independently, so that if one fails, communication through
  the network is not interrupted. The ring network is most predominantly used in local area networks.

6 *Communication model* – Networks can be broadly classified as using
   either a *client/server* or *peer-to-peer* model.

- *The client/server model* (illustrated in Figure 2.7) has become one of
  the central ideas of network computing. It describes the relationship
  between two computer programs in which one program, *the client*,

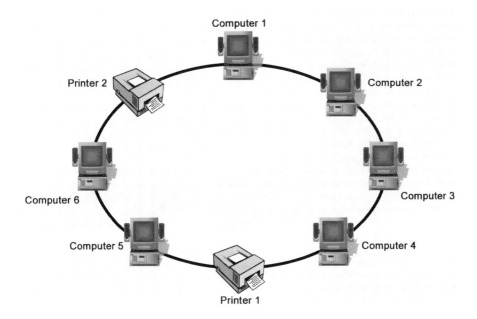

Figure 2.6 Ring network topology

makes a service request from another program, *the server* (sometimes called a daemon, which fulfils the request. The client is the user interface to request or initiate a function and is normally a desktop computer but can also be a laptop, Personal Digital Assistant or mobile-Internet phone. The user generally only interacts with the client application to input or retrieve data. The server provides the client with services. The server can be a mainframe but is usually a specialised server that can store and process data while at the same time performing a range of functions not visible to the users, such as managing network activities. Most business applications use the client/server model.

Relative to the Internet, a Web browser (such as Microsoft Explorer or Netscape Navigator) is an example of a client program that requests services (access to Web pages or files) from a Web server on the Internet. Checking e-mail using an e-mail programme uses a client/server model. Computer transactions using the client/server model are very common. For example, to check your bank account from your computer, a Web browser (client) on your computer forwards your request to a server program at the bank. That program may in turn forward the request to its own client program that sends a request to a database server at another bank computer to retrieve

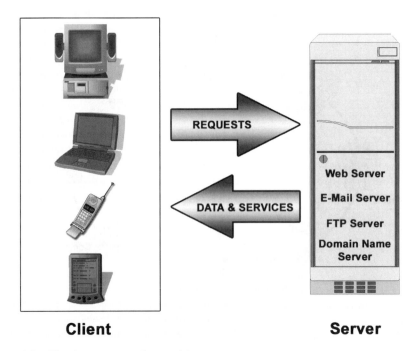

REQUESTS

DATA & SERVICES

Web Server

E-Mail Server

FTP Server

Domain Name
Server

Client

Server

Figure 2.7   Client/server computing model

your account balance. The balance is returned back to the bank data client, which in turn serves it back to the client in your personal computer, which displays the information for you.

- *Peer-to-peer*[16] is where each party in the network has the same capabilities and any party can initiate a communication session. The Internet P-to-P communication model has been highlighted by the cases of Napster and Gnutella, providers of P-to-P networking software. A group of computer users with the same networking program can use the Internet to access and exchange files directly from one another's hard drive or through a mediating server. Napster was the leading on-line P-to-P software provider, enabling users to swap music files. It suffered a barrage of legal attacks from the music industry who accused it of copyright infringement by providing the software that enabled copyrighted music to be swapped freely. Litigation is still ongoing and the majority of legitimate file swapping sites no longer allow the free exchange of copyrighted music. However, corporations are now looking at the advantages of using P-to-P as a way for employees to share files without the expense involved in maintaining a centralised server and as a way for businesses to exchange information with each other directly.

NETWORKS USED FOR E-COMMERCE AND BUSINESS

Another common criterion for distinguishing networks is by the type of users of a network, that is whether it is public or private. There are three main types of network categorised by the type of user and these are:

- *Internet* – a public global network of networks. It is accessible by everybody with the right equipment and because of its size and openness is very difficult to police and control.
- *Intranet* – a private network that is contained within an enterprise. It may consist of many interlinked local area networks and also use private leased lines in a wide area network. Typically, an intranet uses Internet technology and other Internet protocols and includes connections through one or more secure gateways to the outside Internet.
- *Extranet* – extends intranets and links several intranets in different locations using secure hardware and software. This is still a private network accessible only by authorised partners or stakeholders.

The distinction by the type of user is particularly useful from a business management perspective because it involves issues such as identifying business partners, cooperation and resource sharing with stakeholders and also reflects the organisation's corporate policies and business objectives and way of working. Each of these network types and the business implications will be examined in detail in the next part of this chapter.

THE INTERNET

The Internet has been one of the most influential technological inventions of the late twentieth century, and its impact continues into the twenty-first century. The Internet has affected the way business and society communicates and conducts transactions, and has also had an impact on the technological development and concept of networking. This section will cover the development of the Internet, shedding light on why the strengths and weaknesses of its infrastructure exist today.

The history of the Internet can be divided into seven general stages of its development:

1 The early years.
2 Experimental networking.
3 Discipline specific research.
4 General research networking.
5 Privatisation and commercialisation.
6 National information infrastructure.
7 High performance computing and communications.

These stages are charted against a time line in Figure 2.8, which summarises the major events at each stage of the Internet's development. Each of these stages is explained in detail in Appendix 4 and it is advised that this section is read to get a complete picture of the development of the infrastructure that underpins the e-phenomenon.

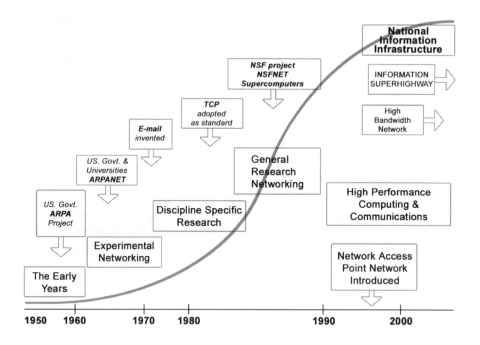

Figure 2.8 A summary of the history of the development of the Internet

So what does the history of the Internet tell us?

The history of the Internet's development is extremely useful for understanding and managing the process of integrating the Internet into an organisation's communications infrastructure. Table 2.1 summarises the facts about the Internet's development and the consequences for managers using the Internet today.

Who manages the internet?

As we have seen, the Internet is a loose and voluntary association of networks that have agreed to use a common protocol (TCP/IP) and so are

TABLE 2.1 Practical lessons that can be learned from the history of the Internet

History of the Internet	Applied lessons for managers
There is no central authority that controls the Internet	Organisations must control, maintain and police their own infrastructure and use of the Internet in terms of content and access
It was designed to be robust and to have a decentralised structure so that, in the event of one node being unavailable, the network as a whole would still be able to function	This underlines the reliability of the network as a commercial and social medium for communications and transactions
It was developed in an academic and research-oriented environment. It was not designed as a commercial channel, neither was security an overriding factor in the design. The primary objective was reliability and efficiency of message transmission and receipt	This underlines the need for each organisation to implement its own security policy and infrastructure to ensure that it protects its assets which become open over the Internet if no protection is put in place
It was initially designed as a medium to share computer resources and used as a tool to collaborate on-line with partners who were geographically distant	This is one of the greatest benefits of the Internet, and organisations should capitalise on this medium to improve collaboration and cooperation between different organisations efficiently and cost effectively
Even in the early days, it was increasingly being used for person-to-person communication (e-mail and newsgroups) and not for its original purpose, underlining human beings' overriding need to communicate with each other by whatever means	This phenomenon continues. No matter how sophisticated the technology and for what purposes it was intentionally designed, users will always find new and different ways of utilising this technology. Organisations should beware of this desire for person-to-person communication and ensure that there are procedures in place to protect against abuse of the medium for which the organisation could be liable (more in Chapter 7)
Technology is continually improving and so the infrastructure of the Internet can also be improved to meet the growing demands of users	Managers must ensure that the investment they make in their infrastructures incorporates flexibility and the ability to add new technology as and when it emerges
In the early days, growth in the use of the Internet was exponential – this pattern of growth continues today	Organisations must factor rapid change in technology development into their overall strategy to ensure they can keep up with technology changes and not be left behind by their competitors

able to communicate with each other. It is often said that the Internet is not owned by any one group. However, since protocols define how networks interconnect and communicate with each other, it can be argued that the organisations setting the protocol standards for these networks manage the Internet.

There is a definite hierarchical structure to the 'independent' organisations, which research and develop protocols and standards that govern the Internet as outlined in Figure 2.9. By examining the individuals who are involved in these 'independent' organisations, a very large majority are based in the USA and affiliated to large multi-national telecommunications or technology organisations such as CISCO and Microsoft, although there is some representation from European commercial and academic organisations. The hierarchical structure of the different organisations involved in determining and developing Internet protocols and standards are detailed in Appendix 5.

Why is this important? Although the Internet is not governed by any one organisation or government, it is governed by the technical standards and protocols that enable it to function as a global infrastructure, and so it is indirectly governed by the representatives of the organisations that develop the technical standards and protocols. This means that these

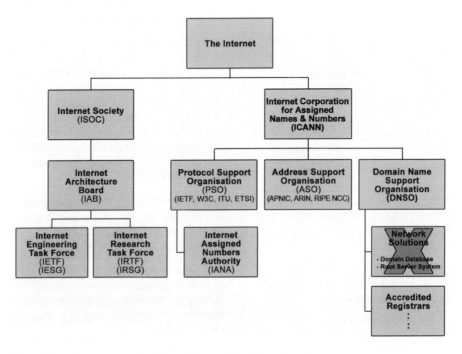

Figure 2.9 Who manages the Internet (www.livinginternet.com)

organisations and the bases from which they operate will always have a technological competitive advantage over organisations and countries not involved in this process – or for as long as the Internet remains so crucial to business and society.

The architecture of the Internet

This section will describe the architecture of the Internet in the context of its infrastructure as it stands today. Figure 2.10 identifies the main elements that make up the Internet.

The backbone Also known as the very high-speed backbone network service (vBNS). It consists of a range of different technologies including cables, satellites, supercomputers, routers and other advanced communications technology. It is a nationwide infrastructure that accepts traffic from designated network nodes that interconnect to it lower down the infrastructure. The backbone is the largest transmission line typically made of fibre optic trunk lines with multiple cables combined together to increase transmission capacity. It can be compared to a motorway, providing high-

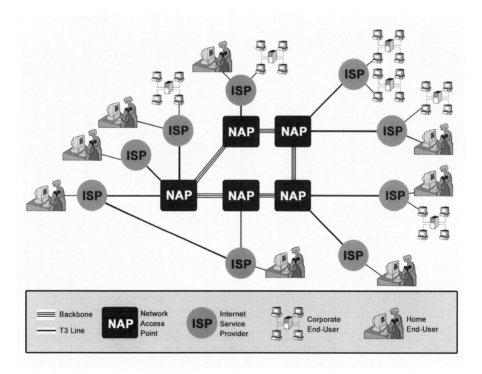

Figure 2.10 Architecture of the Internet

speed connectivity between regions, usually at speeds of at least 155 Mbps and increasing all the time with some operating at up to 4 Gbps. This infrastructure is normally government sponsored since it incorporates the use of national telecommunications infrastructures, but can also be set up and owned by large telecommunications corporations such as UUNET.

Network Access Points (NAPS) These are designated locations where many other different high-level networks can connect to the vBNS. The networks connecting the NAPs to the backbone must operate at speeds of at least 100 Mbps. It is usually private telecommunications companies that are developing these points and have advanced technological infrastructures such as ATM switches for fast packet transfer. Regional, commercial, international, government, education and other networks connect to the NAPs at speeds of 45 Mbps (T3–lines).

Internet Service Providers (ISP) These have a hierarchy within the industry sector itself and are classified by the kind of services they offer. This hierarchy is illustrated in Figure 2.11.

The first of these is the *ISP that is also an infrastructure provider* – these are the multi-million pound telecommunications and cable companies (such as British Telecommunications, AT&T, and Cable and Wireless/NTL) that are involved in building part of the backbone infrastructure. They also provide access to the Internet for a number of end-users that include home users, corporate users and a range of other national regional and local ISPs.

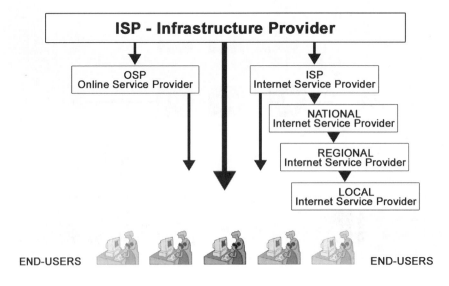

Figure 2.11 Internet access provider industry

National ISPs are dominant players in the Internet access market. They provide Internet access to smaller ISPs and larger organisations through leased lines. These larger ISPs connect to the NAPs at speeds of at least 45 Mbps (T3) and transport Internet traffic across their own networks of routers and switching technology, for example, Demon Internet, PSINet and UUNet.

Regional ISPs offer regional connections to the Internet backbone and are usually customers of the national ISPs. They cannot offer connections nationwide and only offer their services regionally. These types of organisations offer value added support services as well as Internet access.

Local ISPs offer a lower speed service to users confined within a city or metropolitan area. They sublease circuits from regional or national ISPs. Although smaller, they are more flexible and innovative in service offerings.

Although there seems to be a clear distinction between the different types of providers, this is more representative of the early days of the Internet when the cable infrastructure accessing the Internet backbone were still limited. There has since been a shake-out in the market and the service being provided has changed where the majority of ISPs lower down the hierarchy have now become OSPs or on-line service providers.

Online service providers (OSPs) connect to the Internet via the infrastructure providers or national ISPs. They have their own independent on-line content such as America Online (AOL) and offer an extensive array of services and even their own Web-browsers. Some OSPs, such as Microsoft, Freeserve and Virginnet, offer free access to the Internet usually as a means of raising their brand awareness and image.

The end-users   These can either be individual home users or businesses or larger organisations. They connect to the Internet through an ISP but there are a number of ways of connecting to the Internet. Some of these methods and their suitability include:

1   For home and SME businesses using the Public Telephone Network, some of the ways of connecting to the Internet are:

   - *Dial-up modem* with speeds up to 56 Kbps[17] is suitable for low one or two users for home or very small businesses.
   - *ISDN (Integrated Services Digital Network)* uses an adapter that enables telephone wires to carry up to 128 Kbps voice and data at the same time. This is suitable for heavier home users or businesses with up to 10 low-user employees.
   - *DSL (Digital Subscriber Line)* has different upload and download speeds varying from up to 1.544 Mbps download and 128 Kbps upload. With a special modem, DSL uses existing telephone wires;

however, the further the user is away from the central provider the slower the speed of transmission. Also suitable for heavy home users or small businesses with up to 20 users.

2 For home and small and medium-sized businesses using direct connect cable, it bypasses telephone networks and uses the existing cable TV infrastructure with a special modem to access the Internet. It has speeds of around 1.5 Mbps and bandwidth is shared with other users in the area, which means the more users, the slower the speed of access to the Internet.

3 For larger organisations and heavy business users, leased line options are available where organisations can lease a line directly from the telecommunications company exclusively for their use. Leased lines are based on the T-carrier system, introduced by the Bell System in the USA in the 1960s, the first successful system that supported digitised voice transmission. It uses digital pulses with four wires, two for receiving and two for sending at the same time. Originally the four wires were based on a pair of twisted copper wires, but now can include cable and even faster and more sophisticated optical fibre, digital microwaves and other media. The most commonly known options are:

- *T1 lines* span distances within and between major metropolitan areas, and have an overall speed of around 1.544 Mbps. Some Internet access providers connect to the Internet as a point-of-presence (POP) on a T1 line owned by a major telephone network. Some larger organisations connect directly to the ISP using a T1 line.
- *T3 lines* provide transmission speeds of around 45 Mbps, and are also commonly used by Internet service providers. Another commonly installed service is a fractional T–1, which is the rental of some portion of the 24 channels in a T–1 line, with the other channels going unused.

These options are very expensive and only suitable for large organisations with heavy Internet traffic and/or where security is important.

This is only a selection of different methods of connecting to the Internet; it will be an interesting exercise to see how long these methods remain relevant.

So how does the Internet actually work?

Networks and the Internet (being a network of networks) are governed by protocols. Protocols are a set of rules that determine how two computers communicate with one another over a network. A familiar human protocol is saying 'thank you' when receiving something. There is a standardised set of protocols referred to as 'the seven-layer model' set by the International Standards Organisation (detailed in Appendix 1). These seven layers are related functions needed at each end when a message is sent from one party to another party in a network. However, in this case, we will only be looking at Transmission Control Protocol/Internet Protocol (TCP/IP).

TCP/IP is the basic communication language or protocol of the Internet. It can also be used as a communications protocol in a private network (either an intranet or an extranet). TCP/IP is a two-layer program. The higher layer, TCP, breaks down an electronic message or file into smaller packets at source and re-assembles the packets into the original message at destination. The lower layer, IP, formats the packets broken down by TCP and assigns addresses (detailed below) to each packet so that it gets to the right destination. Each gateway computer (that directs packets across a network) checks this address to see where to forward the message. Some packets from the same message can be routed differently than others, and may also arrive in a different order, but are reassembled at the destination.

TCP/IP uses the client/server model of communication in which a computer user (a client) requests and is provided with a service (such as sending a Web page) by another computer (a server) in the network. Other application protocols that use TCP/IP to get to the Internet include: the World Wide Web's Hypertext Transfer Protocol (HTTP), which enables the exchange of multimedia information; Telnet, which enables users to log on to remote computers; and Simple Mail Transfer Protocol (SMTP), which enables the exchange of e-mail. These and other protocols are often packaged together with TCP/IP as a 'suite'.

The Internet addressing system

Since the Internet uses TCP/IP, every computer on the Internet has an IP address. The IP address is numerical and is made up of a series of numbers separated by 'dots', for example 163.52.12.72. IP addresses denote a specific host and network attached to the Internet. A computer acting as a server must have a static IP address – one that never changes. However, when users dial into the Internet via an ISP, their computer is given a temporary dynamic IP address, which changes with each separate log-on session.

Because numeric IP addresses are difficult to remember, the Domain Name System (DNS) was created to pair a specific IP address (such as 163.52.12.72) with an alphanumeric domain name such as www.company. co.uk. In order for IP addresses to be associated with domain names, they must first be registered in the Domain Name System by ICANN accredited domain name registrars. The domain names and related IP addresses (more than one IP address can be associated with a single domain name) are stored on a DNS server maintained by Network Information Centres (NICs). When one uses a domain name, the system must first contact a DNS server to identify the IP addressees associated with the specific domain name, and then contact the target computer using the IP address.

Domain Names The Internet domain-naming infrastructure illustrated in Figure 2.12, is made up of a number of levels interspersed with 'dots'.

Top-level domain (TLD) identifies the most general part of the domain name in an Internet address and is registered by an accredited domain name registrar. A TLD can be a *country code top-level domain (ccTLD)*, which usually indicates the country of origin. For example: .uk – United Kingdom; .fr – France; .de – Germany; .gr – Greece. Organisations in each country are responsible for managing their country's top-level domains, and the subsequent prefixes. Some clever marketers register names with country extensions to spell out a word or a name – for example, www.bla.de or www.pota.to (country extension of Trinidad and Tobago).

The other kind of TLD is the *generic top-level domain (gTLD)*, such as:

- *com* – 'commercial' to indicate a site used for commercial purposes and also for a US company. It is the most used top-level domain, constituting over 50 per cent of all domain name extensions. It is now used for any kind of site originating in any country.

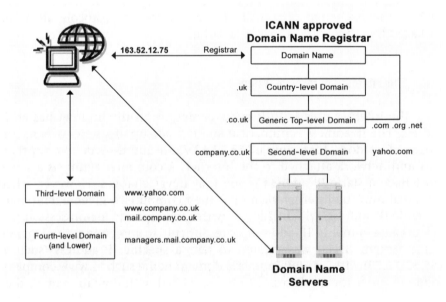

Figure 2.12 Internet addressing system

- *net* – originally intended for Internet Service Providers, but now used for a variety of purposes.
- *org* – originally intended for non-commercial, non-profit making 'organisations', but now used by industry groups as well as others.
- *gov* - reserved exclusively for the Government.
- *mil* – reserved exclusively for the Military.
- *int* – reserved for 'international' organisations established by international treaties between governments, usually NATO sites, but not often used.

These can be used as prefixes to country code TLDs (as in .gov.uk). If there are no following extensions this usually indicates a US institution or organisation: for example, .edu is reserved for educational institutions in the USA granting four-year degrees; .mil is reserved for the US military; .gov is reserved for the US government.

ICANN controls the kinds of TLDs that are available and in 2001 authorised an additional seven prefixes (and is in the process of introducing some more).

.biz – businesses
.museum – museums
.pro – professionals
.aero – aviation
.coop – cooperatives
.info – general information

A second-level domain (*SLD*) identifies the specific and unique administrative owner associated with an IP address. More than one second-level domain name can be used for the same IP address. Second-level domain names generally correspond to their type of activity or company name, for example mycompany.co.uk. SLD names can have up to 61 letters. Any one of these letters may include any of the 26 letters, 10 numbers and the hyphen character (except the hyphen can't be the first or last character). That's 4.33^{95} possible different domain names. However, only a few correspond to recognisable words. Both top-level and second-level domains are part of the domain name that is resolved to an IP address and must be registered by official domain name registrars. Second-level domains can be divided into further domain levels. These sub-domains sometimes represent different computer servers within different departments.

Third-level domain names precede second- and top-level domain names and are created by the owners of the domain names. They are often used to specify the domains for different purposes, such as a domain for Web access (www.company.co.uk) or one for mail access (mail.company.co.uk).

Fourth-level domain names can be used to specify even further domains for different purposes such as separating mail servers into different groups, for example managers.mail.company.co.uk

An intranet is a private network that is contained within an enterprise and is designed in a way that links together different IT systems, hardware, databases and other resources (as illustrated in Figure 2.13). An intranet uses TCP/IP, HTTP and other Internet protocols and in general looks like a private version of the Internet. Typically, larger enterprises allow users within their intranet to access the public Internet through one or more gateway computers protected by firewalls – a combination of hardware and software that maintain the privacy and security of intranets by monitoring all traffic.

The main purpose of an intranet is to share company information and computing resources among employees. This improved capacity for knowledge sharing increases the empowerment of individual employees and

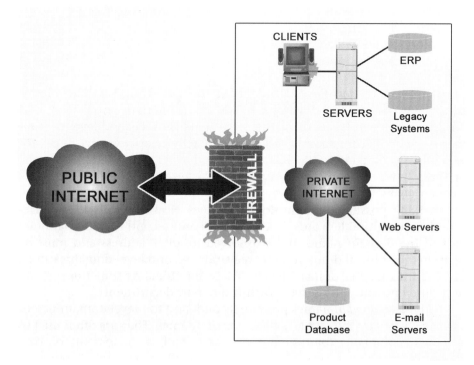

Figure 2.13 Architecture of the intranet

enables them to operate more effectively. It also facilitates group decision-making and improves business processes throughout the organisation, which in turn has an impact on the quality of customer service being offered. The kinds of facilities that are enabled and provided via an intranet are:

- *E-mail and Web facilities* – where corporate, department and individuals can transmit, develop and display information in a Web page format over the intranet.
- *Database access* – Web technology eases the problems of incompatibility, which means that databases (including new and older legacy systems) can be accessed centrally.
- *Search engines and directory facilities* assist key word-based searches, similar to those used on the World Wide Web, making it easier and quicker to find information.
- *Interactive multimedia* enables real-time communication via text, audio and videoconferencing, including telephony over the intranet.
- *Document distribution and workflow*, where Web-based downloads and routing of documents facilitates collaborative working and sharing documents, which leads to improved decision-making and project control and management.
- *Integration* with a number of different applications and systems (including Web-based systems) to manage activities such as purchasing, inventories, interacting with suppliers, providing customer service and tracking orders using enterprise resource planning (ERP) systems.
- *Cost savings* – Sun Microsystems estimate that the reduction of printing and distribution of documents alone saves around US$3.5 million per year.[18]

Other advantages include: reducing paper; reducing errors by not having to re-key the same information several times for individual databases; and central software distribution and control to ensure compatibility of standards across departments. A survey[19] conducted by CIO (part of the research group IDG) on the uses of intranets in over 200 businesses (see Figure 2.14), revealed that the most popular use of intranets by business was publication of information for access by all staff – including product catalogues and manuals, corporate policies and procedures. Business process applications such as purchase orders and order entry were also popular uses, with accounts being the least popular use of intranets.

Despite the fact that some companies have been developing intranets since 1993–4, companies are still in the early days of intranet use. A report by Jakob Nielsen,[20] a leading intranet expert and pioneer, estimates that the total cost of running an intranet per 1,000 employees is US$1.3 million per annum and US$400,000 of that is as a result of users' wasted time

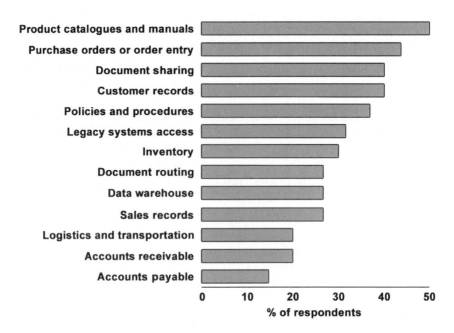

Figure 2.14 Uses of intranets by business

because they cannot find what they want. Having outlined all the benefits of the Intranet, there seem to be some main issues that some organisations are failing to address. As a result, the investment in and the use of intranets is not being maximised. For example:

- *Intranets must be relevant and useful* – often companies design their intranets around what they think employees should know, rather than what employees actually want to know. This results in employees not using the site because there is no meaningful or value added information: 'approach what will be on the Intranet from the employees' perspective. Give them things that will help them do their jobs and don't waste their time.'[21] At Chicago-based Accenture offices, consultants' contribution to the intranet is a part of each employee's performance review. This encourages knowledge sharing even in a highly competitive environment where individuals jealously guard their own expertise and knowledge.
- *Sufficient planning* – there must be a clear and centralised decision-making framework that ensures the intranet is consistent with the organisation's strategic objectives, otherwise each department will devise their own individual site with no continuity or framework. In October 2000, Hewlett-Packard implemented a policy of controlling and centralising the format of their intranet sites, resulting in the

culling of 2,000 sites and saving US$50 million annually because it was able to eliminate paperwork, streamline the travel bookings process, consolidate websites, and reduce printing, fax machine and copier costs.[22]

- *Well-organised material* – as intranets grow in size and depth, resembling a mini-Internet, for some it is becoming increasingly difficult to control the material and also to search it and find the relevant information. So a search engine taxonomy should be put in place to ensure that words or phrases common to the organisation will yield the right results.
- *Intranets need to be backed up by a whole communication programme* where everybody understands the need and use of the intranet in their job and part of their overall skills building strategy. This especially needs commitment from the top: 'Senior executives will embrace the idea of empowering employees by giving them direct access to information . . . but in reality, Intranets tend to flatten the corporate hierarchy and this can be scary to executives.'[23]

Some examples of Intranet use

CASE STUDY

In their Web Business Awards December 2001,[24] CIO voted *Cisco Systems* 'one of the best internal corporate websites ever'. Cisco saves more than US$75 million annually as a direct result of its employee services applications intranet. The Employee Connection caters for Cisco's 26,000 employees, it has an automated expenses reimbursement tool, provides a wide range of technical documentation and keeps track of new and old patents.

Ford Motor Company has an intranet that supports over 175,000 users across 92 countries. The intranet allows employees to customise their site views to get the information and tools they need for their jobs (myford). This then allows staff access to personal information, links to benefits, salary history, employee-specific job information and a range of other services. The company estimates this has saved them millions of dollars and thousands of man-hours, while at the same time improving employees' business acumen by providing information about company performance.

> For Ford, the intranet is not just a tool for employees to manage their benefits efficiently; it's a foundation for the company to become a digital business. In order for Ford to run a successful e-business with customers, suppliers and partners, its employees first had to be adept at using e-business technologies themselves. 'You're not properly doing e-business unless you're doing it inside the company as well . . . It starts on the inside.' Martin Davis, manager of e-portal project.'[25]

The Wharton School of the University of Pennsylvania has an intranet for 5,000 students nicknamed SPIKE.[26] Facilities, which can be customised, cater for each individual's personal needs, including a school calendar, course schedule, e-mail access, Web bookmarks and, most innovatively, a school course auction. To get into a popular, oversubscribed class, students log onto the intranet and bid for a place. The students check the site at the beginning of the semester to see if they have been successful and have the place they wanted. Input, feedback and content is regularly invited from students to make sure that the content is always up-to-date and presented in a way that captures the students' attention.

As organisations become more familiar with intranet technology and the kind of facilities that it enables, there will be more extensive use of intranets as more applications become Web-enabled; legacy applications having Web front-ends and the increase of bandwidth will bring an increased interactivity with the use of sound and video.

WHAT IS AN EXTRANET AND WHY IS IT IMPORTANT?

Extranet = intranet + extension outside the company

An extranet is a private network that uses Internet technology and the public telecommunication system to securely share part of a business's information or operations with authorised users, such as suppliers, vendors, partners, customers, or other businesses. An extranet can be viewed as part of a company's intranet that is extended to users outside the company (as illustrated in Figure 2.15). There are a range of components and participants that make up an extranet, including intranets, Web servers, firewalls and interface software to ensure all authorised and authenticated participants can communicate with each other. When part of an intranet is made accessible to customers, partners, suppliers, or others outside the company, that becomes part of an extranet.

An extranet requires security and privacy both of the users and the data, which travels along the public network. Although this will be discussed in more detail in Chapter 4, briefly this includes firewalls, digital certificates or similar means of user authentication, encryption of messages and virtual private networks (vpn) that use tunnelling to use the public network securely. Tunnelling means that data transmissions across the Internet can be made secure by authenticating and encrypting all IP packets. The tunnelling principle is the basic concept that makes the extranet possible. Extranets can also be implemented using a direct leased line linking all intranets. The uses and benefits of extranets are very similar to those of intranets but also include:

- *Exchange large volumes of data* using Electronic Data Interchange (EDI) on demand across a variety of different locations and from a number of different sources.
- *Share product catalogues* exclusively with wholesalers or those 'in the trade'.

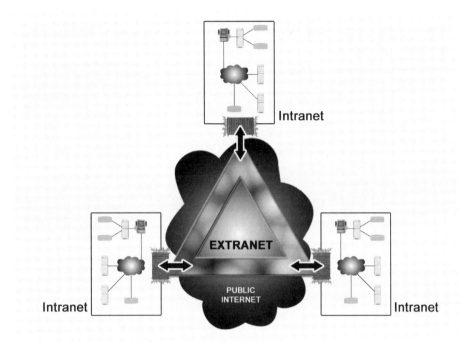

Intranet

EXTRANET

PUBLIC
INTERNET

Intranet

Intranet

Figure 2.15   Architecture of the extranet

- *Collaborate* with other companies on joint development efforts to lower design and production costs while at the same time improving the development process and increasing the time to market.
- *Jointly develop* and use training programs with other companies.
- *Reduce costs* because of reduced errors (input once); reduced travel and meetings expenses, reduced administration and operational costs, and the reduction/elimination of paper publishing and mailing costs.

In a CIO survey[27] of business use of extranets (see Figure 2.16), the most popular use of extranets by business was very similar to that of intranets, with publication of information for access by all partners – including product catalogues and manuals; corporate policies and procedures. Business process applications such as purchase orders and order entry were also popular uses. The main users of extranets included customers, distributors, dealers, suppliers and, interestingly, government regulators, which indicates the level of trust in some industries between government and organisations.

The extranet suffers from the same problems as the intranet; however, an additional problem is the coordination of the different stakeholder systems and ensuring that there is a standard whereby all systems linked to the extranet can communicate with each other. Also the effectiveness of an

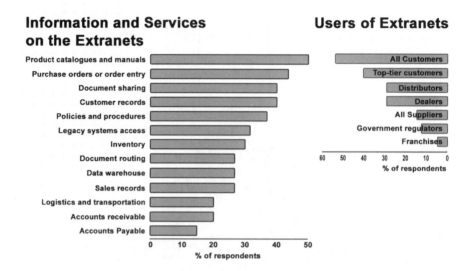

Figure 2.16 Uses and users of an extranet (www.livingnet.com accessed September 2000)

extranet depends on the degree to which it is integrated with legacy systems and databases. In many instances, integrating with legacy systems involves integrating systems network architecture with TCP/IP, the Web backbone. The technical differences between the systems are often sources of conflict and could potentially cause problems with the implementation of the infrastructure.

CASE STUDY

Some examples of extranet use

OM Direct (Owen & Minor) integrated their Internet order-fulfilment system with the product catalogue system of their key supplier, Kimberley-Clark Corp. This means that when any OM customer clicks for more information on a product, there is a direct connection to the supplier's own product information which provides information on safety videos on proper usage; product substitute information and any recall announcements. Thus, OM Direct do not have to maintain a catalogue for that supplier's products and information is up-to-date. There is a very close collaboration and long-term relationship between the two organisations, where they work together to decide how cooperation and technology can help streamline processes and manage inventory more efficiently, and how key customer data that is captured can be shared with both. However, because it takes so much management time to nurture such a close and trusting relationship, OM Direct concentrate on close collaborative relationships with only the top ten suppliers that provide 60 per cent of sales.[28]

UPS Logistics helped Ford Motor Company build a system to track individual vehicles throughout the shipping process by integrating employees of both Ford and

UPS to set up a unit called UPS Autogistics. Ford contributed 27 employees to a UPS staff of 120, using their automotive industry expertise and collaboration of systems and resources. One year after the launch of Autogistics, Ford revealed a 25 per cent cut in delivery times, US$125 million savings in annual carrying costs and US$1 billion a year in inventory reductions.[29]

Intel Corporation's goal is to develop a 100 per cent electronic corporation. Already suppliers can access their account information on-line and see Intel's demand forecasts, engineering changes, orders and invoices. Its factory systems automatically communicate demand, inventory and receipt information to suppliers without the involvement of an Intel buyer. However, Intel feels that this is the easy part – 'once you get past the low-hanging fruit of automation, that's where it gets difficult.'[30] Intel is currently developing their on-line design collaboration system where suppliers are working closely together with raw materials suppliers (such as silicone) and those that build manufacturing equipment. Partners can share documents and files, exchange messages, and track comments and any input or corrections to product design. Tracking is particularly important, to ensure that the exact contribution each person added to a product design is recorded and creates an audit trail, since this could be potentially very contentious for determining final intellectual property rights. This extranet collaboration also improves development with companies in Asia (where over half of Intel's suppliers are) by cutting the number of days in the exchange of work. However, while collaboration in areas such as design is progressing, and processes such as ordering and inventory monitoring have been automated, there is still a problem of compatibility when working with customers such as Compaq and Dell since there are no real industry standards for data transfer between their respective corporate infrastructures.

Sikorsky Aircraft Manufacturers – a single electronic interface was designed to enable the 250-member design team to share resources and work interactively on the design and development of the new Comanche helicopter for the US Army. This eventually reduced design time by 30 per cent.[31]

SUMMARY

E-commerce is based on technology, so in order to effectively manage an e-business, it is necessary to understand how the technology works and its business benefits and limitations.

Networking, computing and telecommunications is at the core of e-commerce and e-business, where the most commonly used infrastructures are the Internet, intranets and extranets. Each type of network has a similar basic architecture, uses Internet-based protocols and standards, and provides similar benefits, such as cost savings, increased efficiency, collaborative working, resource and information sharing. One of the main problems of all these infrastructures is a lack of inbuilt security, which stems from the origins of the Internet, where efficiency and reliability of data delivery was paramount. The major differences between networks are in the types of users and the degree of control.

The Internet is a public network with no limitations to individuals who can access it, so long as they have the correct hardware and software. The information is general, commercial and public – there is no real control over content on the Internet and it is very difficult to police. The intranet is a private and restricted network where only authorised users can access the network. The information is proprietary, controlled by and specific to the organisation. An extranet is also a private network where only authorised users can access it. However, the circle of authorised users is much wider and includes a range of business partners, such as suppliers, customers and manufacturers. The kind of information available over an extranet is controlled by the respective organisations it is shared with.

Technology is no longer the exclusive domain of the IT department. In the world of e-commerce and e-business, managers and decision-makers need to be able to understand the technology in order to make decisions that are consistent with the overall business objectives. This chapter has presented one aspect of that technology. The following chapters will deal with other aspects of the technology.

DISCUSSION QUESTIONS

1 Why is it important for managers to understand networking?
2 What are the different uses and applications of the Internet, intranet and extranet?
3 What are the different ways of connecting to the Internet and what is the advantage for each?
4 What are the problems with the Internet and what changes would you make if you could?
5 Explain what you have learned from this chapter and how you can apply it in a business environment.

REFERENCES

1 'Improving the delivery of government IT projects (HC 65)', Reports by the Committee of Public Accounts Session, 1999–2000 (05/01/00): http://www.publications.parliament.uk/pa/cm199900/cmselect/cmpubacc/65/6511.htm (accessed December 2001).
2 'Improving the delivery of government IT projects: Introduction and Conclusions and Recommendations', Select Committee on Public Accounts First Report: http://www.publications.parliament.uk/pa/cm199900/cmselect/cmpubacc/65/6503.htm.
3 'Litany of hi-tech fiascos', BBC website, 15/02/2001: http://news.bbc.co.uk/low/english/uk/newsid_1171000/1171471.stm (accessed October 2001).

4 'London trading: what went wrong?', BBC on-line, 06/04/2001:
http://news.bbc.co.uk/low/english/business/newsid_703000/703859.stm
(accessed 02/10/2001).

5 'Improving the delivery of government IT projects: Introduction and
Conclusions and Recommendations', Select Committee on Public Accounts
First Report: http://www.publications.parliament.uk/pa/cm199900/cmselect/
cmpubacc/65/6503.htm.

6 M. Bensaou and M. Earl, 'The right mind-set for managing information
technology'. *Harvard Business Review*, 01/09/98.

7 Webopedia: http://www.webopedia.com/TERM/s/supercomputer.html
(accessed December 2001).

8 Webopedia: http://www.webopedia.com/TERM/M/minicomputer.html
(accessed December 2001).

9 whatis.com: http://searchnetworking.techtarget.com/sDefinition/0,,sid7_
gci211941,00.html; http://searchnetworking.techtarget.com/sDefinition/
0,,sid7_gci212737,00.html (accessed December 2001).

10 A connection established and maintained for a limited time duration.

11 A connection that is continuously in place, always on.

12 A dedicated logical connection but the actual physical resources can be shared
among multiple logical connections or users.

13 The transmission of information as light pulses along a glass or plastic wire or
fibre. It carries much more information than conventional copper wire and is
in general not subject to electromagnetic interference and the need to
retransmit signals. Most telephone company long-distance lines are now of
optical fibre.

14 Invented in 1929 and first used commercially in 1941; a copper cable used by
cable TV companies between the community antenna and user homes and
businesses.

15 The most common kind of copper telephone wiring. Twisted pair is the
ordinary copper wire that connects home and many business computers to
the telephone company. To reduce cross talk or electromagnetic, two
insulated copper wires are twisted around each other. Often associated with
home use, a higher grade of twisted pair is often used for horizontal wiring in
LAN installations because it is less expensive than coaxial cable.

16 How does Internet P-to-P Work? The user must first download and execute a
peer-to-peer networking program. (Gnutellanet is currently one of the most
popular of these decentralized P-to-P programs because it allows users to
exchange all types of files.) After launching the program, the user enters the
IP address of another computer belonging to the network. Once the computer
finds another network member on-line, it will connect to that user's
connection. Users can choose how many member connections to seek at one
time and determine which files they wish to share or password protect.
Source: Whatis.com http://searchnetworking.techtarget.com/sDefinition/
0,,sid7_gci212769,00.html (accessed December 2001).

17 The average text e-mail (without attachments) is about 30-40,000 bits (or
30/40 Kb) in size.

18 T. Horgan, 'Developing your intranet strategy' – a presentation by CIO's VP of
Technology; parts of the presentation were provided by Dennis Tsu, formerly
of Sun Microsystems: http://www.cio.com/WebMaster/strategy/.

19 'Intranet use by business', CIO-WebBusiness 1999: www.cio.com/webusiness
(accessed 1999).

20 'The costs of running an intranet – Infrastructure and staffing costs are only the tip of the iceberg', Jakob Nielsen, Nielsen Norman Group, 2001: http://www.darwinmag.com/read/110101/intranet_cost.html (accessed December 2001).

21 Howard McQueen, CEO of McQueen Consulting, an early Internet architect: http://www.darwinmag.com/read/110101/intranet_content.html (accessed December 2001).

22 D. Duffy, 'Why do intranets fail?' – *Darwin Magazine*, November 2001: http://www.darwinmag.com/read/110101/intranet_content.html (accessed December 2001).

23 D. Duffy, 'Why do intranets fail?' – *Darwin Magazine*, November 2001: http://www.darwinmag.com/read/110101/intranet_content.html (accessed December 2001).

24 'Web business 50 awards', *CIO Magazine*, 1 December 2001: http://www.cio.com/archive/120101/winners.html (accessed December 2001).

25 Simone Kaplan, 'Calling all workers', *CIO Magazine*, December 2001: http://www.cio.com/archive/120101/rule_ford.html.

26 Wharton Intranet Interface: http://www.wharton.upenn.edu/spike/auction/ (accessed December 2001).

27 'Extranet use by business', CIO-WebBusiness 1999: http://www.cio.com/ webusiness (accessed 1999).

28 Marianne Kolbasuk McGee and Chris Murphy, 'Collaboration is about more than squeezing out supply-chain costs', *Information Week*, 10 December, 2001: http://www.informationweek.com/story/IWK20011207S0016 (accessed December 2001).

29 Eric Chabrow, 'Collaboration takes different roads: CNF and UPS find success using different approaches to logistics services for major automakers', *Information Week*, 10 December, 2001: http://www.informationweek.com/ story/IWK20011207S0008 (accessed December 2001).

30 Tracy Nielsen, co-manager of Intel's private e-market office. M.K. McGee and C. Murphy, 'Collaboration is about more than squeezing out supply-chain costs', *Information Week*, 10 December, 2001: http://www.information week.com/story/IWK20011207S0016 (accessed December 2001).

31 '2001 innovators in collaboration listing', *Information Week*, 11 December, 2001: http://www.informationweek.com/story/IWK20011207S0015.

Elements of e-commerce: applications

LEARNING OBJECTIVES

- To understand the main elements of a Web-based 'business'.
- To identify the common technological applications that enable and facilitate e-business.
- To be able to explain how each of these applications work.
- To understand how each of these applications is used and implemented by business.

INTRODUCTION

The previous chapter explored the technology of telecommunications, networking and computing and how they evolved to create the Internet. It also looked at the design and development of different network infrastructures and how they are used by business.

This chapter continues the theme of explaining technology to the non-technical. It will focus on the kinds of applications and tools that are used by Web- and Internet-enabled businesses. It will identify the common functions that a Web-based business fulfils and the main tools that achieve its business objectives, explaining how they work and the business advantages and disadvantages of each.

WHAT IS A WEB-BASED BUSINESS?

In this context, a Web-based business is one that explicitly uses the World Wide Web to fulfil one or more business processes. There are many different kinds of business processes, but when we examine how businesses are using the Web we can classify them as fulfilling four major functions: information dissemination; data capture; promotions and marketing; and transacting with stakeholders (customers, suppliers, partners) – for example, sales, delivery, manufacturing. Figure 3.1 illustrates how these business objectives are achieved by the interaction of business systems and Web based applications. 'Front-end' applications are those which are accessible via the World Wide Web and provide a direct user interface with business systems. For example, the front-end application for accessing an on-line bank account and the process of inputting account details via the website. 'Back-end' applications or programs support the front-end services and are the indirect interface with users. Back-end applications have the capability of communicating with a required resource such as databases or legacy systems. For example, once the request for the customer's bank account is received with the necessary details, these would usually be processed via a Web server and then the details retrieved from a database of customer accounts.

Some of the commonly known Web-based applications include:

- *e-CRM (electronic customer relationship management)* – there are over 150 definitions for e-CRM. Briefly, it is a means of enabling '360-degree'

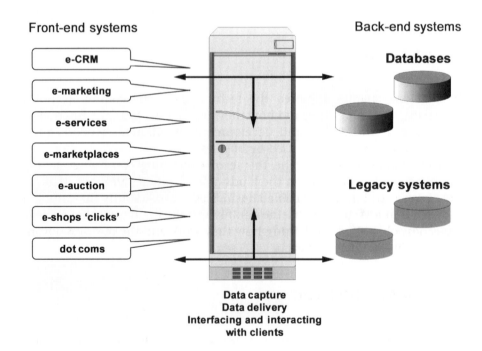

Figure 3.1 An illustration of some Web-based e-business processes

customer visibility by capturing relationships and interaction throughout the customers' lifetime. It is about retaining customers, creating incremental sales, anticipating customer needs, providing customer support, and more timely and personal contact. Traditional CRM has mainly concentrated on point of selection and purchase and less on complaint tracking, delivery, replacement and support. E-CRM has achieved improved knowledge of the customer by fusing information from different communication channels into a single database of information. Integrating all the communication channels means that most of the customer information can be gathered and accessed through websites, feedback forms, website browsing behaviour, transaction behaviour, inbound and outbound e-mail with embedded Web addresses, telephone call centres (the largest part of e-CRM), interactive TV and mobile telephony (SMS[1] and WAP[2]), to name a few.

Mobile CRM

CASE STUDY

Cendres & Metaux (CM) is a medium-sized Swiss company employing around 300 staff who are both office based and external sales staff who service markets in Europe, the USA and the Far East. CM's main activity is processing precious metals such as gold and platinum across its three main divisions which are dental technology, the watch-making and electronics industry, and prestige jewellery.

What makes CM one of the leaders in the industry is its state-of-the art production technology and its high-quality customer service which is underpinned by its IT systems. At the beginning of 2001, CM wanted to improve and streamline its market and customer relationship activities by seamlessly integrating the data from their office-based internal staff with data from their international sales force.

Using SAP, they were able to implement a mobile multi-lingual e-CRM sales system. This system improved customer service by enabling the external sales force access to the same data as the office-based team across all three divisions – so they had customer information at any time, at any place and in any language. The sales teams were then able to prepare their calls and visits more systematically, and retrieve user-specific views of relevant data they needed, to help them deal with their clients more effectively and efficiently. Like the office-based sales teams, the external staff were able to access specific reports and use sales analysis tools on their mobile hardware, and send data to head-office updating central records in real time.

Source: SAP website: http://www.sap.com/solutions/crm/customersuccesses/

CASE QUESTIONS

(a) Do you think this system is central to Cendres & Metaux's e-commerce plans? Explain.
(b) How does the system implemented by Cendres & Metaux enhance long-term customer relationship management?

(c) Identify any weaknesses in the system described in the mini-case study.

CASE STUDY

e-CRM

Villeroy and Boch AG (VB) are a German public company that produce an extensive range of household products, such as wall and floor tiles, bathroom and kitchen fittings, crockery and cutlery, and textiles and accessories. Based in Mettlach in the Saar region of Germany, they have 22 plants, 10,000 employees and revenues of over 940 million euros a year. VB's strategy focuses on innovation and customer orientation and to provide customers with a range of products to complement their lifestyles. In order to do this, they needed to ensure that the sales force had a consistent customer database with a stable infrastructure that enhanced communication between internal and external sales teams.

The solution was an e-CRM system with a Web-browser–based interface which allowed external sales employees to access all customer and project information, status reports, activities and data for bid invitations while they were away from their offices. The sales force can also enter information directly into the database while they are with the client. Communication between the internal and external sales forces has benefited both the organisation and also the customer, by ensuring that any customer queries can be answered faster and the data is more reliable and up-to-date, with no delays in updating information. The e-CRM system has improved customer service, productivity and revenues.

Source: SAP website: http://www.sap.com/solutions/crm/customersuccesses/

CASE QUESTIONS

(a) How has the e-CRM system improved customer service, productivity and revenues at Villeroy and Boch?
(b) What areas of CRM cannot be executed by an electronic system in Villeroy & Boch's case?

- *e-marketing* (*electronic marketing*) – identifying prospective customers, tracking and collecting data on these potential customers and then targeting them. A number of different Web-based technologies and techniques are being used and will be discussed later in this chapter.
- *e-services* (*electronic services*) – a concept first coined by Hewlett Packard (HP)[3] where many business services can be provided to a business or consumer using the Web. HP defines e-services as 'modular, nimble, electronic services that perform work, achieve tasks, or complete transactions'. They are also considered to be customer services supplied over the Internet, providing support and information through determining

customer requirements, acquiring the service or product, after-sales support and support in the disposal of the good or service at the end of its lifecycle.

CASE
STUDY

Professor Voss,[4] Chair in Management Technology and Learning at London Business School, defines e-service as 'the delivery of service using new media such as the Web'. He describes e-service as covering a broad spectrum from pure sales on the Web with little or no e-service content, to pure service as delivered free or as part of a service contract. Some e-services, such as remote bulk printing, may be done at a website; other e-services, such as news updates to subscribers, may be sent to individual computers. Other e-services will be done in the background without the customer's immediate knowledge, where the customer will no longer have to visit a merchant's website to engage their services. E-services are being created to run on any device, each one able to trigger a request that sets into motion a whole range of services devoted to completing a whole process without human intervention. Some of the current examples are UPS's package tracking, MapQuest.com's driving directions, and even banking and brokerage firms are making their services externally accessible.[5] Thus, e-services increase competition, broaden distribution channels, lower costs through easier outsourcing and ease the integration efforts required to implement value added partnerships.

- *e-marketplaces, dot coms, e-auctions* and *e-shops* – all types of organisations that enable the commercial exchange of goods and services with customers over the Internet via a website. These organisations are discussed in detail in Chapters 5 and 6.
- *e-Supply Chain Management (e-SCM)* – involves the coordination of all supply activities of an organisation from its suppliers and partners to develop a product or service for delivery to a customer using Web technology. Supply-chain management is a whole subject in itself and is only touched upon briefly in this chapter in the context of the different Web-based applications that are possible.

CASE
STUDY

e-Supply Chain Management

Carlsberg Group was founded more than 150 years ago and is a market-oriented company with a leading position within the global brewing industry. Carlsberg Denmark is a subsidiary of the Carlsberg Group located in Copenhagen. The Danish brewers have to forecast and deliver over 350 different drink products to over 23,000 customers across Denmark. These have to be coordinated across 3 production sites, 2 main stocking terminals and 16 distribution offices. Carlsberg forecasting must also factor in elements such as seasons, weather, events and promotions to get the fulfilment numbers right. It must also deliver the right product to the right customer at the right time, while keeping inventory low to maximise efficiency. Carlsberg's strategic plans for developing their business is to create a fully integrated, Internet-enabled supply chain.

Carlsberg Denmark had been using standard production-planning functionality to plan for customer demand. They were operating a three-month plan which was calculated and updated once a month. What Carlsberg were looking for was a supply-chain system that would allow users to get a complete overview of the business in a single screen without having to shift back and forth between applications and systems to retrieve data, for example from sales, distribution or manufacturing. This would enable them to improve the accuracy of their forecasting and production planning and so lower costs of inventory and improve delivery to customers. They wanted a system that would integrate the different applications, seamlessly allowing access to information across systems and departments.

The solution was an integrated supply-chain system which enabled every piece of relevant information on every transaction to be updated in every part of the system whenever something happened. Carlsberg input sales history information into the systems daily, to build a long-term forecast for replenishing its retail, wholesale, restaurant and convenience store sales channels over a 12-week period. The company then uses the system's demand planning capabilities to create a short-term forecast for a 10-day period with an additional 3-week forecast. There is also the ability to include other factors such as promotions, with all results being reviewed with the sales force to ensure accuracy. The demand planning system enables sales forecasters and production planners to cooperate together and produce forecasts more easily, faster and with all the relevant information. If the forecast or any conditions change, they are able to build new plans more quickly than before, and send them to necessary production, stocking and distribution centres. This allows them to reduce inventory and get better and more precise information to customers. By implementing this supply chain management solution system Carlsberg achieved a more than 30 per cent reduction in stock and have improved their ability to deliver the correct items at the correct times to the correct customers by 20 per cent.

Carlsberg working with SAP also plan to integrate CRM systems to provide better service to customers by linking customer systems to their own, allowing them to integrate additional customer information (what they have ordered, when they ordered it and what they have sold) into their forecasting and planning system. Carlsberg are also piloting business-to-business procurement systems to integrate the purchase of raw materials (such as glass and packaging) into their forecasts and plans. Their aim is to create a fully integrated electronic supply chain.

Source: Carlsberg and SAP website: http://www.sap.com/solutions/crm/customersuccesses/

CASE QUESTIONS

(a) What areas of the system implemented by Carlsberg contribute to its overall aim of a fully integrated supply chain? Is there anything missing?

(b) How does Carlsberg's infrastructure compare with Bill Gates's conceptual model of the organisation as a digital nervous system, conducting business at the speed of thought (see Chapter 8).

These Web-based e-business applications are bound by the capability of the technology and the data is controlled and manipulated by the organisations' back-end systems. Some of the back-end applications are based on knowledge management processes including:

- *Data warehousing* where data collected from the organisation's various and diverse business systems is collected in a server-based central repository. The data is 'cleansed', which means that it is organised into relevant and appropriate 'metadata' (a summary of data), and is structured as a relational database making it easier to index, search and access by the end users. Data warehousing allows information processing to be offloaded from expensive operational business systems onto lower cost servers and can be made accessible for users over an intranet. Data warehousing is expensive (costs may average US$1 million) and is mainly used by large multinational organisations.
- *Data mining* is an application that can make use of a data warehouse or alternatively information stored in some other large database such as intranet servers. It includes the analysis of data for relationships that have not previously been discovered. The kinds of results yielded include:
  - Associations, where one event can be correlated to another event (for example, train passengers buy newspapers at a certain time).
  - Sequences, where one event leads to another later event (for example, a carpet purchase followed by a purchase of curtains).
  - Classification, where patterns are recognised, resulting in new organisation of data (for example, profiles of customers who make purchases).
  - Clustering, where groups of facts not previously known are found.
  - Forecasting, where patterns in data can be used to make predictions about the future.
- *Enterprise resource planning (ERP)*[6] attempts to integrate all departments and functions across a company onto a single computer system that can serve all different departments' particular needs. ERP organises, codifies and standardises an organisation's business processes and data, to make sure that transaction data is transformed into useful information that can be analysed to support business decisions. This enables various departments to share information and communicate with each other more easily, for example product planning, parts purchasing, maintaining inventories, interacting with suppliers, providing customer service and tracking orders. Typically, an ERP system uses or is

integrated with a relational database system. The deployment of an ERP system can involve considerable business process analysis, employee retraining and new work procedures. The idea is that new technologies will enable the extension of the value chain to ensure that stakeholders can easily 'plug' their internal information systems into the information chain that mirrors the value chain. In this way all the organisations involved in the value chain will truly become part of a networked team of partners dedicated to delivering customer value.

Figure 3.1 illustrates conceptually the interaction between the back-end and front-end applications. They may interact directly with one another, or more typically, interact through an intermediate program (often called middleware) that mediates front-end and back-end activities. One of the most common and difficult problems is integration and compatibility of both front- and back-end systems and also between different back-end systems. The reality is that business systems typically interface with other corporate systems such as accounting and inventory, many of which use legacy software based on older mainframe computers with different programming languages and operating systems, which may not work with the latest Internet technologies. In such cases, the corporation needs to either switch to a new system, or get the old and new systems to talk to each other. Since the former option usually means scrapping the old system, most companies prefer to look at integrating the two.

Integration will only become widespread and useful once a common and universal framework providing a vocabulary and interface to bridge the communication between disparate applications and systems across the Internet and intranets, is implemented. Some multinational IT corporations are providing open source platforms that are freely downloadable, such as Hewlett Packard's 'e-speak'[7] in order to promote it as a universal standard. Other companies such as IBM and Microsoft support comparable structures such as UDDI (universal description, discovery and integration) and SOAP (Simple Object Access Protocol) for facilitating the interaction of e-services.[8]

Creating middleware and achieving compatibility across different systems (new and legacy) and databases is an extremely complex area and is the crux of successful integration of e-business systems. Although only mentioned briefly here, detailed analysis of middleware and back-end system integration is beyond the scope of this book as the area is a topic, which requires a specialist information systems and programming tome in its own right.

The common functions of both front-end and back-end systems are: data capture and delivery; dissemination of information, communication, promotion and interaction; and interfacing with third parties. The Web-based technology that enables and facilitates these functions can be listed as:

- Web pages
- E-mail
- Cookies
- Search engines
- Shopping Carts
- Videoconferencing
- Interactive 'chat'
- Bulletin boards

Although these technologies are usually incorporated into websites to provide an all round functionality, they can also be standalone technologies. The following sections will examine each of these technologies, explain how they work, how they are used by organisations and what kind of common business objectives they can achieve.

WHAT IS A WEB PAGE AND HOW DOES IT WORK?

Web pages are created by a format known as hypertext – a concept and word invented by Ted Nelson, a computer scientist in the late 1960s who wanted to be able to look at a number of related documents while he was reading one. Twenty years later, hypertext was developed into a usable language and infrastructure by Tim Berners-Lee. Hypertext is a specialised kind of database system in which objects[9] (text, graphics, audio, video, programs) can be creatively linked together even though they have different formats through *hypertext links* or *hyperlinks*, which usually appear as highlighted or underlined (hypertext link). Hypertext is the organisation of information units into connected associations that a user can choose to make, and are particularly useful for organising and viewing large databases that consist of disparate types of information.

The actual Web page is a file that is written in HyperText Markup Language (HTML). This defines the structure and layout of a document by using a variety of tags or attributes that are basically a set of directions that tell Web browser software how to display and manage a Web page's text and images for the users – similar to music score which contains instructions that tell a musician how to play a particular song. These instructions (known as tags or markups) are embedded in the source document that creates the Web page or html file. Tags reference graphic images located in separate files and they instruct the browser to retrieve and display these images within the page. Tags can also tell a browser to connect a user to another file or World Wide Web address Uniform Resource Locator (URL) when the hyperlink is clicked. Markup languages are *not* programming languages, they are much simpler and describe the way information is displayed. Programming languages – such as C+ or Pascal – are more complex and deal with writing complex applications such as word processing and spreadsheet applications. Some useful websites have been set up to aid the novice or expert in writing HTML, such as www.pagetutor.com, the World Wide Web consortium (www.w3.org)[10] and the HTML Writers Guilds (www.hwg.org). HTML can embed applets or small programs that can be sent along with the Web page to the user, for example javascript applets which can perform interactive animations, calculations or other simple but specific tasks without having to send a user request back to the host.

HTML is a formal recommendation by the World Wide Web Consortium (W3C),[11] an industry consortium which seeks to promote universal standards and interoperability on the World Wide Web and is generally adhered to by the major browsers, such as Microsoft's Internet Explorer and Netscape's Navigator. However, both have also implemented some features differently and provide additional non-standard codes, which results in some Web pages not being viewable in certain browsers.

There have been some new developments in HTML, such as dynamic HTML which enables more animated and user interactive Web pages, for example changing text colours/fonts as a user passes a mouse over the text or allowing a user to 'drag and drop' an image to another place on the Web page. The biggest obstacle to the use of dynamic HTML is that many users may still be using older browsers, and so a website must create two versions of each site and serve the pages appropriate to each user's browser version, which can slow down user access to a Web page.

Other developments are Extensible Markup Language (XML), also formally recommended by W3C. Whereas HTML describes the content of a Web page in terms of how it is interacted with – for example, a new paragraph is indicated by the letter 'p' placed in mark up tags (<p>) – with XML it describes the content in terms of what the data describes, which would enable a program to identify and use the data in a way it wanted. For example, the word 'telno' placed within markup tags could indicate that the data that followed was a telephone number. This means that an XML file could be processed purely as data (in this case it would dial the telephone number). It can be stored with similar data, or like an HTML file, it can be displayed – depending on the application in the receiving computer. XML is 'extensible' because, unlike HTML, the markup symbols are unlimited and self-defining. It is expected that HTML and XML will be used together in many Web applications.

HTML has actually been reframed to incorporate XML creating XHTML, a particular application of XML for 'expressing' Web pages. Unlike HTML, but similar to XML, XHTML can be extended by anyone that uses it.

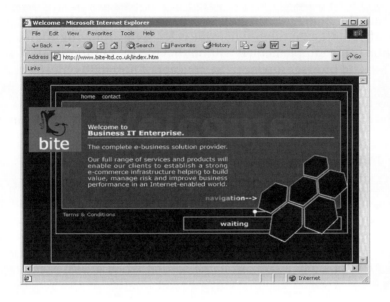

Figure 3.2a   An example of a Web page

Figure 3.2b   HTML code of the above Web page

This means that new tags or attributes can be defined to enable new applications to perform a whole range of functions, making possible new ways to embed content and programming in Web pages. The W3C maintains that this standard will provide 'extensibility and portability'.[12] This means that with extensibility new ideas for Web communication and presentation can be implemented without having to wait for the next version of HTML and browser support. The concept of portability means that with XHTML Web pages can be made simpler allowing access by small devices such as mobile and possibly household devices (such as fridges) that contain microprocessors with embedded programming and smaller memories.

STAGES IN THE CREATION OF A WEBSITE

The stages in the creation of a website are illustrated in Figure 3.3. Once a Web page is created in HTML (or similar) and is linked to other relevant Web pages, then the whole site is stored as a file on a Web server – a computer that delivers (serves up) Web pages. Every Web server has an IP address and possibly a domain name so that when a URL is entered in a browser (e.g. www.tassabehji.co.uk/index.html), this sends a request to the server whose domain name is *tassabehji.co.uk*. The server then fetches the HTML file named *index.html* and sends it back to the browser. Any computer can be turned into a Web server by installing server software and

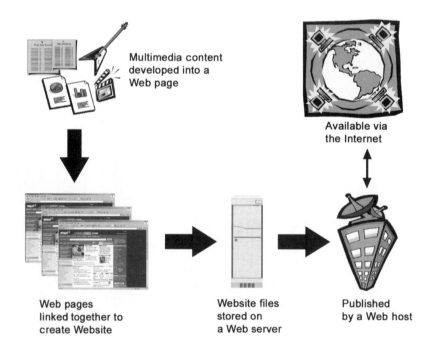

Multimedia content developed into a Web page

Available via the Internet

Web pages linked together to create Website

Website files stored on a Web server

Published by a Web host

Figure 3.3 Stages in the creation of a website

connecting the machine to the Internet. In this instance the Web browser is the client software and the server software runs on a Web host.

Web hosting is the housing, serving and maintaining of files for a website. Hosting businesses have been set up to offer a whole range of hosting services dependent on the size of the website, and the needs and budget of the organisation. The larger multinational corporations tend to have their own Web servers that are managed and maintained in-house; however this is expensive and beyond the resources of the majority of companies who have alternative options for outsourcing the provision of Web-hosting services. More important than the computer space that is provided for website files is the fast connection to the Internet. Most hosting services offer connections on faster and higher capacity T-carrier system lines (T1 or T3), which for an individual business hosting its own site would be too costly. Using a hosting service lets many companies share the cost of a fast Internet connection for serving files. The options include:

- *Virtual Hosting* – this is where a website is published on a 'virtual server', which allows the organisation to have its own domain name and set of e-mail addresses, but is in fact published on third-party Web servers provided by an outsourced hosting company providing file storage and directory setup facilities. This is suitable for small companies or individuals that do not have the resources to purchase and maintain their own Web server and connection to the Internet. The website owner and user of the virtual Web hosting need only to have a file transfer protocol program for exchanging files with the virtual host.
- *Dedicated Hosting* – this is the provision of a dedicated server machine that is rented to and used exclusively for the purposes of the single company by an outsourced third-party hosting company. Dedicated servers typically include a Web server, related software, connection to the Internet and housing, maintenance and service by the Web-hosting company. Typically, a dedicated server is rented on the basis of pre-agreed amount of memory, hard disk space and bandwidth (i.e. the number of gigabytes of data that can be delivered each month). This solution is usually needed for a medium- to larger-sized company that has a website (or set of related company sites) that may attract a considerable amount of traffic – for example, a site that might handle up to 35 million requests for Web pages a day. The server can usually be configured and operated remotely from the client company. The advantage of dedicated hosting for companies is that it removes the additional problems and cost of increased demand on the organisation's network infrastructure, Internet connections, security system and network administration.
- *Co-location* – this is where host providers allow a client company to purchase and install its own computer server at the host provider's

physical site. The company could also offer facilities management and other services. For example, a website owner could place the site's own computer servers on the premises of the Internet Service Provider (ISP). Or an ISP could place its network routers on the premises of the company offering switching services with other ISPs. Companies that specialise in website hosting sometimes provide co-location.

THE WORLD WIDE WEB IS *NOT* THE INTERNET

The World Wide Web is the universe of network accessible information, and the Internet is a public global network of networks. Although often incorrectly used interchangeably, the World Wide Web is the information and the Internet is a way of accessing that information.

Tim Berners-Lee, an Oxford University physics graduate, proposed a global hypertext project in 1989 while he was at CERN, the European Particle Physics Laboratory in Geneva, Switzerland. Based on his earlier work, this project, later to be known as the World Wide Web, was designed to allow people to work together by combining their knowledge in a Web of hypertext documents. Berners-Lee wrote the first World Wide Web server, 'httpd', and the first client, 'WorldWideWeb', a what-you-see-is-what-you-get (wysiwyg) hypertext browser/editor which ran in the NeXT-Step environment.[13] This work started in October 1990, and was made available on the Internet at large in the summer of 1991. His initial specifications of URLs, HTTP and HTML were increasingly developed and refined as Web technology spread to the wider community. In 1994, Berners-Lee founded the World Wide Web Consortium at the Massachusetts Institute of Technology (MIT). He has said:

> It's a very simple idea and the simplest ideas have the greatest effect – the universe of all information, all of mankind's knowledge as one abstract information space . . . I thought of a lot of things to call it but the thing I liked best was the World Wide Web. (Open University Programme on BBC)

It is interesting to note that one of the 'things' he considered calling his global hypertext system was 'Mine of Information' (MOI) but thought it might be 'un peu egoiste' (a little egotistical). He abandoned the name 'The Information Mine' (TIM) for the same reason, and didn't use 'Information Mesh' because he thought it sounded too much like 'mess'. Tim Berners-Lee has never profited directly by creating the World Wide Web, giving away his proprietary rights in the belief that the Web needed to be an open system if it was to grow and become universal. He was right.

As well as HTML (discussed in the previous section), which covers how Web pages are formatted and displayed, another standard that controls how the World Wide Web works is Hypertext Transfer Protocol (HTTP). HTTP is the set of rules for exchanging files (text, graphic images, sound, video and other multimedia files) on the World Wide Web.

HTTP is called a *stateless* protocol because each command is executed independently, without any knowledge of the commands that came before it. This is one of the chief drawbacks to the HTTP protocol since it is difficult to implement websites that react intelligently to user input without being able to know what command has gone before. However, programmers have developed a number of techniques and technologies to overcome this problem, for example cookies, JavaScript and ActiveX,[14] all of which provide some sort of interactivity within the HTML Web pages. Relative to the TCP/IP suite of protocols (the basis for information exchange on the Internet), HTTP is an application protocol, which defines how messages are formatted and transmitted, and what actions Web servers and browsers should take in response to various commands. A Web server machine contains an HTTP daemon,[15] a program that is designed to wait for HTTP requests and handle them when they arrive, in addition to the HTML and other files it can serve.

A Web browser is an application program with a graphical user interface that provides a way to look at and interact with all the information on the World Wide Web. Technically, a Web browser is a client program that uses the Hypertext Transfer Protocol (HTTP) to make requests of Web servers throughout the Internet on behalf of the browser user. When the browser user enters file requests by either 'opening' a Web file (typing in a URL or Web address), or clicking on a hypertext link, the browser builds an HTTP request and sends it to the IP address indicated by the URL using TCP/IP. The HTTP daemon in the destination server machine receives the request and, after any necessary processing, the requested file is returned. The first Web browser, called Mosaic, was launched in 1993. This was then developed into the first widely used browser, Netscape Navigator. Microsoft followed with its Microsoft Internet Explorer. These two browsers are the most dominant and widely used browsers; however, others such as Lynx and Opera are also well regarded, though not widely used.

HOW TO MAKE WEBSITES MORE EFFECTIVE

There are whole modules and volumes of books that concentrate their efforts on how to make websites more effective and attractive. This section looks very briefly at the concepts of Web design and highlights the major areas that should be concentrated upon to make a website work for the business.

In a study of the responsiveness to web-based service delivery, Voss[16] identified a set of metrics that could be used for assessing e-service quality, such as *security/trust; response time; response quality; navigability; download time; fulfilment; pp-to-date information; availability; site effectiveness and functionality.* These can be usefully extended to develop a set of basic website design rules:

- *Consistency* – in both design and navigation throughout the website. Menu buttons, logos, colour and design schemes should not only be consistent throughout the website but should also be consistent throughout the organisation's other promotions and marketing media. The website should reflect the image and the brand of the company. Site maps should also be clearly and consistently displayed to ensure users can see the overall map of the website.
- *Density* – Web pages should have less text but without compromising content and information quality. Text should be broken down into small chunks, allowing users to create their own sequences and the option to download more in-depth information if they require it. For example, multimedia video or audio files of interviews, messages, demonstrations or even marketing events such as fashion shows. Also small graphics files with large impact should be used to minimise download times rather than have high intensity graphics websites that take too long to download.
- *Content* – information put on a website should be valuable to visitors and should be kept up-to-date and constantly renewed to ensure the return of visitors for more. Information should answer visitors' queries and questions. FAQs (frequently asked questions) are a useful and easy way of providing visitors with information in a format and place that is easy to find and based on other visitors' information needs. This reduces customer service time and is useful in building up a database of issues or questions often raised by customers. This facility should also offer customers the opportunity to log new questions that have not been answered or raised – but this, as with the rest of the information on the website, needs to be updated regularly.

Links within the websites should be kept to a minimum and all should be tested regularly to make sure they work and they are not out of date or links to a changed website. In one instance a website link I recommended to students was to an e-commerce information site. Within months the domain name had expired and had been acquired by a pornography site.

Websites should also provide a means of building up dialogues with customers or visitors and so there should be some interactivity with customers – such as feedback forms that enable the customers to choose the reason for the feedback; on-line surveys covering specific topics (but these should not be obligatory to customers); discussion boards; an on-line forum such as chat facilities; contact details for e-mail queries; and a 'contact me' facility which enables the visitor to request that the company calls them at a convenient time. This can only be effective if there is the staff to carry out the request, otherwise it will prove detrimental to the organisation's reputation and lose rather than attract customers.

- *Accessibility* – websites should be accessible to everybody, including people with disabilities. The US 'Center for Applied Special Technology' (CAST) is an educational, not-for-profit organisation that uses technology to expand opportunities for all people, including those with disabilities. Websites can be passed through CAST's Bobby software or website (www.cast.org/bobby) to make sure that Web-page authors can identify and repair significant barriers to access by individuals with disabilities. For example, for those who are visually impaired, providing text equivalents for all images and multimedia, such as animations, audio and video, and ensuring colour combinations are legible.

  Translation facilities would also be useful – altavista.com enables users to type in a Web address which is then converted into a range of languages including English, Spanish, German, Chinese, Japanese, Italian, Portuguese, Russian and Korean. Powerful search engine technology within the site should be included to enable users to locate pages or relevant information they require easily within the site.

- *Three-click rule* – one of the rules of Web design that provides accessibility and ease of use as well as effectiveness is the *three-click rule*. This rule states that a well-designed website should allow the visitor to access the information they require within three clicks of the mouse.

Customers should have what they want when they want it and where they want it. We don't have a choice – the 24 hour society is inevitable. (Peter Simpson of First Direct)

USE OF WEBSITES BY CORPORATIONS

Earlier in the chapter, four main business functions of Web-based technology were identified: information dissemination, data capture, promotions and marketing, and transacting with stakeholders. This section will take each of these business functions and discuss how websites achieve these objectives.

Information dissemination

Organisations can publish information that is relevant to respective stakeholders such as shareholder/investor information, product specifications and details, privacy policies and corporate ethos. A particularly innovative and useful way of using the website is as part of its crisis management policy. Every organisation has the potential for some sort of problem to arise – whether as sellers of services or products, there is the possibility that something may be defective or harmful, or as public entities, where some disaster has struck. So organisations have two options when problems do arise and disasters strike – either they can cover up or they can go public and warn or inform stakeholders about the problem and how it can be overcome. In order to be prepared with a contingency plan, organisations need to create a 'dark or black' site that remains unpublished but readily available, covering any potential disaster/problem that might strike – anticipating the worst possible case scenario and providing details and information on how to deal with it.

CASE STUDY

Example of using dark sites

In October 1996, a 16–month-old baby died from an infection of e-coli bacteria after having drunk apple juice from a California-based juice company which was suspected of being the source. Within 12 hours, the management had set up a website with information on the incident, containing a statement by the management, a frequently asked questions page (FAQs) on e-coli bacteria, and links to the Food and Drug Administration, while a team of experts was on-line to calm frightened customers. Although another 66 cases of infection were registered, a survey afterwards showed that almost 90 per cent of customers were still willing to drink their apple juice in the future.[17]

Similarly with the Swiss Air crash in Halifax, Canada in 1998. Swiss Air had published a press release on the website within hours: they included important telephone numbers and a condolence page, and more information was released as it became available, including the radio contact between the tower and the pilots. Nearly four years later, the information is still available on the Swiss Air website and there is still updated information about the crash investigation as it progresses over the years.[18]

Data capture

There are a range of techniques and technologies that can be used in association with websites to collect information about customers in order to be able to profile them and develop marketing strategies. There are two main ways of capturing data, either as a result of *manual input* or *automated* programming or scripting.

Manual input comes from the visitors themselves through completion of on-line questionnaires, surveys, feedback forms or compulsory/voluntary registration forms. The quality of this data is potentially dubious as very few Internet users give correct personal details – even when compelled by some sites that send user passwords or usernames upon completion of the registration process. Many Internet users are setting up free e-mail accounts that they use specifically for this kind of registration process or for 'junk' e-mail. Even so, with registration this enables websites to identify 'unique' if anonymous users and thus attribute them with Web-usage characteristics.

Automated collection of data by using server *log files* and other means such as *cookies* can enable Web owners to track and profile users and visitors to the website in order to develop a whole range of marketing and business strategies.

Server log files   Web servers maintain log files listing every request made to the server. In its basic state this type of visitor profiling is known as *counting*, which works on the basis of Web-server file logs keeping track of users accessing its Web pages by saving the action into a log file. Some of the problems are that: special servers allow access to websites and save them in temporary memory or cache; and ISPs and other on-line services save copies of Web pages and images on specialised servers and provide data from their servers rather than where the website is hosted. In both cases, this improves performance for other users that access the same server. This means that potentially thousands of visitors might be accessing a website but this could appear as having been accessed by only one person.

Also, search engines send out automatic agents that go around the different websites and create indexes of websites. This would appear as a person accessing the website but in fact it has been a robot visiting the site. With the increasing number and intensity of search engines this could considerably inflate user access figures. Some of these problems can be overcome by using cookies (which enables Webmasters to log even more detailed information about how individual users are accessing a site: discussed below) and special software, which can detect the difference between proper users and robot agents.

One of the best ways to overcome these problems is *auditing*. Log files can be analysed by software tools that create reports with tables and charts indicating where users have come from (by IP addresses and domain names), which sites they have come from (by Web address stored in their browser's cache) and the kind of search engine, browser, operating system being used, how often they return and how they navigate through the site. This analytical software spots trends and patterns of users on the website and detects problems that users might be experiencing, such as difficulty in finding certain information, error pages and so on. However, problems with IP addresses could arise; for instance, one IP address does not necessarily identify a single user or visitor, but could represent many users. Similarly different IP addresses could represent a single user – for example, dynamic IP addresses are assigned to users by their ISPs every time they log onto the Internet through the ISP, giving the same user many IP addresses.

CASE STUDY

Example of analysis of server log data

Figure 3.4 shows an example of software that analyses data collected on server logs into data that is easily understood. The kind of information is seen on the left-hand side, and includes access statistics which illustrate the most popular pages and files, and the most popular days and times that the website is accessed. Other information includes technical information which gives details of error pages and miscellaneous errors, informing the website manager of any errors that might be occurring. The referrer information shows the most popular sites from whence visitors come. In one instance, the referrer information showed a large number of visitors to a company website selling kitchen units were found to be coming from a Star Wars fan's website. It emerged that the Star Wars website designer had erroneously entered the Web link pointing to the wrong website.

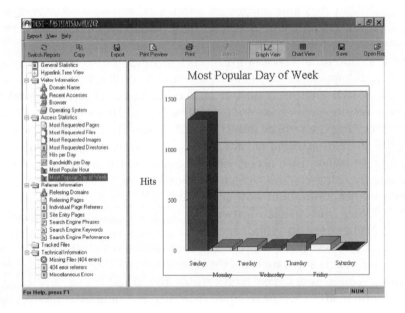

Figure 3.4 Faststatsanalyzer package analysing server log data

Rating agencies use specialist software, which is actually installed on the users' machine and monitors the activity of each user including website visits, on-line chats and other Internet services. Everything here is monitored on the user level rather than service level and this is useful for profiling and monitoring niche groups, rather than achieving a representative sample of users and gaining demographic information. This is similar to the software used that monitors TV ratings.

Cookies   As already mentioned, using HTTP means that each request for a Web page is independent of all other requests. Thus, the Web server has no memory of what pages it has sent to a user previously or anything about previous user visits. A cookie is a mechanism that allows the server to store its own information about a user on the user's own computer. A cookie is a small piece of information that is sent to a browser – along with an HTML page – when a website is accessed. The browser stores the cookie/message in a text file called *cookie.txt*. The cookie/message is then sent back to the server each time the browser requests a page from the server. Cookie data is stored in a series of 'name = value' pairs where cookie-producing common gateway interface (CGI) scripts[19] actually store information that will later be transferred when a user returns to the site. This information can be any number of things: items placed in a shopping cart, a username and password for a 'members only' website, a unique tracking number, the last time a user visited the site, the user's favourite site, and so on.

Example of cookies

Figure 3.5 shows a number of cookie files collected from a number of websites that were visited using a Web browser. The size of the cookie file is limited to 1KB and the format is a simple text (displayed using MS Windows 98 Operating System). Some of the file names state the name of the site visited (for example, guardianunlimited.co[1] and amazon[2]), others just give the IP address of the website (for example, 207.136.66[1]).

CASE STUDY

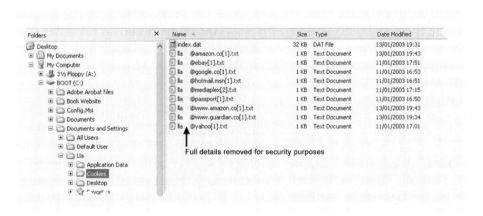

Figure 3.5   Cookie files

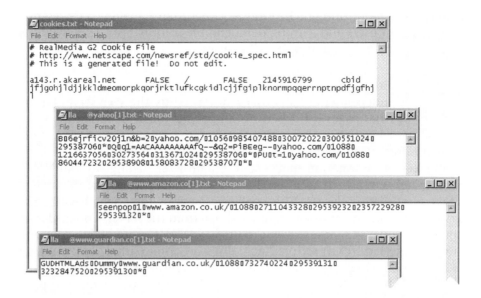

Figure 3.6 Content of cookie text file

Figure 3.6 shows the content of the cookie file – it is difficult to decipher exactly the content of the file, but the user is assigned a session ID which identifies them for the duration of their visit to the site; the IP address of the user is also taken and the date and time of the session and whether pop-ups have been 'seen'.

The main purpose of cookies is to identify users. They usually store information such as username and password of a specific site so that the user does not have to fill it in again the next time they visit the site. A cookie is generally associated with a specific domain and so no other site can request it. Some cookies have expiration dates so that when a cookie expires, the browser will simply erase it from the user's hard drive. A cookie that doesn't contain an expiration date will only last as long as a browser stays open. These are called 'session cookies'. When a browser is closed all session cookies disappear. Cookies can be disabled through the browser, but increasingly more websites will not allow the user access unless they accept cookies. Cookies are stored in different places according to the browsers used – for example, Internet Explorer stores each cookie as a separate file under a Windows subdirectory; Netscape stores them in a single cookies.txt file; while Opera stores them in a single cookies.dat file. These files can be deleted either manually by the user or by using some software such as 'Cookie Cutter' or 'Cookie Dog'.

Some of the commonly used data metrics for assessing the criteria of user profiles and visits to a website have been categorised by FAST (a body set up by advertising industry stakeholders to discuss and develop the on-line future of advertising).[20] They introduce three main measures that are logged in a log file by the site server with programs like Web Trends that can read the log, abstract meaning from it, and generate a report about site usage. These are activity, reach and frequency.

Activity   To track usage at a website, for example:

- *Visits* – a sequence of page views performed by a single visitor.
- *Page view* – the successful download of an HTML page. A page view differs from a hit by counting only the number of times a page has been accessed, whereas a hit counts the number of times that all the elements in a page, including graphics, have been accessed. Page views are increasingly complex metrics because of the increasingly complex Web pages that might include frames that divide pages into separate parts.
- *Ad view* – there can be multiple ad views per page views. View counting should consider that a small percentage of users choose to turn the graphics off (not display the images) in their browser.
- *Ad impression* – number of banner views on a certain Web page. The term 'impression' is sometimes used as a synonym for 'view', as in *ad view*. On-line publishers offer and their customers buy advertising measured in terms of ad views or impressions. Since a single Web page can contain multiple ads (depending on its design), a site usually registers more ad views per unit of time than Web pages per unit of time.
- *Ad click* – number of clicks on a banner for a certain Web page.
- *Click stream* – in Web advertising, a click stream is the sequence of clicks or pages requested as a visitor explores a website.

Reach   To identify the number of unique visitors to the website during a period of time, for example:

- *Hit* – a single file request in the access log of a Web server. A request for an HTML page with three graphic images will result in four hits in the log – one for the HTML text file and one for each of the graphic image files. While a hit is a meaningful measure of how much traffic a server handles, it can be a misleading indicator of how many pages are being looked at.
- *Visit* – a Web user with a unique address entering a website at some page for the first time during a pre-specified period of time. The number of visits is roughly equivalent to the number of different people who visit a site.

- *Visitor* – a unique visitor is someone with a unique address who is entering a website for the first time during a pre-specified period of time. Thus, a visitor that returns within the same day is not counted twice. A unique visitor count indicates the number of different people in the 'audience' during the time period, but not how much they used the site during the period.
- *User session* – someone with a unique address that enters or re-enters a website each day (or some other specified period). A user session is sometimes determined by counting only those users that have not re-entered the site within the past 20 minutes or a similar period. User session figures are sometimes used, somewhat incorrectly, to indicate 'visits' or 'visitors' per day. User sessions are a better indicator of total site activity than 'unique visitors' since they indicate frequency of use.

Frequency How often a visitor comes back and how much the visitors interact with the site. Frequency is often the result of dividing one of the metrics for activity level and total reach:

$$\text{Frequency} = \frac{\text{activity level}}{\text{total reach}}$$

These are particularly useful metrics since they provide some indication of trends and patterns of usage.

- *Click through rate* – in Web advertising, the click rate is the number of clicks on an advertisement, on an HTML page as a percentage of the number of times that the advertisement was downloaded with a page. Thus, the click rate on a particular page with an advertisement would be 10 per cent if one in ten people who downloaded the page clicked on the advertisement.
- *Average basket transaction order* – takes the value of the shopping carts and divides it by the total number of transactions.
- *Average clicks to order* – looks at the total number of clicks to order a product and divides it by the total number of orders.
- *Non-completion of transaction rate* – the total number of abandoned and non-completed transactions divided by the total number of transactions.

Different measurements taken can tell a different story. For example, one visitor can be equivalent to 5 visits, 20 page views and 75 hits, while one ad click can be equivalent to 1,000 ad impressions. It is therefore important to understand how the Web-server log files are being analysed and also the limitations of different metrics that might be used.

Promotions and marketing

There are a number of ways that websites can be used for promotions and marketing, including:

- *Banner advertising* – typically a banner is a rectangular advertisement placed on a website either above, below or on the sides of the host website's main content and is linked to the advertiser's own website. In the early days, banners were static adverts with text and graphic images, but with more dynamic technologies, banners can be multimedia audiovisual mini-productions. There are three main types of banner advertisements,

  - *Interstitial* (meaning *in between*) – an advertisement that appears in a separate browser window as a Web page is loading. Interstitials tend to contain large graphics, with multimedia presentations. These, however, can slow access to destination websites for some users.
  - *Hyperstitial* technology is an application that runs alongside a browser, allowing advertisers to present full-screen advertisements during the delay of web page downloads. As users wait for the content of a website to be displayed, or downloaded, hyperstitial 'ads' are displayed in a similar manner to television commercials. Viewers are subjected to the advertisements, which are more difficult to ignore than the common banner advertisement.
  - *Superstitial* advertisements are highly interactive, non-banner ads that can be any size on the computer screen and up to 100K in file size, featuring full animation, sound and graphics. They are pre-loaded and play only when a break in the user's surfing pattern is detected, such as a mouse click.

  There are two types of banner management agencies: banner exchange, which allows companies to exchange banners on each other's websites; and banner selling, where space is sold for banners to be published on very popular sites that are used many times daily for a certain period of time, for example www.ft.com. This provides an additional source of revenue for websites.

  However, Web users are increasingly getting more irritated with intrusive banner adverts and 'mouse trapping', where a number of pop-up advertisement boxes appear on the screen one after the other and, in some extreme cases, the user has to shut down the computer to close all the boxes. So banner advertising should be used with caution because it could potentially backfire on the advertiser and cause users not to return to the website.

- *Affiliate programmes* – this is similar to a reseller network. There are a number of ways in which this can be used. For the host that joins an affiliate programme, this can extend the range of goods or services that they are offering the customer, by adding third-party service products or information. For example, Amazon.com's affiliate programme has thousands of members who place a link to Amazon on their site. The benefits for Amazon are that it increases its brand awareness and its customer base with a minimum of marketing effort. The benefit for the affiliate is not only extending the range of goods or services, but also earning extra revenues since Amazon pays a fee when customers are re-directed from affiliate sites and a percentage of each sale that is achieved. A list of affiliate networks is available from www.refer-it.com.

- *Registration with directories and search engines* to ensure that the website can be found. Search engines will be discussed in more detail later in this chapter.
- *Opt-in e-mails and e-newsletters* where visitors themselves can register and elect to receive offers from the organisation and informative newsletters by e-mail.
- *Websites enable companies to cater for a mix of niche and mass markets* – companies can split up their marketing offensives into narrow target markets that correspond to zones or channels. So products or services can be customised for certain communities and presented in a way special to them. For example, if a company sold children's clothes and a large group of customers were fans of Teletubbies or Batman then a special area could be set up to provide information or goods that are relevant to them. Also with newspapers, each individual can customise the kind of information they wish to receive and where they wish to receive it – for example by e-mail or Web browser or mobile phone.
- *Traditional marketing strategies* still apply in promoting the website and encouraging visitors to visit and become customers. Issues such as raising awareness of the company, its products or services and publicising events are all important. The new technology enables more channels for marketing and promotion – for example, showing events live on-line. However, companies must be sure that they have the capacity in place to be able to cope and maintain the service they are providing – whether selling or promotions.

For example, Victoria's Secrets in February 1999 broadcast a fashion show of its lingerie live on the Internet, but they underestimated the number of visitors to the site and the server crashed – an estimated 250,000 copies of Realplayer (the video player) were downloaded per hour on the day of the event.

In 2002, there are still examples of this type of bad planning. In the UK, the results of the 1901 census were published and promoted on the BBC and in the British media. The result was that the technology was unable to cope with the demand, so the service was taken off-line and

An extract from the 1901 Census Website Message Page

Overwhelming public interest in the 1901 Census Online service resulted in sustained levels of hits which far exceeded design capacity during the first days of operations. Based on carefully benchmarked market research of similar genealogical sites, the site was actually specified to be able to cope with a sustained 1 million visitors a day, with a peak of 1.2 million averaged over 24 hours. Behind the 1901 Census website front end web-services is a very large searchable database and eCommerce elements which, given time and cost, could be scaled up to meet the exceptionally high levels of demand seen during the first days of operation. The PRO and QinetiQ are keen to enhance the site, but will not be able to increase capacity so dramatically as to cope with the levels of demand seen before. The investment required would be prohibitive and would result in unreasonable charges to the public for the paid services.

The following enhancements are being made to the Census Online:

- Increased ISP bandwidth
- Addtional firewalls within the ISP, both to protect the 1901 site and also to avoid impact on other sites hosted by the ISP
- Improved handling of traffic to divert overloads.
- Addtional database server to enable more concurrent searches

As a result of work and technical evaluation over the past week, it has become clear that further work needs to be undertaken to enable the site to function well under general internet access. In particular, a way of dealing with potentional overload is being devised, which has to be fully tested...

Even with these improvements, the site will not be able to service the levels of demand encountered on the first few days, and we ask users to continue to be patient.

PLEASE HELP

Once we are back on line, as happened during the first few days of operation, continual attempts to access the site by using the browser "refresh" button will only serve to compound the problems of site access and we would be grateful if you could avoid doing this.

Figure 3.7   UK 1901 Census website

Source: http://www.censushelpdesk.co.uk/ (accessed January 2002)

the message duplicated in Figure 3.7 was published explaining how the demand had exceeded their calculations based on census website traffic in other countries. (See www.tassabehji.co.uk for full details).

Transacting with stakeholders

One of the main uses of a website is for generating revenue through the direct selling of products and services. One of the major benefits of a website is that a whole range of products and services can be displayed on the Web and cross-selling strategies can be easily implemented to ensure that maximum value is obtained from a customer. Products and services can be cross-referenced in a way that when a customer buys one thing they are automatically presented with a range of other goods or services. For example, Amazon.co.uk produces a list of books by the same author and also indicates what other books customers had bought when they have bought the same book.

The reactive and dynamic nature of the Internet and websites means that businesses can react to competitive offers and pricing at the click of a mouse. Websites can be personalised to cater for each individual customer and so prices can be customised for every single customer. Different pricing schemes and mechanisms are discussed in more detail in Chapter 5.

Websites provide customer-service facilities through on-line queries, e-mail and FAQs, which if used properly can improve performance, products and services through feedback. However, regardless of whether on-line transactions include selling, delivering or customer services the process must work as promised otherwise all the positive forces of the Internet and the Web would then be working in opposition, to the detriment of the organisation.

Having identified the business objectives of a website and explained the technology, the remainder of this chapter will deal with the technologies that can be incorporated within a website or used as a stand alone measure to achieve similar objectives of information dissemination, data capture, promotions and marketing, and transacting with stakeholders.

HOW DOES E-MAIL WORK AND HOW CAN IT BEST BE USED?

Since the creation of the Internet, e-mail was and still is the most used application. E-mail messages are made up of binary data, a standard that enables any computer to read the text regardless of the operating system. Files can be attached to e-mails, including pictures, sound, video and executable (program) files. However, e-mails and attachments have to be encoded into a format that will enable it to be sent over the Internet using TCP/IP protocols. E-mail software automatically encodes messages being sent and un-encodes messages received and the majority of mail programs such as Pegasus Mail and Microsoft Outlook allow users to specify both an SMTP server and a POP server. This information can be obtained from the Internet Service Provider or the e-mail service provider.

SMTP (Simple Mail Transfer Protocol) is a TCP/IP protocol used for transferring e-mail messages between systems over the Internet and provides notification of incoming mail. SMTP is limited in its ability to queue messages at the receiving end, and so it is usually used with one of two other client/server protocols, which act as mail handlers, putting messages into server mailboxes. These protocols are Post Office Protocol 3 (POP3) or Internet Message Access Protocol (IMAP).

POP3 allows a workstation to retrieve e-mail from the mailbox on the server, and download it onto the user's local workstation. Once the mail is read and downloaded it is no longer maintained on the server. POP3 is built into the Netscape and Microsoft Internet Explorer browsers. POP can be thought of as a 'store-and-forward' service.

Alternatively, IMAP is used when e-mail is received and held in a mailbox on the server. IMAP allows the e-mail client to view and manipulate e-mail messages on the server remotely, for example, users can view the heading and sender of the e-mail and then decide whether to view the mail; folders can also be created and manipulated or messages deleted. IMAP requires continual access to the server (and thus the Internet) when the user is using e-mail. IMAP can be thought of as a remote file server.

Thus, an e-mail program typically uses SMTP for sending e-mail and either POP3 or IMAP for receiving messages that have been received in mailboxes on their local server.

BUSINESS USES OF E-MAIL

There are a number of ways in which e-mail can and is being used by e-mail:

- *Marketing and promotions* for example,

    - *Spam* is unsolicited e-mail on the Internet. From the recipient's point of view, it is a form of junk e-mail. From the sender's point of view it is a form of direct marketing, sending bulk mail to a list of e-mail addresses obtained either from Newsgroups or bought from companies providing e-mail distribution lists. Web hosts are very much against spam and will tend to immediately stop the mail services of clients who do use spam unless it is agreed beforehand. Although not yet illegal in Europe, it is considered unethical and against the etiquette of the Net.

CASE STUDY

The disadvantages of spam far outweigh the advantages and it is worthwhile considering the following proposition. If a company sends out 5 million e-mails and only 0.2 per cent (10,000) are interested, then directly reaching numbers of potential customers is much higher and cheaper than by any other traditional methods – so maybe some companies might consider the rewards outweigh the negatives. However, if 99.98 per cent of the recipients of spam are unhappy, that is 4.99 million potential customers who have been lost and the brand name tarnished. Furthermore, if only 5 per cent of the total recipients of spam sent an e-mail back complaining or requesting to be taken off the distribution list (as is their right under the Data Protection Act), then this is a total of 249,500 e-mails of complaint being received – which not only is bad for the organisation's reputation, but also receiving that volume of e-mail has the danger of increasing the likelihood of transmitting a virus, increased network traffic and capacity for the mail servers to handle, and increased administration necessary to deal with the e-mails.

    - *Opt-in mailing lists* are the solution for overcoming spam. Visitors should be given the option of receiving 'junk' e-mails or newsletters based on their having actively selected to do so. However, one common ploy is to have an option box at the bottom of a page, which usually indicates that unless action is taken by the visitor (i.e. a box is ticked) then junk mail will be sent. Also when e-mail is sent, there is always the option for the recipient to opt-out of the mailing list; for example, 'If you wish to cancel or subscribe to any of our other e-newsletters, please go to: http://website.com/unsubscribe'.

● *E-mail databases of customers* can be built up to send customers special product or service offers, or to encourage interaction with

TABLE 3.1 E-mail advantages and disadvantages

Advantages of e-mail	Disadvantages of e-mail
● Instantaneous and fast access, where at the click of a button, an e-mail is sent and often received within minutes ● Sound, video and graphics files can be sent	● The recipient controls their e-mail access and so might access their e-mail once a week, once a month or once a year ● E-mails may get 'lost' and never arrive at their destination ● It may take anything from minutes to days for e-mails to arrive ● E-mail is the most effective way of spreading viruses and malicious rumours ● A source of unsolicited junk mail and information overload
● Worldwide geographic reach ● Relatively easy and inexpensive to set up ● Inexpensive to use	● The recipient must have access to the Internet, e-mail software, and an e-mail address and software ● Computer hardware and software must be available ● E-mail must be connected to an Internet Service Provider (ISP) which provides access to the Internet
● Computer-to-computer delivery so that the e-mail is received directly by the addressee ● Reduced paperwork and increased automation of processes	● E-mail software must be compatible with the senders' in order to decode the files ● Dependent on the user's practices and the degree of integration of e-mail into business processes. For example, some managers allow their secretaries to access their e-mail and then print them
● Other services can be incorporated into this, e.g. fax to e-mail and e-mail to fax	● E-mail to fax is dependent on the technological set-up of the fax machines ● There is currently no legal or commercial support infrastructure for e-mail communications and document transfer ● In practice, e-mail is often used as a private form of communication by employees who may exchange disparaging comments about individuals or competitors. This can bring about legal action, as in the case of Norwich Union, who were ordered to pay nearly £500,000 in damages and costs after being found guilty of committing libel by e-mail for the first time in legal history. (see Chapter 7)

TABLE 3.1 *continued*

Advantages of e-mail	Disadvantages of e-mail
• Value-added facilities can be combined with the basic e-mail service, e.g. security, virus checking, conversion to/from fax	• Currently e-mail is untrustworthy because there are no security or authentication standards which allow the possibility of: *Repudiation* (denying that a message was sent or received) *No confidentiality* – anyone who has access to the user's e-mail box may read the message *No integrity checks* – the message received may have been intercepted, changed and forwarded without detection *No authentication* – where a user can masquerade as and send e-mail purporting to be another person without detection • Another increasing trend of e-mail usage is information warfare and sabotage. Whereas previously viruses were largely transferred through sharing unsafe software, now with e-mail and the Internet, transfer of viruses is becoming easier and more harmful. Viruses can propagate themselves, find information of interest and send it to a specified location via the Internet. One virus – Picture.exe – targeted America Online, where it stole user names and passwords and e-mailed them to an address in China. Similarly the Happy.exe virus hidden in an electronic greeting card copied e-mail logs from the user and mailed itself out with every new e-mail. Thus, the security needs of organisations using e-mail have to incorporate new and modified means of attack and threat.

customers to get updates or product information via e-mail, including attachments with software patches or Web addresses for downloads. But companies operating throughout Europe must comply with the European-wide Data Protection Act.

• *Market research* – this provides an extra channel for researching users by sending survey questionnaires by e-mail.

• *Communication* with stakeholders both within the organisation and outside the organisation. The Internet was created for the main purpose of sharing information and collaborating with geographically disparate partners. In a study by Professor Palme of Stockholm University in 1997, the benefits of e-mail to business were measured in practical terms of time and cost.[21] The report found that the average business letter takes 30 minutes to produce, while the average business telephone call lasts 20 minutes, ignoring unsuccessful attempts to reach the intended person. In comparison, the average e-mail takes just under 5 minutes to prepare and send and is much less costly.

Information sharing with stakeholders – e-mail allows partners to send electronic documents, graphics, audio and video files between each other with no financial or other limitations on the numbers of people to whom they are sent. E-mails arrive almost immediately and collaborative partners can work iteratively on a document and changes can be tracked and passed on.

There are a number of advantages and disadvantages of the use of e-mail and these are summarised in Table 3.1.

HOW DO SEARCH ENGINES WORK AND HOW CAN THEY BEST BE USED?

A search engine is a program that searches documents for specified keywords and returns a list of the documents where the keywords were found. Web pages have meta-tags that supply information about a Web page, which search engines retrieve and index. There are many types of meta-tag but the 'description' and 'keywords' tags are important for search engines. These two tags are used to summarise what the site is about (description) and what keywords are relevant to search queries. Most of the major search engines index meta-tags, although what weight they give them varies from engine to engine. Meta-tags are placed within the 'head' tags of a Web page and the following is taken from the BBC website:

> < meta name = "description" content = "BBCi offers a varied range of sites including news, sport, community, education, children's, and lifestyle sites, with TV programme support, radio on demand, and easy to use web search from the BBC."/> <meta name = "keywords" content = "BBC, BBCi, Search, British Broadcsting Corporation"/>

These tags are important because they offer a means of supplying search engines with relevant keywords if they do not appear elsewhere on a Web page. For example, if the website's home page contains a graphical link and no plain text, then meta-tags will be the only place where programs can find any meaningful text. Also, the meta-tag description is displayed as the description of the page in search-engine listings. Without the description meta-tag, the search engine will display the first few lines of text found on the Web page, which can often be inappropriate.

There are a number of different types of search engines and these can be categorised into three main groups: *web crawlers* or *spiders*; *directories*; and *meta-search engines*.

Web crawlers or spiders were first created in 1993 and are known as the World Wide Worm. Spiders are typically programmed to visit sites that have been submitted by their owners as new or updated. Entire sites or specific pages can be selectively visited, indexed and stored in a large database. Spiders are so called because they usually visit many sites in parallel at the same time, their 'legs' spanning a large area of the 'web'. Spiders can crawl through a site's pages in several ways. One way is to read all the pages and visit all the links within the site and to other sites until all the pages have been read. Another program, called an *indexer*, then reads these documents and creates an index based on the words contained in each document. Each search engine uses a proprietary algorithm to make sure that only meaningful results are returned for each *query*. Crawlers perform a very useful task but consume a large part of network bandwidth – they retrieve a document and then recursively retrieve all documents linked to that particular document. The robots crawl the Internet 24 hours a day and try to index as much information as possible. To keep information up-to-date it revisits links to verify if they are still up and running or have been removed. The spiders generally adhere to the rules of politeness for Web spiders that are specified in the Standard for Robot Exclusion (SRE). Some of the rules include the spider asking each Web server which files should be excluded from being indexed; not going through firewalls; and using a special algorithm for waiting between successive server requests so that it does not affect response time for human users. Some examples of a Web crawler search engine are Altavista, Excite and Lycos.

Directories or indexes contain a structured tree of information where information is organised into major subject and sub-topics. With directories, information is entered by the Webmaster or directory administrator who check submitted Web pages. Entries to directories can be made directly by the user and are increasingly charged but can be free. This, however, will not guarantee entry to the directory. Examples include yahoo.com and yell.co.uk.

Meta-Search Engines work with Web crawlers and directories to find information. Meta-search engines send out a request to search its own databases of information from Web crawlers and directories. For example, Ask Jeeves incorporates results from other search engines, limiting results to a maximum of 10, while Dogpile incorporates results from Looksmart and Goto search engines

As well as complete Web-based search engines, there are a number of different specialised search engines that perform specialised content searches and are programmed to be selective about the part of the Web that is crawled and indexed. There are also even more specialised search engines that only index and retrieve the content of their own site. Some of the major search engine companies license and sell their search engines for use on specialist individual sites.

As the Internet grows, sometimes the results yielded from a single request could be in the millions of returns, especially since keywords could yield very imprecise words. Search engines tend not to search image, sound, video or special format files and tend to concentrate on text.

However, this is changing with the introduction of international search engines, which are programmed to recognise different typescript characters.

BUSINESS USES OF SEARCH ENGINES

One of the most important and effective ways of locating a corporate website on the World Wide Web is by using a search engine. Users tend not to look beyond the top twenty links returned by a search engine and thus it is imperative for companies to optimise their position in the list of results yielded. However, useful as meta-tags are, they do not guarantee a company the much sought after top-ten listing of results yielded by the search engine query. This still depends on overall design of the website, choice of keywords and a range of other increasingly more sophisticated and costly techniques. Some tips recommended by submit-it.com,[22] which offers advice on submission to search engines, include the following:

- It is more difficult for search engines to detect sites that use Frames, Dynamic URLs, Flash, Image Maps and JavaScript for navigation.
- The keywords chosen to appear on Web pages determine how easy it is for target audiences to find the website using search engines. Those responsible for the website need to ask the question: 'When someone searches for a site like mine, what would they type into a search engine?' For example, if a website is about e-commerce then the word 'e-commerce' might be suitable as one of the strategic keywords. This actually yielded 3.29 million results using google.com in January 2002. However, if the website is about e-commerce in the UK then the keyword could be modified to 'uk e-commerce', which yielded 821,000 results also using google.com. This is an extreme example of a very popular keyword; however, the dramatic reduction of results that were yielded illustrates the importance of keywords in refining search results. Another example would be for a shoe retailer, instead of using a keyword of 'shoes', to use 'handmade leather shoes', which would be more targeted.
- The title tag should be 50–80 characters long including spaces; although different search engines accept different lengths, this is the median for all. It is also important to avoid listing all the keyword phrases in the title because search engines will blacklist the website and consider it as spam. Title tags like keywords should be enticing and each page in the site should have its own title tag and keywords.
- Web pages should consist of at least 200 words of copy (text) and, within this, the keywords and phrases. The layout should be logical and

should include additional copy-filled pages to the site, such as tutorials, how-to and FAQs, to increase the number of links to the site.

- Images should be linked with keywords or phrases by adding the 'alt' attribute to the image, for example: < IMG SRC = "myimage.gif" width = "10" height = "10" alt = "R. Tassabehji great e-commerce book" >
- Care should be taken to ensure that search engines do not regard the website as spam and so reject it. Some examples of this would include: not submitting identical pages of the website – Web pages should be called different file names and submitted separately; not making the colour of the text and background the same; not submitting the page more than once every 24 hours; and not using meta-tags that do not relate to keywords or Web page content.

Some companies have been set up to optimise company positions to websites and they use a number of these techniques – however, care should be taken. Submit-it list the lead times for a site to appear after it has been submitted (see Table 3.2)

Developments are being made in search engine technology to create more intelligent, autonomous agents (or programs) that travel between sites collecting information according to a set of criteria that have been pre-specified by the user. These 'knowbots' work with specific and easily changed criteria that conform to, or anticipate the needs of, the user or users. Its results are then organised for presentation, but not necessarily for searching. An example would be a 'newsbot' which visited major news-oriented websites each morning and provided a summary of stories (or links to them) for a personalised news page. Another example of an intelligent agent is to sort unwanted e-mail from a user's inbox to get rid of spam or junk mail. This kind of information delivery is known as push technology, where information is brought to the user rather than the user going

TABLE 3.2 Search-engine submission times

MSN	Up to 2 months
Google	Up to 4 weeks
AltaVista	Up to 1 week
Fast	Up to 2 weeks
Excite	Up to 6 weeks
Northern Light	Up to 4 weeks
AOL	Up to 2 months
HotBot	Up to 2 months
iWon	Up to 2 months

Source: How Long Does it Take to Get Listed?: http://www.submit-it.com/subopt.htm?tipq = 8 (accessed January 2002)

out to find it. Offering this type of service is one way in which value can be added to customers.

WHAT ARE SHOPPING CARTS AND WHAT ARE THEY USED FOR?

On a website that sells products or services on-line, the 'shopping cart' is the name given to the software that imitates the real-life shopping process, acting as an on-line shop's catalogue and ordering process. Typically, a shopping cart is the interface between a company's website and its back-end infrastructure, allowing consumers to select merchandise, review what they have selected, make necessary modifications or additions and purchase the merchandise. The processes involved in on-line shopping are illustrated in Figure 3.8. Typically, customers select any products or services they wish to order and then proceed to a page where the total order is placed and confirmed. The programming that provides a website with the ability to build a catalogue, and its associated database that provides users with the ability to shop, is shopping cart software. The elements necessary for this process include: a database full of product information; the Web interface to the applications, for example ordering system, inventory and payment processing, customisation/configuration tools; payment facilities

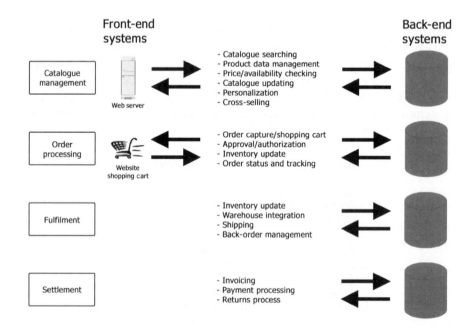

Figure 3.8   On-line shopping processes

supporting several payment models for different customers (such as credit card, cheque, postal order); search engines for customers to find what they want with one mouse click; electronic shopping basket for collecting products customers want to order; and the terms and conditions governing the site.

Shopping carts can be sold as independent pieces of software so that companies can integrate them into their own unique on-line solution, or they can be offered as a feature from a service that will create and host a company's e-commerce site:

- *Option 1: renting space in an e-hosting solution* – this is useful for smaller companies with limited technical and financial resources. This option allows them to rent an on-line shop from a third party ISP with the technology and skills infrastructure to operate the on-line shop for the company. The shop is administered through a Web front-end and no other software is required. Although it is difficult to integrate this with an existing order-fulfilment system, smaller companies will probably have lower sales volumes and therefore are less likely to have automated fulfilment systems, which is why it is suitable for smaller organisations. One example of this is Yahoo Store (see Figure 3.9).

Figure 3.9 Yahoo! Store (www.yahoo.com)

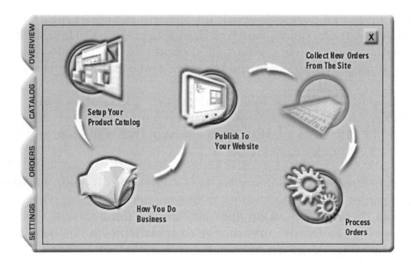

Figure 3.10 Actinic shopping cart software – overview of the process of setting up the shopping cart

- *Option 2: buying a ready-made solution* – this solution is more suitable for organisations with the technology and know-how to install and maintain it. It is relatively expensive because it involves integration with an existing IT infrastructure. In this case, however, companies have total control over their systems. But this software must be customisable, and

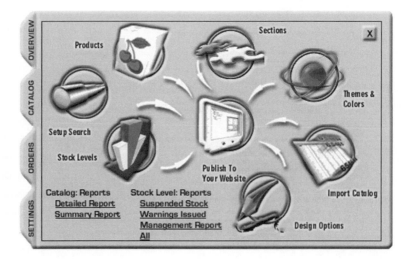

Figure 3.11 Actinic shopping cart software – the stages in building up the catalogue and inventory management of products or services, including the types of management and other reports, and the theme and colours of the website

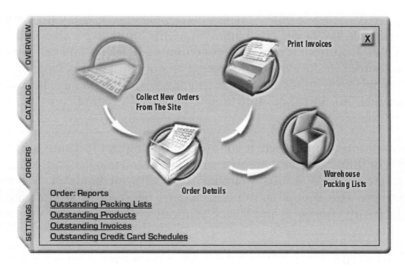

Figure 3.12 The shopping cart order process – includes documentation, inventory and account management, and invoicing

able to grow and expand. One example of this software is Actinic Shopping cart software, which is an extremely comprehensive package that automates the whole process, including building up a catalogue, publishing the website, and collecting and processing orders. The different stages are illustrated in Figures 3.10, 3.11, 3.12 and 3.13.

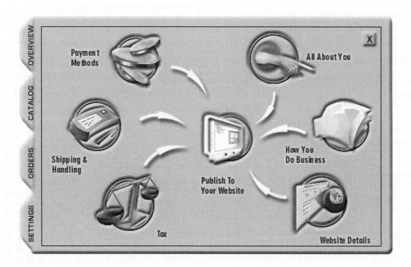

Figure 3.13 The different elements that must be considered to set up the whole shopping cart and accounts management systems (such as rates of tax, payment methods allowed and credit terms, shipping and handling terms, conditions and costs)

- *Option 3: a bespoke system tailored to corporate requirement* – this solution is suitable for larger companies. It is the most expensive and most complex solution. It involves programming language and can either be outsourced or developed in-house if the organisation is large enough. This system requires regular maintenance and upgrading and will be designed to integrate into the company's existing systems infrastructure.

A primary consideration when choosing shopping cart software is whether it will continue to serve a website's needs as its catalogue and volume of orders grow. There is also a similar issue with all kinds of Web-based application: the shopping solution has to be compatible and able to interface with enterprise and legacy applications.

WEB-BASED INTERACTIVE COMMUNICATION AND ITS USES

One of the main disadvantages of using Web-based technology, and an often-heard complaint from stakeholders, is that there is no longer a sense of the human contact with the organisation offering the goods or services. One of the ways in which this can be improved is enabling Web-based interactive communication technology by the organisation. This adds value to the customer-service offering, while at the same time minimising costs and enjoying all the other advantages that come with the Internet. Web-based interactive communication technology includes:

- *On-line 'chat'* – having live keyboard 'conversations' with other people. Text appears in real time on the participants' screens so each party can see the words as they are being typed. Internet Relay Chat (IRC) is one of the most popular methods of 'chatting' – it follows the client/server model, which means both client and server software are needed to use it. The IRC client (usually downloaded onto the user's computer) communicates with an IRC server (connected to the Internet), as illustrated in Figure 3.14.
      Although the term 'chat' seems to indicate a trivial use of this software, it can be used seriously for collaborative working. Additional functionality is available which enables instant file exchange; whiteboards/drawingboards, where drawing and design facilities can be used by 'chat' participants in real time; collaborative Web browsing; Internet telephony allowing international conference calling over the Internet; and sharing programs and other resources. These facilities are the basis for what the Internet was built for.
- *Videoconferencing* – the sending and receiving of audio and video signals in real time. Video cameras, microphones and special server hardware

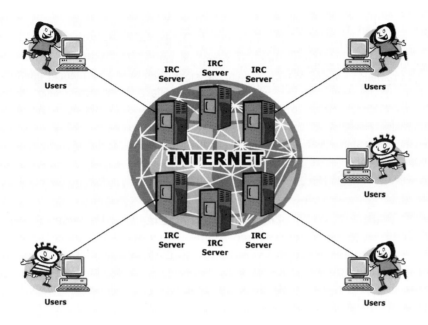

Figure 3.14 On-line chat process

and software are needed to host live videoconferences. Videoconferencing operates on the client/server principle where the client software from the sender converts video image to digital data, compresses it, encodes it and sends it through the server. The receiver client software then decodes the digital data and converts it back to video image.

Web conferencing

CASE STUDY

BASF (Germany) is one of the world leaders in the chemical industry, operating production facilities in 38 countries and employing around 93,000 people worldwide. Its product line includes high-value-added chemicals, plastics, colorants and pigments, dispersions, automotive and industrial coatings, crop-protection agents, fine chemicals, oil and gas. In 2001, sales reached 32.5 billion euros.

As well as the large number of employees across the world, BASF also maintains contact with customers in more than 170 nations. BASF runs a host of training programmes for its sales-force employees and customers throughout the world. BASF were looking for a way in which to make: employee training more effective; reduce the amount of travel required by employees; and expand customer training into a revenue generator. The solution was to use Web-conferencing software to deliver this training to both customers and employees. With only a telephone, Internet connection and Web-browser, all customers and employees could access the training sessions at any time and anywhere (where the equipment was available). BASF found that the interactivity offered by the Web-conferencing facilities made the training more effective because it could be broken down into more regular and smaller 'chunks', and employees no longer had to attend a couple of large training sessions each year which would often disrupt their and the organisation's work schedule. In one instance, BASF held an on-line conference for training experts and customers where they reviewed material, which normally takes a week, in a day and a half. This saved on travel, hotel and meeting-room costs, and staff were also able to continue their sales function without losing opportunities.

Source: BASF website (www.basf.com).

Video data is sent across the Internet using User Datagram Protocol (UDP), which is more resource-efficient for larger files. Like TCP, UDP uses the Internet Protocol to transfer a data unit (called a datagram) from one computer to another. Unlike TCP, however, UDP does not provide the service of dividing a message into packets and reassembling it at the other end. Specifically, UDP does not provide sequencing of the packets that the data arrives in as this would be too resource-intensive to do. This means the application program that uses UDP must be able to make sure that the entire message has arrived and is in the right order. Client software tries to cut down the amount of data being transferred by sending only part and not the entire image. For example, if one party only moves their head, then only the head movement is transmitted with the remaining background staying the same. Video-conferencing requires more bandwidth than text and audio files, and so sometimes there is a problem of quality and speed of the final image. This, however, will change as telecommunications capacity and quality improve.

- *Newsgroups or bulletin boards* – based on 'old' technology and similar to physical bulletin boards, where somebody can post a notice or message on the bulletin board and others can read it and respond. The electronic version of bulletin boards or newsgroups allows asynchronous meetings and discussions on the Internet where once posted messages can remain until they are deleted or archived by the administrator. This allows groups to stay in contact on a regular basis at their own pace. Graphics, text and multimedia files can be posted to newsgroups as attachments. Newsgroups can be moderated or unmoderated. In the former case, the moderator would initiate topics for discussion, and police messages to ensure they do not contravene any laws or regulations such as decency, libel and incitement. Topics are arranged in hierarchies and sub-categories where replies to particular topics are called 'threads'. Newsgroups can be public or private within an organisation or in association with a company's partners or customers where they are particularly useful in the exchange of information and opinions, which might impact on the business.

BUSINESS USES OF INTERACTIVE COMMUNICATION

One of the main uses of interactive communication is the ability to conduct virtual meetings with partners and colleagues. In this case, 'meetings' can be saved to files and so there is a permanent record of the actual proceedings without the problems of third-party interpretation or quality of note-taking. It is also highly cost effective and time efficient because travelling is eradicated, enabling people across the globe to interact effortlessly in real time.

However, because it is based on technology and the Internet, this could be intermittent and unreliable, which would negate the benefits of speed and efficiency. Also, from a physiological point of view, using nonvoice and sound 'chat' means that it is sometimes difficult to interpret text without hearing voice intonations and observing gestures. There are also issues of typing speeds, spelling and delays when 'conversing' textually in real time. The more people involved in the 'chat', the more difficult it is to coordinate, and so there is a need to have a moderator and a clear set of rules on the procedures of contributing.

Interactive communication enables direct contact with customers, which improves customer services by being able to deal with customer queries almost instantaneously.

This technology also allows customers to communicate with each other by providing a forum for discussion and the exchange of experiences and ideas. This could be potentially dangerous because it could be a channel for 'subversive' or 'bad' comments from disgruntled people. However, the benefits outweigh the disadvantages, because it is also a cost-effective opportunity to 'hear' what customers are saying, improve products and services accordingly, and add value in an increasingly competitive world. The most effective way of promoting a company on the Web is through positive word of mouth or viral marketing, and this is one way in which it can be achieved.

WHAT IS NETIQUETTE?

In order to use the Web as a tool for communication and information dissemination, it is crucial to understand that there is a host of 'unwritten' rules or recommendations made by the Responsible Use of the Network (RUN) Working Group of the IETF under RFC1855.[23] This underlines

Netiquette

:-) Laughing and Joking

:) Laughing and Joking for lazy people without noses

:-(Sad, unhappy or unsatisfied

;-) Winking smilie – you don't mean it

(-: Left handed smilie

:-* Kissing smilie . . .

CAPITALS (or UPPERCASE) – this is shouting and considered rude

Figure 3.15 Netiquette symbols

the need for using etiquette for Web-based communication – known as *netiquette*. The need for a sense of netiquette arises mostly when sending or distributing e-mail, posting on newsgroups or bulletin boards, or chatting. A set of typescript symbols representing tongue-in-cheek emotions have been developed to overcome some of the difficulties in determining hard to convey nuances of text. Some of these symbols are shown in Figure 3.15.

Netiquette covers not only rules to maintain civility in discussions, but also special guidelines unique to the electronic nature of forum messages. Netiquette advises users to use simple formats because complex formatting may not appear correctly for all readers. It makes recommendations on the use of mailing lists, moderator and administrator guidelines. In most cases, netiquette is enforced by fellow users who will vociferously object if rules of netiquette are broken; however, in some cases poor netiquette can lead to legal action.

CASE STUDY

In 1997 Dr Laurence Godfrey requested that Demon Internet, a UK Internet Service Provider (ISP), remove allegedly defamatory material containing damaging allegations of a personal nature, posted on a newsgroup (soc.culture.thai), which Demon hosted. He asked Demon to remove the message but the ISP refused. The message was copied to its servers around the world and many others containing newsgroup messages. Dr Godfrey received damages and costs amounting to £250,000 after settling the matter with Demon out-of-court in March 2000.[24] According to UK law, ISPs and Web hosts are not held to be publishers of defamatory material in such cases so long as they have proven they took reasonable care to ensure defamatory material was not published, and once alerted to a problem, took steps to resolve it.

'*Flaming*' is expressing a strongly held opinion, often resulting in a personal attack on another participant, which is insulting and bordering on the libellous. Usually this is seen on a newsgroup but it could be on a Web forum or even as e-mail with copies to a distribution list. Flaming is considered poor netiquette and could potentially lead to legal action. The legal issues are discussed in more detail in Chapter 7.

SUMMARY

In this chapter the main functions and objectives of a Web-based business were identified as information dissemination, communication, data capture, promotions and marketing, and transacting with stakeholders (customers, suppliers). These are similar in relevance and importance to traditional 'bricks and mortar' business, but the means of achieving them are dominated by technology. The major Web-based technologies that are being used include:

- *Websites* that incorporate other kinds of technologies such as banners for promotion, shopping carts to enable transactions, interactive communication to add value to the product and service offerings.
- *E-mail* to improve and facilitate communication and information dissemination and capture.
- *Search engines* for promoting corporate websites and improving the process of information dissemination and finding information.
- *Interactive communication* for enabling collaborative working with stakeholders and improved communication and service delivery to customers.

However, one of the most important issues that arises as a result of using and implementing Web-based technologies is that of compatibility with existing infrastructures. Increasingly all business is reliant on information as its lifeblood for growth and competitive advantage. Many techniques and applications have been introduced such as data mining, data warehousing, e-CRM and others to enable organisations to store, manipulate and transfer information across different business functions within and between organisations. In order to make this happen, it is crucial that compatibility between front-end Web-based technology and older databases, applications and legacy systems is achieved to optimise the benefits of Web-based business applications.

1 What are the major benefits of Web-based business applications?

2 Identify one organisation that you know and list a set of keywords and a phrase that you think would describe that organisation. Visit the organisation's website and note the meta-tags used for description and keywords (from the Web browser select View/Source). How do these compare to your keywords and description? What impact does this have on search-engine listings?

3 Discuss the impact of a website that does not work.

4 Compare the type of data an organisation can collect about its customers on-line and in the 'real' world. Discuss the difference and the impact this would have on the organisation.

5 How would an organisation be able to use the data collected through its Web-based business in other parts of its business. Discuss the impact this data would have on the different business processes and functions within the organisation.

REFERENCES

1 Short Message Service is a service for sending messages of up to 160 characters to mobile phones.

2 Wireless Application Protocol is a specification for a set of communication protocols to standardise the way that wireless devices, such as mobile telephones and radio transceivers, can be used for Internet access, including e-mail and the World Wide Web.

3

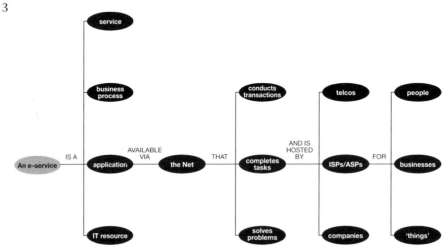

Source: http://www.hp.com/solutions1/e-services/understanding/index.html (accessed 10 October 2001)

4 C. Voss, 'Developing an e-service strategy', *Business Strategy Review 2000*, Volume 11, Issue 1, pp. 21–33.

5 J.R. Borck, 'Transforming e-business: E-services', InfoWorld, Framingham; 9 Oct 2000: http://proquest.umi.com/pqdweb?Did = 000000062486195&Fmt = 4&Deli = 1&Mtd = 1&Idx = 96&Sid = 5&RQT = 309

6 The ABCs of ERP compiled from reports by Christopher Koch, Derek Slater and E. Baatz: http://www.cio.com/research/erp/edit/122299_erp.html (accessed September 2001).

7 E-speak provides an open platform for building distributed, open systems for widespread, service-oriented brokering and delivery over the Internet. Based on open standards, it enables self-registration, advertising of service capabilities, security, protocol, and transport mechanisms, and brokering, management and monitoring. These allow one service to autonomously seek out and employ other services. The e-speak platform establishes a universal language with common vocabulary that is published along with company specific details of service offerings, such as cost and billing, input/output specifications and communication protocols to local repositories and other market-relevant e-speak engines on the Internet. E-services can then search, locate and negotiate with other e-services beyond the local core, regardless of underlying technology. The entire process is handled automatically and transparently to the end-user, who sees only the final outcome – namely, a wealth of new services that enrich the vendor's business offerings.

8 J.R. Borck, 'Transforming e-business: E-services', InfoWorld, Framingham, 9 Oct 2000: http://proquest.umi.com/pqdweb?Did = 000000062486195&Fmt = 4&Deli = 1&Mtd = 1&Idx = 96&Sid = 5&RQT = 309

9 An object is any item that can be individually selected and manipulated ranging from physical shapes and pictures that appear on a screen to less tangible entities such as software. Often used in object-oriented programming, to describe a self-contained entity that consists of both data and the functions that can be applied to data.

10 http://www.w3.org/pub/WWW/MarkUp/MarkUp.html

11 W3C is funded by industrial members, but is vendor-neutral and its products are freely available. The Consortium is international, jointly hosted by the MIT Laboratory for Computer Science in the USA and in Europe by INRIA, who provide both local support and performing core development. The W3C was initially established in collaboration with CERN, where the Web originated, and with support from US DARPA and the European Commission.

12 World Wide Web Consortium: http://www.w3.org/MarkUp/

13 T. Berners-Lee, Biography: http://www.w3.org/People/Berners-Lee/Longer.html

14 ActiveX controls are a set of rules for how applications should share information

15 A program that runs continuously and exists for the purpose of handling service requests. The daemon program forwards the requests to other programs (or processes) as appropriate. Each Web server has an HTTPD or Hypertext Transfer Protocol daemon that continually waits for requests to come in from Web clients and their users.

16 C. Voss, 'Developing an e-service strategy', *Business Strategy Review 2000*, Volume 11, Issue 1, pp. 21–33.

17 D. Amor, *The E-Business (R)evolution*, Hewlett Packard Professional Books, Prentice Hall, 2000.

18 D. Amor, *The E-Business (R)evolution*, Hewlett Packard Professional Books, Prentice Hall, 2000.

19 *Common Gateway Interface*, a specification for transferring information between a World Wide Web server and a CGI program or script. A CGI

program is any program designed to accept and return data that conforms to the CGI specification.

20 'Audit metrics and methodology – a recommendation to the FAST Audit Subcommittee 3/9/1999': http://www.fastinfo.org/pages/index.cgi/metrics (accessed January 2002).

21 P. Palme, 'E-mail cost benefit study': http://www.su.se/palme (first accessed September 1997).

22 http://www.submit-it.com/subopt.htm

23 Netiquette Guidelines RFC 1855: http://marketing.tenagra.com/rfc1855.html (accessed January 2002).

24 'Demon settles net libel case', BBC On-line, 30 March 2000: http://news.bbc.co.uk/hi/english/sci/tech/newsid_695000/695596.stm

Security and e-commerce

LEARNING OBJECTIVES

- To identify the kinds of breaches possible in e-commerce.
- To explain what security is and how to develop a security policy.
- To gain knowledge of the different kinds of security measures available.

INTRODUCTION

This chapter continues the 'technical' theme of the previous chapters in Part I of this book. Security is one of the biggest and highest-profile issues related to e-commerce since its ubiquitous adoption. Security impacts on all areas of a business and it is crucial that all managers and students of management – both technical and non-technical – understand its importance. This chapter will identify some of the security breaches that can occur and explain some of the strategic and technical measures that can be taken to minimise these breaches.

WHY IS SECURITY AN ISSUE?

Looking back to the early stages of the Internet's origins, the focus was on resilience, efficiency and robustness of message transfer, open systems and network infrastructure, rather than on data or information security. One of the original goals of the Internet project (ARPAnet) was to create a network that would continue to function by automatically rerouting network traffic, if major sections of the network failed or were destroyed. The

ARPAnet protocols (the rules of syntax that enable computers to communicate on a network) were originally designed for openness and flexibility,
not for security. The ARPA researchers needed to share information easily,
so everyone needed to be an unrestricted 'insider' on the network. ARPA-
net users comprised a small group of people who generally knew and
trusted each other. Although ARPAnet users at the time used to carry out
minor security breaches it was part of the spirit of the environment in
which they were working. The first real international security breach
occurred in 1986, when Cliff Stoll uncovered an international effort that
was using the network to connect to (military and government) computers
in the USA and copy information from theses sites. He published his
experiences in a book called *The Cuckoo's Egg*.[1] This was the first major
security incident that exposed the destructive vulnerabilities of the
Internet.

Thus, from the beginning, the Internet was designed to be robust
against denial-of-service attacks, but is fundamentally lacking in inherent
security. The exponential growth of the Internet (illustrated in Figure 4.1
by the growth in number of hosts, i.e. computers with IP addresses) and its
continuing trend means that the millions of entry points worldwide and
the tens of thousands of interconnected networks compound the problems
of securing the Internet infrastructure.

Not only this, but there have been similar rates of growth in the
number of users worldwide and the commercial use of the Internet,
resulting in an increased reliance on the Internet and more sophisticated
and complex uses for it. The projected value of e-commerce is estimated to
rise from US$657 billion in 2000 to US$6.7 trillion by 2004.[2] With this rate

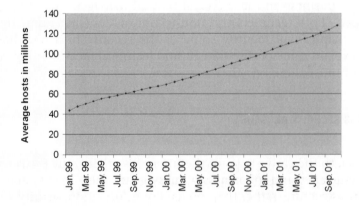

Figure 4.1 The size of the internet and the rate of its growth (1999–2001)

Source: 'Evaluating the Size of the Internet': http://www.netsizer.com

of growth and the increase in valuable transactions (whether data or financial), the Internet has become an attractive target for various people and organisations driven by any number of motives, such as:

- *Criminal activity* to gain money fraudulently by capturing payment/bank account details.
- *Industrial/political espionage* to gain access to sensitive and critical information.
- *Revenge* by aggrieved (ex-)employees or business partners to steal, reveal or destroy important information.
- *Sabotage* by teenage or other intruders as a challenge, curiosity or pure mischief to reveal, access or destroy unauthorised systems or information.
- *Vandalism* to incapacitate systems for any number of reasons – industrial/political or, again, just pure mischief.

Depending on the kind of security breach, the consequences could potentially lead to legal action taken by partners or customers for disclosing confidential or sensitive information, failure to finish contracts on time because of lack of resources or corrupt/stolen data, high costs to retrieve or re-create information or data, or other financial loss.

In the early days of consumer Internet e-commerce, there was a strong perception that the Internet was insecure largely because of the invisibility, speed, complexity, intangibility and lack of user authentication when using the Internet. This perception actually inhibited users from making financial transactions on-line. However, as users are becoming more familiar with the Internet, a larger proportion of users are making purchases on-line. A report by Ernst & Young[3] found that 75 per cent of UK Internet users had purchased on-line in 2000 and that even more (86 per cent) expected to purchase on-line in 2001, despite half of the users claiming they were concerned about credit card security.

So in order to address the issues such as fraud prevention, risk and the creation of trust, security is the responsibility of each organisation and each must take measures to reduce the security risks if e-commerce is to flourish.

WHAT KINDS OF SECURITY BREACHES ARE THERE?

As the Internet and its use for critical organisational tasks increases and as commerce, government and individuals grow increasingly dependent on networked systems, so there have been changes and increases in the number and sophistication of security breaches. It is very difficult to get accurate and exact figures on the numbers of network-related security breaches that have occurred since the inception of the Internet. Some of the organisations that have experienced breaches are either unaware that a breach has occurred, or are reluctant to publicise it – largely because of the potential damage it could do their organisation through destroyed trust or ruined reputation. However, the increasing trend of security incidents is keeping pace with the growth in the Internet.

Figure 4.2 charts the annual growth of the Internet and the corresponding growth of network-related security incidents reported to the CERT® Coordination Centre[4] in the USA. Because of the problems mentioned, the figures represent a small subset of the total number of incidents that actually occur, and are a representative of a trend rather than an exact measure of the increase in activity over time.

In the late 1980s and early 1990s, the typical intrusion was relatively simple, involving the exploitation of poor passwords, system configurations and known vulnerabilities to access systems. There was little need to be more sophisticated because these techniques were effective. For example, vendors deliver systems with default settings that many system administrators did not have the time, expertise or awareness to change. According to CERT®, over the years, there have been progressive changes in

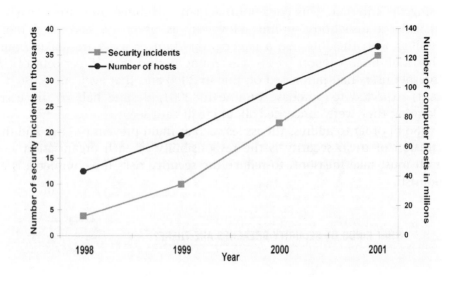

Figure 4.2 Rate of growth of network-related security breaches (1998–2001)

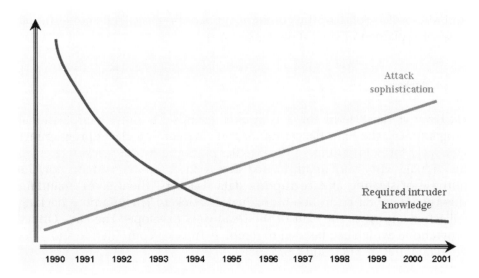

Figure 4.3 Relationship between attack sophistication and knowledge required by attackers

intruder techniques, increased amounts of damage, increased difficulty of detecting an attack and increased difficulty of catching the attackers. As both the number of Internet users grows and intruder tools become more sophisticated and easy to use, the kind of knowledge needed by potential intruders to execute attacks has fallen. One of the reasons is that the few intruders with the technical knowledge have developed new ways to exploit system vulnerabilities and have created software tools to automate attacks. This information and software is being disseminated and shared openly on the Web. This means that potentially more Internet users could perpetrate 'attacks' on the Internet with the minimum amount of expert knowledge – the relationship is shown graphically in Figure 4.3.

TYPES OF SECURITY BREACHES

Numerous types of security breaches can occur, ranging from social engineering – for example, manipulating key and legitimate people to reveal passwords or act in a way that unknowingly breaches security – to sophisticated automated systems attacks. The Systems Administration Network and Security (SANS) Institute[5] regularly publishes lists of the most critical Internet security vulnerabilities agreed by a panel of 'security experts'. They provide information on how to detect and protect against the vulnerabilities for different kinds of systems applications (such as UNIX and Microsoft). Some of the common types of breaches and the terminology are explained in the following sections.

Hackers

Hacker is a slang term for a computer enthusiast. Among professional programmers, the term hacker implies an amateur or a clever programmer who lacks formal training. In the popular press and media 'hacker' refers to individuals who gain unauthorised access to computer systems for the purpose of stealing and corrupting data. Hackers, themselves, maintain that the proper term for such individuals is cracker.[6] The infamous hacking collective known as the Cult of the Dead Cow developed the Back Orifice programme, which can be used to remotely hijack a computer, to show the vulnerabilities of Microsoft's products.

Crackers

Cracker was a term coined in the 1980s by hackers wanting to distinguish themselves from someone who breaks into a computer system (often on a network), bypasses passwords or licenses in computer programs, or in other ways intentionally breaches computer security. A cracker can be doing this for profit, maliciously, for some altruistic purpose or cause, or because the challenge is there. Some breaking-and-entering has been done ostensibly to point out weaknesses in a site's security system.

Phreaking

Phreaking is closely related to hacking, using a computer or other device to trick a telephone system. Typically, phreaking is used to make free calls or to have calls charged to a different account, which makes it more difficult to track down the perpetrator of a computer crime.

Physical infrastructure attacks

Physical infrastructure attacks involve attacks on the physical infrastructure of the network, for example cutting a fibre optic cable, destroying or stealing a server. The physical attack may involve individual corporate systems, which could potentially stop the organisation from functioning or the Internet infrastructure as a whole, which would affect a portion of the Internet but would not affect the whole of the infrastructure because traffic could be re-routed quickly (which was what the creators of the Internet originally intended).

Probing or scanning

Phobing or scanning is where usually an automated tool is used to attempt to find system vulnerabilities and exploit them to gain access or discover information about the system. This can be a prelude to some kind of attempt to alter or steal data or launch a more serious kind of attack, such as a denial-of-service attack. Increasingly home users are unknowing victims of scans that detect unprotected ports, allowing attackers to gain access to their data and even sometimes take control of the computer – this is usually motivated by curiosity and malice by the attacker.

Sniffer program

A *sniffer program* monitors and analyses network traffic or data. A network router reads every packet of data passed to it, determining whether it is intended for a destination within the router's own network, or whether it should be passed further along the Internet. A router with a sniffer, however, may be able to read the data in the packet as well as the source and destination addresses. Used legitimately, the program can detect bottlenecks and problems with the network. Used illegitimately it can capture data such as user names, passwords or other text being transmitted over a network, for example by eavesdropping on Telnet (port 23) or HTTPD[7] (port 80) traffic. This is often an easy process since passwords used to log on to Telnet sessions or transmitted over HTTPD are not always encrypted. FTP and e-mail, (POP and IMAP) protocols are also susceptible to this type of exploit.

Password attacks

Password attacks are the most common and successful kinds of attacks, because once attackers have the user's password, then they can legitimately access all the user's privileges. Every year thousands of computers are illegally accessed because of weak passwords. Users often make a hacker's task much easier by the poor password practices they use, for example:

- Writing down a password on a sticky note placed on or near the computer.
- Using a word found in a dictionary.

- Using a word from a dictionary followed by two numbers.
- Using the names of people, places, pets, or birth dates.
- Sharing a password with someone else – managers with secretaries and work colleagues are particularly guilty of this practice.
- Using the same password for more than one account, and for an extended period of time.
- Using the default password provided by the vendor.

Apart from social engineering tactics such as tricking somebody to reveal their password or even being able to physically see it, the most common types of password attacks are:

- *Brute-force attack or password guessing* – many users choose simple passwords (such as important dates, people's names) and rarely follow guidelines of selecting at least eight mixed alphanumeric characters because they are difficult to remember. Attackers usually use pro- grammed scripts (widely available free cracking programs) that run through a number of different words or names (based on a dictionary of several different languages and may include words from popular culture such as films, novels or sport) or the different combinations of date sequences. This technique is defeated for login to systems because of the system administration features that lock out users if they try too many invalid password (usually three attempts). Some systems admin- istrators make it even easier by not changing default passwords, or setting easily guessable root/administrator passwords ('password', 'administrator', 'love', 'wizard').
- *Password cracking* – this is a method used by attackers who already have a relatively high degree of access and can launch a brute-force diction- ary attack to find out encrypted passwords. Common words (found in dictionaries) are encrypted and compared to stored encrypted pass- words until a match is found, thus revealing the encrypted password. The success of this attack depends upon the application (i.e. the completeness of the dictionary of encrypted passwords) and the pro- cessor power of the machines being used to crack the passwords.

IP spoofing

IP spoofing, also known as source address spoofing, means finding an IP address of a trusted host (source computer) and then modifying the packet headers (which give the address of the data packets' destination) so that it appears the packets are coming from that trusted host.[8] This technique is used to gain unauthorised access to computers, making it easy for an attacker to modify source data or change the destination of information.

The technique is also effective in disguising an attacker's identity, preventing victims from identifying the culprits who breach their systems.

Denial-of-service (DoS) attacks

The goal of *denial-of-service attacks* is not to gain unauthorised access to machines or data, but to cause maximum disruption and cost by depriving legitimate users of a network service they would normally expect to have, for example e-mail, a Web server or network connectivity. A denial-of-service attack can also destroy programs and files in a computer system, but it mainly involves the sending of a large number of data packets to a destination causing excessive amounts of local and global network bandwidth to be consumed, thus denying users normal network-based services. A denial-of-service attack can come in many forms and exploit a number of different vulnerabilities in the Internet protocol infrastructure. Some more common attacks include:

- *Buffer Overflow Attacks* – this is when more data is sent to a network address than can be stored in its data buffer (temporary data storage area). The buffer overflow or excess data overflows into other buffers, corrupting or overwriting valid data already held in them. An additional fear is that the extra data may contain codes designed to trigger specific actions, for example damaging the user's files, changing data or disclosing confidential information. Buffer overflow attacks are usually as a result of system vulnerability because of poor programming practices or programmer error (not anticipating the size of the buffers needed). In July 2000, a vulnerability to buffer overflow attack was discovered in Microsoft Outlook and Outlook Express, making it possible for an attacker to execute any type of code they wanted, merely by the recipient downloading the mail message from the server. Microsoft has since created a patch to eliminate the vulnerability.
- *A distributed denial-of-service (DDoS)* attack is one in which a number of compromised systems attack a single target, flooding it with incoming messages forcing it to shut down. A hacker/cracker begins a DDoS attack by exploiting one computer system and making it the DDoS 'master'. The master system is used to identify and communicate with other systems that it can compromise. Widely available cracking tools are then loaded onto the compromised systems, which are all activated to simultaneously send messages to the specified target. The target is then overwhelmed with packets, causing a denial-of-service. While the press tends to focus on the target of DDoS attacks as the victim, in reality there are many victims in a DDoS attack, including the 'innocent' systems controlled by the intruder.

Despite the care, resources, and attention spent on securing against DoS attacks, Internet-connected systems will continue to face threats from DoS attacks because of two fundamental characteristics of the Internet. The first is that all computer networks (including the Internet) consist of finite and consumable resources, such as bandwidth, processing power and storage capacities – all of which are targeted by DoS attacks in some way. The second is that Internet security is highly interdependent on the different computer systems connected to it. Since DoS attacks are typically launched by compromising one or more systems connected to the Internet and unrelated to the attacker, no matter how well guarded and protected an individual network system is, its susceptibility to DoS attacks is dependent on the security of the remaining systems connected to the Internet. More details about the specific kinds of DoS attacks can be found at CERT® Co-ordination Centre website.

Viruses

Viruses are increasingly the most common and high-profile type of attack. A virus is a manmade program code usually disguised as something else, often designed to automatically spread to other computer users. Some viruses are harmless to the end user, for example the William Shakespeare virus that is activated on 23rd April and displays the message 'Happy Birthday, William!'. Other viruses can be very harmful, erasing or corrupting data, re-formatting hard drives, or flooding the network with high volumes of traffic, creating a denial-of-service attack. Some viruses inflict damage as soon as their code is executed by, for example, opening the attachment. Other viruses lie dormant until circumstances (for example, the passing of a time or date) cause their code to be executed by the computer. Viruses can be transmitted by downloading/accessing infected websites or transfer from a floppy disk or CD.

CASE STUDY

The '*I LOVE YOU*' Virus.

This virus initially came as an e-mail attachment (a VBScript .vbs program), with "I LOVE YOU" as the subject title, in May 2000. When opened the virus was executed, sending the same message to everyone in the recipient's Microsoft Outlook address book and deleting certain files, such as graphics (JPEG) and music (MP3), on the recipient's hard disk. It also reset some Windows settings and spread further through some chat programs. Because of the widespread corporate and home use of Microsoft Outlook, the virus spread rapidly affecting some 45 million users worldwide in a single day. In the UK it is estimated that 10 per cent of organisations were affected, including the House of Commons, British Telecommunications, Vodafone, Barclays Bank, Scottish Power and Ford UK, some of whom were forced to shut down their network to control the spread of the virus.[9]

The most effective transmission method is as an e-mail attachment because, not only does this spread the virus by e-mailing it out to other users, but it also circumvents the advice to beware of e-mails that come from unknown users, since the majority of viruses actually use the recipient's own address book to send the virus and so it seems to be coming from a familiar and trustworthy source. Most viruses can replicate themselves repeatedly. This quickly uses all available memory and brings the system to a halt. An even more dangerous type of virus is one capable of transmitting itself across networks and bypassing security systems.

Some people distinguish between general viruses and *worms*. A worm is a special type of virus that can replicate itself and use memory, but cannot attach itself to other programs. Generally, there are three main classes of viruses, the damage done by each depending on the code written within the virus:

- *File infectors* attach themselves to program files, usually .COM or .EXE files. Some can infect any program, which is executable so that when the program is loaded, the virus is also loaded. Other file infector viruses arrive as wholly contained programs or scripts sent as an e-mail attachment.
- *System or boot-record infectors* infect executable code found in certain system areas on floppy disks or on hard disks. When the operating system is reloaded (either from the floppy or hard disk) then the virus will be triggered off, making it impossible to use the hard drive.
- *Macro viruses* are among the most common types of virus, estimated to be around 75 per cent of all virus attacks.[10] Macro viruses embed a macro (a list of commands or actions) into a document, which is executed each time the document is opened. Once a machine is infected with a macro virus, it can embed itself in all future documents created with applications that support powerful macro languages, such as Microsoft Word and Excel. Computers become infected when users receive a particular e-mail and open a Word document attached to it. One of the first was the 'Melissa' virus in 1999, which was distributed by e-mail attachment (with the suffix list.doc) and subject header 'Important Message From . . .'. Once the document was launched a program was created which disabled a number of safeguards in Word 97 or 2000, and replicated the e-mail sending it to the first 50 people in each of the user's Microsoft Outlook address book. Figure 4.4 shows the screen of a computer which had contracted the Melissa virus, as

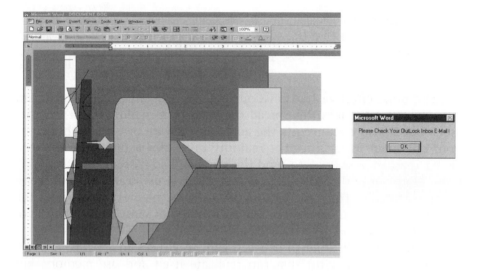

Figure 4.4 The screen of a computer with the Melissa virus[11]

Source: http://www.sophos.com/pressoffice/imggallery/virusimg/index2.html

duplicated by Sophos – a UK computer security company. While it did not destroy files or other resources, Web servers were overburdened with the huge volumes of replicated e-mails, disabling some corporate and other mail servers as in the case of Microsoft and Intel.

Empirical evidence from a number of security surveys[12] identifies some of the types of security breaches mentioned. Although there can be no agreement on the actual figures and percentages, the different surveys do actually show similar trends and patterns of security breaches. This gives a useful snapshot of the state of network security at a certain point in time (2001). The most common type of attack is from viruses, followed by hacking or unauthorised access to networks resulting in vandalism of websites and theft of equipment (mainly laptops). Denial-of-service attacks were less frequent than viruses, with financial fraud and theft of information being the lowest kind of security breach experienced. However, it should be noted that the latter two breaches would be hard to detect in the short term.

The majority of the perpetrators of the security breaches committed were external hackers, closely followed by disgruntled employees, with competitors and 'foreign' governments featuring in the minority. Again, with the difficulty of locating and identifying Internet criminals, this information should be used with caution and as a guideline only.

The breaches described are just a sample of the kinds of attacks that can occur. They all underline the fact that Internet security is a problem because security is not a design consideration but often an afterthought. The kinds of vulnerabilities that exist in hardware, software and the infrastructure of the Internet as a whole are many, so it is necessity for each organisation to take responsibility for its own system security.

WHAT IS SECURITY?

In this section, security will be discussed from the point of view of the organisation, and will relate specifically to electronic data and systems security. As has already been determined, security is the responsibility of each organisation. In order that security breaches are minimised, it must be seen as a total system that is relevant throughout every process and part of the organisation. This is often what many organisations miss, as a result of concentrating on security fire-fighting and technology, rather than developing a complete infrastructure and framework that pervades all parts and functions of the organisation.

The *Financial Times* Computer Security and Prevention Audit[13] outlines the areas for carrying out a security audit on an organisation's information system. The following section draws on the principles of the security audit. Figure 4.5 summarises the main areas that are involved in the security of an organisation and illustrates the processes necessary to develop, implement and maintain security within an organisation. Four main areas of a business are relevant and crucial to developing a security framework:

1 *Corporate policies* govern and control how the business runs and include areas such as management accounts (to show the financial performance of the organisation), audit and other committees. It should also include security policies and security audit practices detailing the kind of committees and responsibility of key personnel and the decision making powers they have.
2 *Business controls* deal with operational issues such as the amount of credit granted to specific customers, levels of stock before re-stocking is required. With regards to security this should include details of systems access and privileges, authentication and verification of users and disaster-recovery issues (defining what a disaster is and procedures to put in place when it happens).
3 *System controls* deal with automated or manual processes for collecting, manipulating and storing data, including systems applications. From a security point of view, this includes ensuring security policies and procedures are carried out and are kept up-to-date and compatible with other systems throughout the organisation.

4 *Infrastructure controls* deal with the actual computing and communications networks and include issues such as networks, operating systems, transaction processing and procedures for developing and maintaining these.

Most security focuses on the fourth and final infrastructure layer in the pyramid illustrated in Figure 4.5. However, no complete security infrastructure will be totally successful unless all the layers are included and begin from the top corporate policy downwards. Each of the layers is dependent on the layer above it and no layer can be dealt with in isolation. Security is about getting commitment from the top down and ensuring that key people throughout the organisation understand various security measures and that security systems are implemented only when they support business systems and objectives.

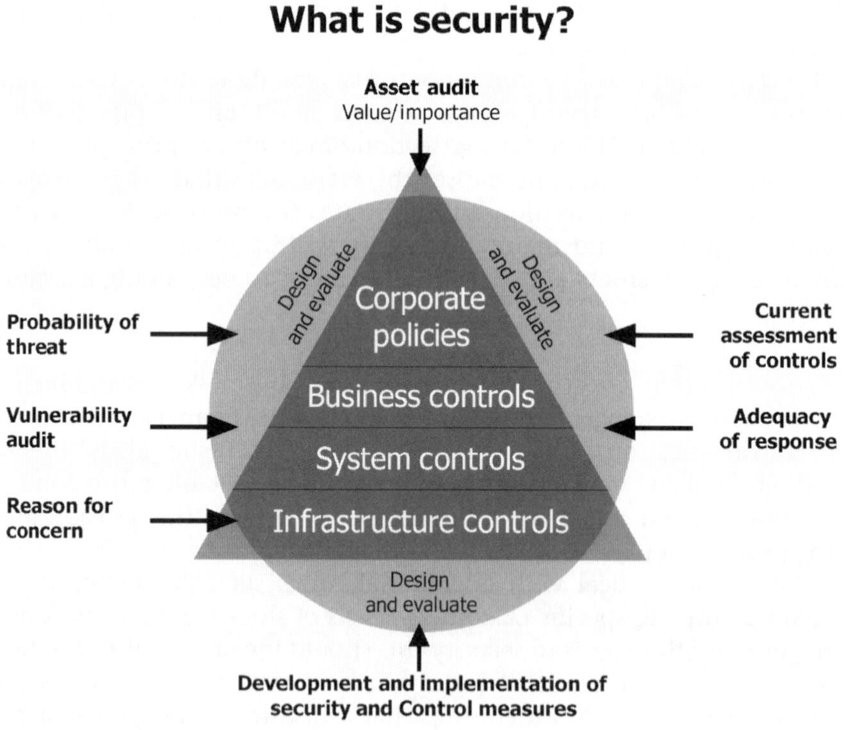

What is security?

Asset audit
Value/importance

Probability of threat

Design and evaluate

Corporate policies

Design and evaluate

Current assessment of controls

Vulnerability audit

Business controls

Adequacy of response

System controls

Reason for concern

Infrastructure controls

Design and evaluate

Development and implementation of security and Control measures

Figure 4.5   Major areas of security in organisations

In order to be able to design and evaluate the policies and controls throughout the organisation as they relate to security, an audit first must be carried out to identify the key areas of the organisation's business and technical infrastructure. This process can be organised into the following stages:

1 *Asset audit* – to determine what kind of assets the organisation has, including both physical and intangible assets, which might not show up on a balance sheet (such as information, brand name, innovative, flexible organisational culture). The value of each asset must be determined in both financial and non-financial terms and in terms of its importance to the organisation.

2 *Vulnerability audit* – to determine the vulnerability of each asset by looking at a number of features such as:

- *Identifying the source of threat* – the majority of security breaches are as a result of direct or indirect human interaction, and thus all parties and systems that have direct or indirect access to each of the assets must be identified, for example IT managers, members of staff, external consultants. The probability of each source of threat becoming a reality must also be assessed.

- *Ascertain the type of damage* that can occur to the asset – for example valuable information could be modified or stolen by individuals, or it could be destroyed by an attack or system failure, or it could inadvertently fall into the wrong hands (for example, costing sheets could erroneously be sent to customers or competitors). This analysis must include system and process controls within the business where potential breaches could occur and the impact of that breach. The probability of the threat becoming a reality must also be assessed.

- *Determining why there is a concern* for the asset to be protected from threat. For example, legislation – the latest Data Protection Act in the UK lays down regulations for ensuring that data collected by organisations is held securely and is protected against unauthorised disclosure, alteration or destruction; the costs of reproducing destroyed or stolen information; whether breaches in security will result in loss of trust, impact on reputation, fall in sales, breaching of insurance conditions or legal action because contracts could not be fulfilled on time or sensitive information was published.

3 *Current assessment of controls* – this would involve an analysis of the current systems controls. For example, do existing controls guard against the threats identified at the vulnerability analysis stage, and what systems would be affected and what would the impact of changing controls make on related systems?

4 *Adequacy of response* – this stage of the audit would be to assess the kind of response that is appropriate to each asset and its vulnerability.

Lindup and Reeve identify five broad categories into which different response measures taken can be classified.[14] These are:

a) *Preventive* – logical and physical access controls, which ensure undesirable events do not occur. Most controls are designed with this in mind (for example, access controls to buildings).

b) *Detective* – invoked once the threat has occurred to initiate corrective action procedures (for example, a smoke alarm).

c) *Damage limitation* – ensures that disaster recovery and contingency measures are in place once the threat has occurred. In the case of a denial of service attack, disconnecting a server from the network.

d) *Investigative* – records details of actions which enables a profile of the potential incident to be re-created to determine how and why it happened. For example, access logs for systems, journal entries in accounting, or black-box flight recorders in the aviation industry.

e) *Confirmatory* – confirm that the desired action has taken place or that an asset or person exists. For example, a confirmation that an e-mail has been received, or a signature when a registered packet has been received in the post.

5 *Development and implementation of security and control measures* – this stage is the final culmination of all the data collected from the previous stages. This stage involves the analysis of the different kinds of security and control measures that should be applied to each of the assets identified in stage one, and the vulnerabilities and implications of these to the organisation. There are five major areas where measures are needed, and these include physical measures, technical, personnel, procedures and documentation. Although these are not mutually exclusive and the areas do overlap, each of these measures will be discussed in more detail in the next section.

Thus, as we can see, security for the organisation is a whole infrastructure and a system which includes all aspects of an organisation, including its people, its policies, its business processes, its physical and network infrastructure. In order to minimise security breaches, the organisation must have many layers of security so that if one layer is breached then the next layer will stand up, and so on. The more layers, the more difficult it will be to breach ultimate security without detection.

WHAT SECURITY MEASURES ARE THERE?

The security measures identified in the previous section were divided into physical measures, technical measures, personnel, procedures and documentation. This section will deal with the commonly used, widespread and high profile measures used by organisations.

Physical measures

Physical measures are very much tangible and apparent and so are widely adopted by a large number of organisations. There are numerous physical security measures that can be implemented. Some of these include access controls in buildings, with authorised users gaining access via 'swipe cards'; electronic keypad codes; smart cards; even biometric devices such as face geometry, iris or fingerprint recognition. Other measures include bolting or chaining computing equipment to desks or floors; storing back-up tapes of corporate data in fireproof and bombproof safes; infra-red identification markers; intruder detection systems, such as CCTV cameras; and motion detection alarms.

Technical measures

Technical measures are the most common and widely used security measures, and the ones most organisations focus on are those related to system security.

Password Access Passwords are often the very first lines of defence in the protection of systems. As already discussed, passwords are open to attack for a variety of reasons, the majority of which are as a result of people. Bruce Schneier,[15] a leading security expert and inventor of a number of encryption algorithms, cites a study which found that 16 per cent of user passwords were three characters or less and 86 per cent were easily crackable. Passwords technically can only be secure if dictionary attacks are prevented. Long and strong passwords (i.e. a minimum of eight characters and a selection of upper and lower case and alphanumerics and symbols) can be secure because they would not be susceptible to dictionary attacks and a brute force attack would take a long time and a large amount of processing power, by which time the password should have changed. Thus the generation of long and strong passwords and the regular changing of passwords (every 30–60 days, not allowing previously created passwords to be re-assigned) should be automated. Unfortunately, people are not accustomed to remembering difficult passwords and the ever-increasing number of passwords required to work in today's world makes this problem worse. Many people have compensated for this problem by writing down their password and keeping that information in an unsecured area, for example stuck to a computer screen, which is an issue discussed later on in the chapter.

Other measures to protect password integrity are:

- Activating an automatic system lockout after 3–10 erroneous password attempts at logging in to systems or accounts.

- Disabling 'auto-complete' facilities in some software applications, such as Microsoft Explorer and even some 'cookies' that save passwords and account numbers to prevent keying these details in at every login.
- Schneier suggests non-computer manual interfaces, a distinction which very few systems designers make. A non-computer interface is one which requires the physical presence of an individual at the terminal, for example cash machines. The four-digit PIN could be easily cracked in less than a second, but an individual would have to stand at the cashpoint terminal to manually input all 10,000 possible PINs. Similar systems are in operation for electronic door locks, burglar alarms and others where there is also an inbuilt lockout system that is activated after more than three attempts. These systems work because the attack (as yet) cannot be automated. So although a weak four-digit PIN is secure with a manual interface, similar PIN-like passwords are totally insecure on systems with a computer interface such as Web systems.

Viruses   Viruses are the most common form of security attack. Technical measures that can be used to counteract them include:

- *Virus detection software* – more than 500 new viruses are discovered each month, although many more are released. Anti-virus software should be applied both locally and centrally, where the software is automatically activated to scan all data that either passes through the gateway servers of a network and/or locally at each individual terminal. This includes e-mail attachments, websites, downloads and other files and data from a storage and readable device such as floppy, CD-ROM, DVD, zip drive. Because of the proliferation of new viruses on a daily basis, virus software must be updated regularly (weekly, if not daily). Reputable software companies send e-mail alerts of new viruses and provide automated download facilities every time the virus data files are updated to accommodate new virus discoveries. There are also databases[16] of viruses that can be accessed to see the profile and threat of certain viruses if there is a suspected infiltration.
- *Configuring the e-mail gateway* to block file types such as VBS, SHS, EXE, SCR, CHM and BAT or file types with 'double extensions', such as .txt.vbs or .jpg.vbs, which are usually viruses attempting to disguise their executable nature. It is unlikely that organisations will ever need to receive files of these types from outside and so the best policy is to block them.
- *Disabling Windows scripting host*, which disables the running of VBS scripts (the usual language of viruses). Windows Scripting Host is automatically loaded on installation of Windows. Disabling it (Windows Scripting Host in Windows 98 and VBScript in Windows NT and

2000) prevents viruses such as VBS/LoveLet-A[17] being launched. Related to this is the disabling of applications (such as e-mail programs) from automatically executing JavaScript, Word macros or other kinds of executable code included in messages.

- *Change the CMOS boot up[18] sequence*, so that rather than booting from drive A, which is the default of most computers, automatically boot from drive C instead. This will stop all pure boot sector viruses from being launched if a floppy disk containing the virus is left in the drive.
- *Good practice measures by users* – for example, not opening unexpected e-mails with attachments, even from senders known to them; not down-loading/accepting files from unknown or dubious sources; using anti-virus software regularly; upgrading anti-virus software regularly; not forwarding virus alerts or 'chain letters' to other users.

Firewalls Firewalls are a very common technical measure used by organ-isations to protect their IT systems from unauthorised access. Bruce Schneier[19] explains the origins of the term firewall. In the past, train drivers shovelled coal into the engine of coal-powered trains, which produced highly flammable coal dust as a by-product. Occasionally the coal dust would catch fire, causing an engine fire that spread to the travellers in the passenger cars. In order to prevent the fire from spreading, iron walls were built and thus got the name firewall.

In the world of network security, a firewall performs a similar function. As a combination of hardware and software, it is located at a network gateway[20] server protecting the private network from unauthorised out-siders. A firewall works closely with a router,[21] examining each message or packet, and blocking those that do not meet the criteria specified in the firewall configuration. By installing measures which restrict and examine network traffic, this inevitably impacts on the widespread usage of fire-walled intranets. For instance, for mobile users, firewalls allow remote access into the private network only by using secure logon procedures and authentication certificates. Mobile users would not be able to log onto the network using an ISP because the IP address of the host (which is dynamic and changes with each login session) would not be pre-configured in the firewall records and so access would be denied.

There are different kinds of firewalls. *The network level firewall* is one of the most common, which functions like a packet filter system. This is where all network traffic is tested against a pre-defined set of rules, which either allows the data into the network or rejects it. One of the rules would be: only allow packets to pass that come from previously identified and configured domain names and IP addresses. The set-up of the network level firewall is illustrated in Figure 4.6.

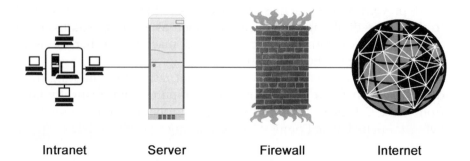

| Intranet | Server | Firewall | Internet |

Figure 4.6   Network-level firewall

An organisation with an intranet that allows access to the Internet uses a firewall to prevent outsiders from accessing its own private data and resources. It can also control internal access to external addresses and resources (such as sites that contravene decency laws, or public chat facilities). A firewall is often installed on a specially designated computer separate from the rest of the network, so that the intranet is protected from external dangers by ensuring all network traffic passes through the firewall first. Although firewalls are fairly effective, they are often difficult to configure correctly and it is these misconfigurations which lead to security vulnerabilities. Schneier underlines other weaknesses, for example the firewall does not modify packets, which means that once a packet gets through a firewall it can do what it wants, which is what happens with some e-mail viruses such as the I Love You bug. Network level firewalls are also susceptible to IP spoofing (disguising the true source of the packet) which Schneier compares to a guard trying to stop a flow of dangerous letters into a castle by looking at the envelope.

Another type of firewall is the *proxy* or *application level firewall*. This kind of firewall adds more layers of security; Schneier compares it to placing a guard inside the castle walls and another outside the walls. Neither guard knows anything about the environment of the other, but merely passes messages to the other. The configuration rules for allowing data to pass through each application firewall are specific to that application. Anything not conforming to that application's rules would be rejected. For example, a packet containing information from a website would be rejected by the e-mail or ftp server firewall. The proxy server acts as an intermediary between users and application servers; making requests on their behalf, it intercepts all messages entering and leaving the network. This then filters all the requests to and from the users, adding an extra layer of security and also hiding the true source (network address) of the user, as illustrated in Figure 4.7.

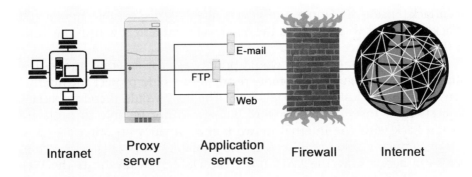

Figure 4.7 Application-level firewall

One of the problems is that application level firewalls are even more difficult and complex to configure correctly, and they also have a tendency to slow down the network even more than network layer firewalls. Schneier states that 'some of the best firewall professionals I know don't even bother with firewalls, they believe that a well-configured router with strong security at the end points is more secure than a firewall . . . Certainly firewalls have given the corporate walls a false sense of security.'[22]

A demilitarised zone (DMZ), coined from the setting up of a buffer zone as a result of the conflict between North and South Korea in the 1950s, describes the use of two firewalls to protect an area of the network, which consists of dispensable public services. Carrying on with Schneier's castle metaphor, he compares DMZ to the area of the castle between inner and outer castle walls. Inside the outer walls was an area for the stables, servants' quarters and other resources that were dispensable in the event of

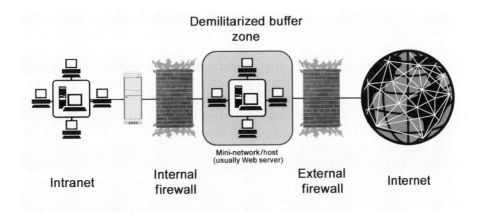

Figure 4.8 Firewalls creating a demilitarised zone

an attack. Inside the inner walls were the less dispensable nobility. If attacked, soldiers would defend the outer walls but retreat within the inner walls if their defence failed.

In the DMZ, one firewall would protect against external attack. The other firewall configured with more restrictions would protect the internal network. This is illustrated in Figure 4.8. The DMZ would therefore receive requests from the internal network but would not be able to initiate a session back with the internal network and provides no other access to private company resources. Users of the public network outside the company can access only the DMZ host. The DMZ typically hosts the Web server so that the corporate website can be accessed by the outside world but the rest of the network is separate and secure. In the event that an outside user penetrated the DMZ host's security, the Web pages might be corrupted but no other internal company information would be exposed.

OVERLOOKED OR MISUNDERSTOOD SECURITY MEASURES

Still continuing with the theme of technical security measures, one of the things that organisations often overlook is the security of their data or information. Information is the lifeblood of all organisations and one of its most valuable assets, especially in the increasingly paperless and net-worked economy. Often information is left unprotected behind layers of systems security already mentioned. The major foundations which con-stitute electronic data or information security include:

- *Confidentiality* – ensuring that information and data is accessible only to those authorised to access it.
- *Integrity* – ensuring that data is in its original format and unchanged whether it is stored or transmitted. If data has been tampered with, forged or altered in any way (whether accidentally or intentionally), then there are measures that can detect this and inform the recipient or owner of the data not to trust it.
- *Non-repudiation* – ensuring that when data is delivered to a recipient, that recipient cannot deny having received the data. Also ensuring that the sender of the data cannot deny having sent the data.
- *Authentication* – ensuring that entities (whether individuals, hardware or software) can be authenticated as being original and genuine, mak-ing sure the entities are who they claim they are or appear to be.
- *Trust* – ensuring the security infrastructure engenders trust, in both the technical and in the procedural measures that are being used.

The technical infrastructure that provides the functionality for data security is *Public Key Infrastructure (PKI)*. PKI incorporates four elements,

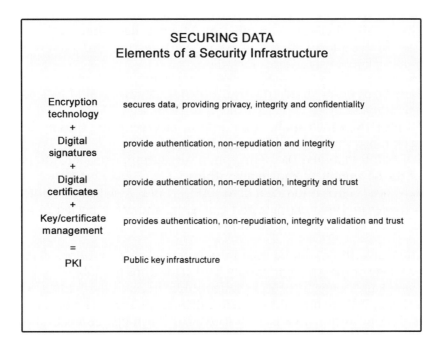

Figure 4.9   Elements of public key infrastructure (PKI)

each of which provides one or more data security functions (as summarised in Figure 4.9).

Encryption technology

Cryptography or encryption is the conversion of data into an illegible form (known as ciphertext) using a mathematical formula (known as an algorithm). Decryption is the conversion of ciphertext back into its original legible format. Encryption and decryption have been used since the beginning of human communication, including in times of war to keep messages secret from the enemy. The first known use of a modern cipher was by Julius Caesar for communicating secretly with his governors and officers. He created a system in which each character in his messages was replaced by a character three positions ahead of it in the Roman alphabet.

Since then, cryptography has developed into an extremely complex technology based on complicated mathematics. An explanation of the mathematics is beyond the scope of this book, but those interested should read *A History of Algorithms from the Pebble to the Microchip*,[23] which gives an interesting account of the development and usage of algorithms as a good starting point. There are a number of different algorithms with varying degrees of complexity that can be used to encrypt text. Some of the commonly known algorithms include:

- Data Encryption Standard (DES), which originated at IBM in 1977 and was adopted by the US Department of Defense.
- 'Triple DES', which applies three keys in succession and thus makes DES even more secure.
- IDEA (International Data Encryption Algorithm), considered to be one of the best publicly known algorithms.
- Advanced Encryption Standard (AES)[24] and Blowfish (invented by Schneier in 1993) are new and emerging, and are expected to replace the old DES and IDEA algorithms.

All these algorithms can be used in symmetric key encryption (explained below). One of the most commonly used algorithms for public key encryption (explained below) is the RSA algorithm invented by mathematicians Ron Rivest, Adi Shamir and Leonard Adleman in 1977. The RSA Laboratories website (http://www.rsasecurity.com/rsalabs/faq/sections.html) is an excellent source of further information.

In very simplistic terms the encryption software works by:

(a) *Generating unique user keys* – a key is a digital value. This is generated when the user's passphrase is converted into a unique value by the algorithm in the software. The length of this key (the number of bits in the digital value) determines how secure it is from attackers trying to crack the code. The longer it is, the more difficult it would be to crack.

The details of Figure 4.10 are generated from the estimates of a number of cryptography experts. They give an indication of the degree of difficulty in breaching the security of each of the respective

Key size (bits)	Number of alternative keys	Time required at one decryption per microsecond	Time required with specialised hardware
40	1.1×10^{12}	6.36 days	0.2 seconds
56	7.2×10^{16}	1,142 years	3.5 hours
128	3.4×10^{38}	5.4×10^{24} years	10^{18} years

Figure 4.10 Security of encryption key sizes

key sizes, even if the algorithm is known. These figures are a guideline and there are other factors, such as the type of algorithm being used, which impact on the speed at which they could potentially be cracked. For example, with a key size of 40 bits there are over a trillion different combinations (1.1×10^{12}) that the original key could be. If a cracker was trying to guess the original key size by using a brute force attack, working at one decryption (i.e. one key combination) per microsecond, it would take over six days to crack this code. However, using specialised hardware with the processing power equivalent of 20–100 computers, it would take about 0.2 seconds to crack. With a 128 bit key, there are even more potential combinations and even with specialised hardware it would take much longer to crack the code.

However, as the price of technology falls, processing power increases, 'cracking' information and tools become more widely available and crackers become more sophisticated, so the time it takes to crack keys will fall. This presupposes that encryption technology is standing still, which it is not. Algorithm creators are also becoming more sophisticated and developing more complex algorithms, which they usually publish with a cash prize for the first person that cracks the code. The reality is that there is a relative status quo between the crackers and the inventors.

(b) *Applying the unique user key* with the algorithm to convert the clear text or message into illegible ciphertext; the process is similar to decrypting the ciphertext back into legible text.

Both these processes are carried out by the software, with the user initiating the process with the click of a mouse.

There are two main types of encryption systems – *symmetric (or private) key encryption* and *asymmetric* or *public key encryption*.

Symmetric key encryption is where a single private key is generated and this is the sole key that is used both to encrypt and decrypt a message. One of the main disadvantages of symmetric key encryption is the problem of distributing the single private key to other parties in a secure manner. If the key is sent by e-mail then this compromises its security, so it must be exchanged in a very secure way, the most secure being face-to-face. Furthermore, this type of system relies on all users operating identical high standards of security to maintain the integrity and security of the single private key shared by all.

Asymmetric or public-key encryption is the foundation on which PKI is based. In this system (illustrated in Figure 4.11), two keys are generated – *one private key*, which is unique and private to the user and is used to decrypt a message, and *one public key*, which is also unique but is published in a public directory, is accessible to all and is used to encrypt a message.

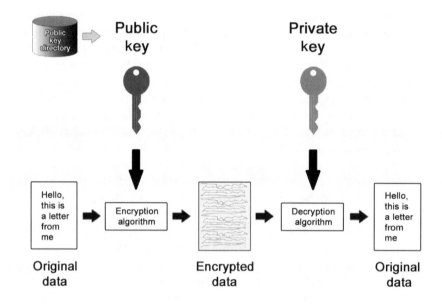

Figure 4.11 The process of public key encryption

For example, David wants to encrypt a message to Victoria. He first downloads Victoria's public key from a public key directory (similar in function to a public telephone directory). David then encrypts the message using Victoria's public key, which ensures that only Victoria will be able to decrypt it. Once Victoria receives the message, using her private key, which is unique to her, she then decrypts the message and can read it. If the message were accidentally sent to Alex, he would not be able to decrypt the message because it was only encrypted using Victoria's public key and not his. However, a single message can be encrypted for a group of people using each individual person's public key to encrypt the message.

So encryption technology provides privacy and confidentiality, where only the person for whom the message was encrypted can decrypt it, and a modicum of integrity, since encrypted messages if intercepted cannot be decrypted, so they cannot be changed.

Digital signatures

Digital signatures are electronic signatures that can be used to authenticate the identity of the originator of a message in a similar way that a handwritten signature authenticates the signer. By sending a message or receiving a message that is digitally signed, the sender or receiver cannot later deny having sent it because the digital signature is unique to each

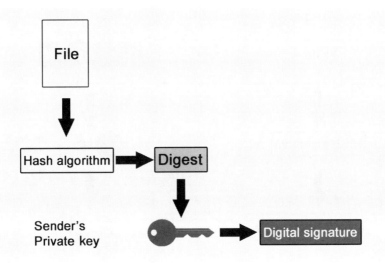

Figure 4.12   Components of a digital signature

individual user. A digital signature can be used with an encrypted message if confidentiality is needed or a clear text message as proof of identity and also integrity.

Again in very simple terms (illustrated in Figure 4.12), a digital signature is created by using special software which:

(a)   Converts the electronic message, file or data into a mathematical summary (hash or digest) using a special mathematical algorithm (hash algorithm).
(b)   This digest is then encrypted using the originator/sender's own private key.
(c)   This then creates an encrypted value, which is the digital signature. Each digital signature is different each time it is used on a different and new message.

To ensure that the digital signature is valid and that the message has not been altered from its original format, the signature undergoes a verifying process (illustrated in Figure 4.13). The verifying process carries out the following steps:

(a)   Using the same software, the recipient converts the received electronic message, file or data into a mathematical summary (hash or digest) using a special mathematical algorithm (hash algorithm).
(b)   Using the sender's public key, the message digest or summary is decrypted.
(c)   If both the digest created by the recipient matches the digest decrypted by the recipient match, then the signature is both genuine and the

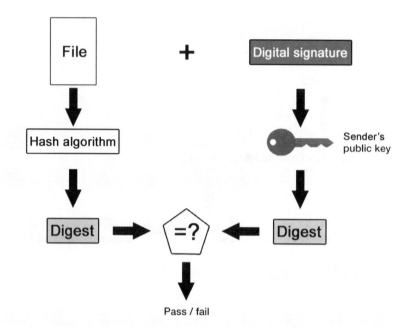

Figure 4.13 Verifying a digital signature

message is original and has not changed. If they do not match, then the recipient knows not to trust the message.

Digital certificates

Following from the procedures we have discussed so far, data can be encrypted and signed, with the recipient of the data being confident that it is confidential, in its original state and signed by the person or entity that has created the signature. However, one element of trust is missing – ensuring the entity or person is who they claim to be. This is where digital certificates come in.

A digital certificate is an electronic identification card that establishes a user's authenticity in the electronic world. It is issued by a certification authority (CA) or Trusted Third Party (TTP) after going through a series of validation procedures to verify that the entity is who they say they are. The digital certificate (conceptually similar to a credit card) contains information, such as name, e-mail address, a serial number, expiration dates, a copy of the certificate holder's public key and the digital signature of the certificate-issuing authority so that a recipient can verify that the certificate is real. Some digital certificates conform to a standard X.509, but this is not yet a widespread standard and so some certificates issued by some CAs may not be compatible with or readable by those running different software and issuing different forms of certificates. Digital certificates can be kept in public directories so that users can check the validity and authenticity of other parties' public keys.

Key/certificate management

This is the final and critical piece in the public key infrastructure. CAs or TTPs provide the element of trust on which the whole PKI system must be built (see Figure 4.14). A CA can have a number of different roles. These include:

- *Verification of users* – there are different levels of verification ranging from *insecure* (issuing a digital certificate based on an unverified e-mail address) to more *secure* (for organisations this could involve verification of a business address and business name by checking against Companies House registration details, letter-headed paper, written references from banks or trading partners, visiting the business address and meeting with the management, verification of employees by checking their staff identification cards, for non-business users, this could also involve using passports or personal identification cards to prove that

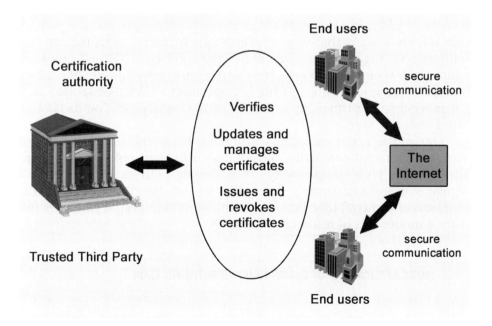

Figure 4.14 Certificate management and delivery system

individuals are who they claim they are). The process of verifying users in some cases is carried out by a registration authority (RA), which in turn passes this information to the CA.

- *Issuing key pairs and digital certificates* once the users and their details have been verified and validated. This provides the authentication by a trusted entity that the key and certificate are genuine and match the owner.
- *Managing and maintaining* the public key and digital certificate directory. The public keys and certificates must be made publicly available and accessible to ensure that encryption keys can be downloaded and certificates checked. Part of the process of managing and maintaining trust in the whole system is maintaining the integrity of the user information by keeping it up-to-date. If certificate holders' details change or if it is found that the details are wrong or expire, then certificates will be revoked (just like blacklisted credit cards) and so subsequent users of the public keys will know not to trust them.

CAs can be internal to and run by an organisation itself, in which case it would manage all the stages in the PKI itself and would also verify and manage the process for its partners to make sure they have a compatible infrastructure.

CAs can also be external to an organisation and independent of it. These are known as Trusted Third Parties (TTPs). In the UK TTPs are regulated by the Electronic Communications Act of 2000; this ensures that there is an additional element of trust in the external CAs, and the pattern that has emerged is that large organisations or public organisations are setting up CA organisations. One of the first and largest TTPs is Verisign,[25] which has a number of associates and partners worldwide, including British Telecommunications in the UK operating a CA called Ignite[26] and ChamberSign,[27] a partnership with the British Chambers of Commerce and Royal Mail.

One of the major problems with PKI is that there is not yet a single standard. Different companies have different PKI technologies and there are problems with compatibility when dealing with external and non-regular stakeholders. Until a standard is agreed upon there will remain problems of compatibility. But as a technological solution, it addresses the main requirements of information security.

SOME APPLICATIONS OF ENCRYPTION AND AUTHENTICATION

Encryption and authentication is also a solution to prevent IP spoofing, by securing transmission packets and establishing screening policies. Point-to-point encryption will prevent unauthorised users from reading the packets. Authentication can prove that a legitimate source, and not a spoofed middleman, sent the contents of the packet. In either case, any attempt to tamper with the packets would leave some telltale sign to warn system administrators.

There are numerous methods of securing transactions over the Internet, the majority of which are based on encryption and authentication. This section will cover a small selection of the more popular security measures. The majority of secured Web based e-commerce transactions are based on the principles of authentication and encryption. One of the most common security protocols used is SSL (secure sockets layer), developed by Netscape. SSL is included as part of both the Microsoft and Netscape browsers and most Web-server products. SSL uses the public-and-private key encryption system from RSA, which also includes the use of digital certificates which authenticate the Web servers. When a browser connects to a Web server using SSL, the server sends the browser its public key and certificate verifying the Web server is the one it claims to be, then data such as credit card or order details are encrypted and sent to the server by the client. By convention, Web addresses that require an SSL connection start with *https:* instead of *http:* and display a locked padlock icon in the bottom right of the Web page. The advantages of SSL are that it is relatively mature as a protocol, simple and widely used. The disadvantages are that only the Web server and not the client (user) are authenticated, and encryption of data is only from client to server across the Internet.

Another similar protocol is Secure Hypertext Transfer Protocol (S-HTTP), which is designed to transmit individual messages or files securely. It also allows the client (browser) to send a digital certificate authenticating the user but this feature is optional. AOL, Compuserve and IBM all support S-HTTP. Whereas SSL creates a secure connection between a client and a server, over which any amount of data can be sent securely, S-HTTP is designed to transmit individual messages securely. SSL and S-HTTP are seen as complementary rather than competing technologies. Both protocols have been approved by the Internet Engineering Task Force (IETF) as a standard.

MORE OVERLOOKED SECURITY MEASURES

Physical and technical security measures have already been discussed in detail. This section will look at other security measures and controls, which often are not dealt with fully – namely people, procedures and documentation.

People security measures

Surveys, reports and personal experience repeatedly show that many of the security breaches that occur are as a result of people. A survey by the UK Department of Trade and Industry[28] in March 2000 found that 40 per cent of companies reporting security breaches were due to operator or user error and over 30 per cent of organisations not recognising their business information was either sensitive or critical. A comment made to the author by a business manager also underlines the lack of awareness of general users about security issues: 'We are very trusting really – other than passwords we don't really use any other security measures internally.'

A security system is only as good as its weakest link – which in many cases are the people in the organisation. Thus people need to be made aware of the issues that surround security and how easy it is for breaches to occur because of poor general practice and lack of awareness. Organisations must embark on awareness raising education and training programmes to ensure all members in the organisation, from those in the lowest position to the highest, are aware of potential security breaches and how to avoid them. This would include dealing with issues such as passwords and the importance of keeping them confidential, changing them regularly and making them more difficult to guess. Other issues to be dealt with are virus awareness restricting the use of unauthorised or unchecked disks, using virus-checking software locally and being vigilant about attachments and deleting any e-mails from people they do not recognise.

Security policies and procedures

There is a necessity for developing and maintaining policies and procedures which must be followed by people, systems and apply to technology. The kind of information that must be included in a security policy is:

- *Access* – determining who has access to systems and files, who is allowed access, the nature of the access and who authorises access.
- *System maintenance* – who is responsible for carrying out the various maintenance tasks and the procedures. Some of the tasks of systems maintenance include making regular and several backups of corporate data, regular checks on security measures installed and how effective they are, upgrades and patches for hardware and software such as anti-virus, operating systems, server and other applications.
- *Content maintenance and upgrade* – who is responsible for content accessible on the intranet and Internet and how often it should be checked and updated.

- *Responsibility for complaints and requests* – this is a responsibility for both internal and public systems, determining who is responsible for complaints or requests, how they will be dealt with and by whom, and whether they comply with the organisation's overall policies for complaint handling.
- *System and software testing and evaluation* – procedures and responsibility for checking new systems or software, conducting pilots or laying down criteria for evaluating each of these.
- *Reaction to security breaches and incidents* – deciding what the procedures would be in the event of specific types of security breach, who would be responsible for carrying them out, measures for reporting them, and so on.
- *Updating the security policy* – how often and who would be responsible for updating the security policy and measures taken to ensure that the security policy and the data published in it is relevant to the changes in technology.

Documentation and security

As part of the complete security infrastructure it is necessary to have documentation laying down all the procedures and controls as a source of reference. To aid organisations with this process, an internationally recognised Information Security Management Standard ISO 17799[29] has been published (December 2000). This is based on the British Standard BS7799 (part 1) and is the only 'standard' devoted to Information Security Management in a field generally governed by 'guidelines' and 'best practice'. As such it is useful in providing a benchmark and standard against which an organisation can develop and manage its own information security and also be confident that other organisations complying to the same standards have similar systems in place. For some organisations in industries requiring a high degree of assurance, gaining ISO 17799 certification could become mandatory. For other organisations it is a useful brand-building and marketing tool. The main areas laid down by ISO17799 should and do duplicate the procedures and issues already mentioned earlier in this chapter and in particular in the security policy. Very briefly, ISO17799 covers areas such as:

- The necessity for a security policy document including ownership and review.
- The need to address organisational security as a management framework to identify the kinds of roles that are needed (for example, security officer) and the processes where responsibilities and access controls are determined.

- Asset classification and control, again dealing with issues such as responsibility and access to assets.
- Procedures to ensure personnel security, such as screening employees, training, access and responsibility.
- Physical security access and responsibility.
- Communications and operations management to ensure security is maintained, for example by segregating and rotating security-related roles to prevent the development of collaborations.
- Business continuity planning testing and ensuring that systems can still function in the event of an interruption.
- Checks to ensure compliance with legal regulations (software copying or protection of data), contractual obligations or other security procedures such as upgrades.

These are just a few of the major areas that are set out in the ISO standard; for organisations interested in establishing a completed framework for information security, ISO17799 is a must.

SUMMARY

One of the highest barriers to e-commerce and one that is least addressed as an organisation-wide issue is security. Referring to a number of reports based on empirical data, and examining the kinds of network security breaches that are possible (the most frequent of which are virus attacks), security breaches are on the rise. This is compounded by the fact that the Internet infrastructure has many fundamental security design problems that cannot be addressed quickly. Software producers continue to release software with a range of vulnerabilities, including vulnerabilities that are well known (for example, buffer overflows in denial-of-service attacks). The complexity of protocols and applications attached to the Internet is increasing, as is the reliance upon it, the number of users and the readily available information and tools for a non-expert but enthusiastic user to initiate an attack.

This chapter has focused on security in organisations as a complete system. Using an audit-type framework, it underlines the concept that security is a holistic system interrelated with a whole range of business processes and entities and cannot be taken in isolation. The main areas of security are identified as being physical, technical, human, procedures, processes and documentation. It is almost impossible to eradicate security breaches, mainly because the majority of them are as a result of human malice, error or lack of awareness. All that organisations can do is minimise security breaches. This can be done by introducing different layers of security in an organisation to ensure that, once all the measures are in place, if one layer is breached then the next layer will stand up and so on, until either the impact of the breach is at best detected and disarmed or at worst causes minimum damage.

DISCUSSION QUESTIONS

1 Why is the Internet increasingly susceptible to more security breaches?

2 What are the different ways of protecting an organisation from attack?

3 'We had all the recent viruses, but we do have a Firewall so they were all caught before they caused any problems' (a quotation from a business manager). Is this statement true of false? Why?

4 Develop a security-awareness training session for a group of employees from the accounts and marketing departments.

REFERENCES

1 C. Stoll, *The Cuckoo's Egg: Tracking a Spy through the Maze of Computer Espionage*, Doubleday, New York, 1989.

2 Forrester Research Report: http://glreach.com/eng/ed/art/ 2004.ecommerce.html (accessed December 2001).

3 Global online retailing, January 2001, Ernst & Young: http://www.ey.com/ global/gcr.nsf/UK/Consumer_Products_-_Press_Release_-_Global_Online_ Retailing_Survey_2000–01 (accessed December 2001).

4 http://www.cert.org/meet_cert/meetcertcc.html

5 The SANS (System Administration, Networking, and Security) Institute: http:// www.sans.org/newlook/home.php

6 E.S. Raymond, *The New Hacker's Dictionary*, 2nd edn, MIT, 1993.

7 HTTPD is the protocol that manages the behaviour of the ports and buffers used by Web servers for Internet access.

8 IP spoofing definition: http://www.webopedia.com/TERM/I/IP_spoofing.html

9 'Love bug bites UK', BBC online: http://news.bbc.co.uk/hi/english/uk/newsid_ 736000/736080.stm

10 Macro-virus definition: http://www.webopedia.com/TERM/m/macro_virus. html

11 wm97/Melissa AG and wm97/Melissa-V Source: www.Sophos.co.uk

12 Information Security Magazine, Industry Survey October 2001, p. 34: http:// www.infosecuritymag.com/articles/october01/images/survey.pdf; Computer Security Institute 2001, CSI/FBI Computer Crime & Security Survey, Vol. VII, No. I, Spring Issue: www.gocsi.com/pdfs/fbi/FBIsurvey.pdf; CBI Cybercrime Survey 2001: Making the information superhighway safe for business: www.cbi.org.uk

13 K. Lindup and L. Reeve, *The computer security and fraud prevention audit: an in-depth security check on your computer systems and the information they hold*, Pearson Education Ltd, 2000, SRI edition.

14 K. Lindup and L. Reeve, *The computer security and fraud prevention audit: an in-depth security check on your computer systems and the information they hold*, Pearson Education Ltd, 2000, SRI edition.

15 B. Schneier, *Secrets & Lies – Digital security in a networked world*, John Wiley & Sons, 2000.

16 These databases are usually provided by the software vendors, or alternatively by organisations such as Central Command – AntiViral Toolkit Pro Virus Encyclopedia: http://www.avpve.com/

17 http://www.sophos.co.uk/virusinfo

18 The sequence which initiates a series of checks once a computer is first switched on.

19 B. Schneier, *Secrets & Lies – Digital security in a networked world*, John Wiley & Sons, 2000.

20 A gateway is a network point that acts as an entrance to another network.

21 A router is a device or software that determines the next network point to which a packet of data should be forwarded en route to its final destination.

22 B. Schneier, *Secrets & Lies – Digital security in a networked world*, John Wiley & Sons, 2000, p. 192.

23 J. Chabert, *A History of Algorithms from the Pebble to the Microchip*, trans. Chris Weeks, Springer, 1999.

24 For more information on AES and a range of others, a good starting point is the RSA security web site.

25 www.verisign.com

26 www.ignite.com

27 http://www.chambersign.co.uk/

28 Information Security Survey 2000, Department of Trade and Industry: www.dti.gov.uk (accessed December 2000).

29 www.iso.ch

Business and e-commerce

E-business models

- To define business models for electronic commerce.
- To identify the different kinds of e-business models that have emerged.
- To understand the different frameworks for analysing Internet business models and their respective characteristics.

INTRODUCTION

This chapter will look at business models in the context of e-commerce. It will explore what business models are and the different kinds of business models that have emerged in the e-commerce environment. Different methods of classifying business models will then be identified and the benefits of each method will be discussed.

WHAT IS A BUSINESS MODEL?

Business models are one of the most discussed, most hyped and least understood aspects of the World Wide Web. The perception is that a business model is a concept arising out of e-commerce and the Internet era. This, however, is not the case – the concept of a business model is as old as business itself. It is a method of doing business whereby an organisation can sustain itself in the short term, and develop and grow in the medium to longer term. A well-planned and successful business model will, in the longer term, give the business a competitive advantage in its industry, enabling it to earn more profits than its competitors.

Research into Internet-based business models is still in its infancy. However, some academics, such as Affuah and Tucci[1] and Mahadevan,[2] have suggested a framework where a business model can be divided into three major areas that impact on the sustainability and growth of an e-business. These are the revenue stream, the value stream and the logistical stream. None of these operate in isolation but each area interacts with and impacts on the others, as can be seen in Figure 5.1. Each of these categories will be discussed separately and in the context of Internet-based business.

One of the more prominent effects of e-commerce and the Internet that impacts on business models are transaction costs. This theory was developed by the leading economist Ronald Coase, editor of the *Journal of Economics and Law* and Nobel Prize winner in Economic Sciences. Coase studied the nature of transaction costs and their implications on the existence and structure of companies and firms: 'In order to carry out a market transaction it is necessary to discover who it is that one wishes to deal with, to conduct negotiations leading up to a bargain, to draw up the contract, to undertake the inspection needed to make sure that the terms of the contract are being observed, and so on.'[3] Briefly, this refers to the transaction cost of providing some good or service through the market, which includes:

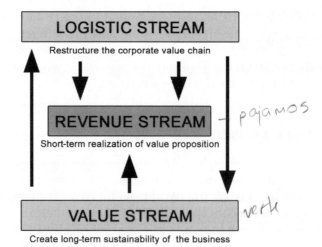

Figure 5.1 Components of a business model

- Searching for and obtaining information both in terms of time and the resources necessary for the search process.
- Participating in a market.
- Policing and enforcing transactions, ensuring that they conform to the organisation's processes and buying policies.
- Bargaining and decision costs which include the costs of carrying out the negotiations, the time, effort and financial cost it takes to finalise the decision, which might include comparison of different products/services.
- The actual cost of buying or selling the product or service.

Different products, services and markets have different transaction-cost profiles. For example, buying a bar of chocolate would involve finding the nearest retailer and the actual cost of the chocolate bar. However, buying a computing system would involve finding out about the different models and specifications of machines, comparing different manufacturers and prices, evaluating the different offers in terms of requirements and price, and negotiating with the supplier on cost and time of delivery – physical cost is only part of the total transaction costs. The higher the cost of the product/service and the more specialised, complex and bespoke it is, the higher the transaction cost.

The remainder of this chapter will show the impact that the Internet and World Wide Web have had on transactions costs and business models.

WHAT IS A VALUE STREAM?

A business value stream is the potential benefit for various business stakeholders of offering something distinctive from their competitors. This can arise out of reduced transaction costs, lower product costs, improved product or service, brand name and reputation, complementary products or services. This value creation can be achieved by a number of different means; the following are examples of four value streams.

Creation of/participation in an e-marketplace to reduce transaction costs

In its very broadest definition, an e-marketplace is an 'Internet based broker of goods or services in a community of many buyers and sellers',[4] where by using the Internet, transaction costs can be reduced drastically both directly in terms of cash saved and indirectly in terms of improved efficiency in the buying/selling process (for example, through automated and/or integrated purchasing/sales processes). The economics of e-marketplaces are similar to those of 'traditional' free markets, where markets will grow and develop if stakeholders are benefiting and if there is equal unrestricted and free movement to enter and exit the market. An e-marketplace can be set up and managed by a supplier or a buyer or run by an independent organisation.

Initially suppliers must offer differentiated products or services to attract buyers. The e-marketplace acts as a 'technology translator' so that an organisation does not need to allow for the different technology platforms of its trading partners or customers. This means that facilities provided by e-marketplaces can be automated or integrated into the respective organisation's purchasing/selling process relatively easily. This increases efficiency, and reduces lead times for fulfilling and completing business transactions. As more suppliers join in the market, they expand the benefits and choices for buyers. The increase in product/service choice attracts more buyers. As more buyers join in, benefiting from the reduced transaction costs, so suppliers benefit from a wider and accessible customer base and so experience lower customer search costs. This in turn translates into improved services and products, reduced transaction cost and improved convenience to buyers. So a virtuous cycle (illustrated in Figure 5.2) is created where value is created for the participants in the marketplace.

An example of an e-marketplace is ChemConnect, an on-line chemicals exchange which set up an on-line exchange floor, where 5,000 to 7,000 companies negotiate to buy and sell specialised chemical products in password-protected negotiation rooms, where they can deal with issues such as product quality, warranties, shipping and price. In exchange for enabling such negotiations, ChemConnect charges annual subscription fees ranging from US$300 to more than US$100,000. In 2001 they handled transactions valued over US$1 billion.

Creation/participation of virtual communities

This involves the bringing together of members of a community where they can exchange ideas or information, adding value in a number of ways. Larger communities mean larger sources of knowledge and information. For example, LloydsTSB Bank have the 'success4business' website where business customers can interact directly with each other, exchanging specialist and expert information and ideas freely, sharing information and reports provided by the organisation and sharing in a range of other activities exclusive to the community of on-line members. Microsoft have set up their website to enable customers to download software patches to upgrade their systems and application software, at the same time improving their products and providing an excellent aftercare service. ISPs such as AOL have also set up an on-line community for AOL members to share

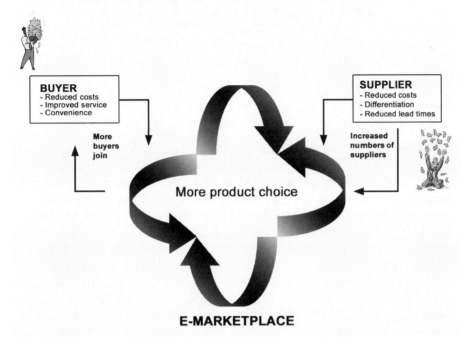

Value Stream
A description of the potential benefits for the various business actors or stakeholders

BUYER
- Reduced costs
- Improved service
- Convenience

SUPPLIER
- Reduced costs
- Differentiation
- Reduced lead times

More buyers join

Increased numbers of suppliers

More product choice

E-MARKETPLACE

Figure 5.2 Value creation of an e-marketplace

resources, facilities and exchange information with each other. CISCO engineers can access and assess their customers' infrastructure from their own location using the Internet, improving customer service with minimum investment.

Additional value offers

Value is added by improving the product mix being offered by widening the variety of product or service offering, for example by introducing the concept of a one-stop shop where customers can access everything they might need from a single source. Widening the product mix can be achieved through association or partnership with other organisations offering complementary services or products. These organisations should also be complementary in terms of brand name, image and business styles.

For example eBay, the on-line auction company, offers a range of services, such as fraud protection if products are paid for but not received, dispute resolution services, and security and trusted third-party escrow

A customer visits your site.. ..then shops at amazon.co.uk.. ..and we pay you.

Figure 5.3 Stages in Amazon's Associates Programme Scheme

Source: Amazon.co.uk[5]

services where the buyer's money is held in trust by a neutral third party until the seller sends the merchandise to the buyer who accepts it.

The Customs and Excise office in the UK also allow businesses to submit their VAT forms on-line but need to apply for a digital certificate from a recommended provider before this can happen. There are links to these providers (Chambersign and Equifax) from the Customs and Excise website.[6] Value is added by enabling businesses to submit their returns on-line seven days after the deadline, and this can be done instantaneously.

For Internet-based businesses, widening product mixes through links with partners can be achieved at a minimum cost, by joining an associate programme. The complementary product/service provider can integrate links into the host's website and receive micro-payments for a referral (typically valued from as little as £0.001 to a maximum of £5 or £10) or a percentage if a sale is made. One of the first Internet-based businesses to set up such a scheme is Amazon's Associates Programme (see Figure 5.3). If customers link to Amazon.co.uk then Amazon handle all the customer service, delivery and tracking of sales generated from the associate's website – Amazon even build the links and provide a number of methods to select the link such as placing an amazon.co.uk search box on the associate site.

Exploitation of information

E-commerce and the Internet economy is founded on information and, as discussed in Chapter 3, this is either consumed, collected, analysed, disseminated or manipulated in some way for a number of different functions. Value can be added in many ways by using this information – for example, capturing data to provide a personalised and customised service or product for individuals, as in the case of personalising Web pages specifically for individuals, enabling them to include only the resources that interest them. This adds value by improving customer satisfaction and enabling customers to customise products or services as per their requirements. Amazon.com also use data gathered on its customers to suggest personalised choices for them.

The Web also facilitates setting up information that targets different customers demographically, geographically and linguistically. For example, websites can be replicated relatively cost effectively in different languages or for different countries (to include different prices, delivery and other terms and conditions) commensurate with different laws. This adds value to the organisation by broadening their potential customer base and being able to cater for different user needs. For example, Amazon has a number of sites catering for the Japanese, French and German markets amongst others.

Over the centuries, business has profited from the lack of information symmetry between buyers and sellers. There has been a lack of information amongst buyers and sellers about each other, which leads to an inability to compare prices and locate alternative business partners easily. This means that numerous buyers, with a range of resources available to them, and numerous sellers, having perishable products or services spread over a wide geographical area, did not have access to each other mainly because there was no centralised and immediate source of information enabling buyers to meet and transact with sellers. E-marketplaces and communities of value can be used to reduce this information asymmetry, allowing buyers to post requests for proposals (RFP) for suppliers to answer.

In some instances, particularly in the hotel, travel, tourism and food industry where there is a wide variety of product offerings, a high level of uncertainty about consumption and a high rate of perishability, businesses have been set up to exploit this information asymmetry. These businesses are sometimes known as infomediaries. One of the first examples is Web-based priceline.com, where the website allows customers to input the maximum price they are prepared to pay for a product or service. Priceline.com then tries to match the offer made to information from a number of different 'brand name' providers of services, such as airlines, car rental and hotels. If the customer's offer is accepted then the transaction is confirmed within minutes.

The examples of value streams identified above are not mutually exclusive and are interlinked. For example, the benefits of virtual communities, infomediaries and added-value offerings all include reduced transaction costs. The measures taken to add value create opportunities for the long-term sustainability of the business, which in turn impacts on revenue streams and the structure of the organisation.

WHAT IS A REVENUE STREAM?

The revenue stream is the source of income for the organisation and is the financial realisation of its success year on year. Revenue streams for Web-based business can be *Direct*, as a result of what the organisation produces to sell, or *Indirect*, as a result of facilities that provide an additional source of income that are not core to what the organisation does.

Direct revenue stream

A number of strategies can be used to increase revenue from the direct sale of the organisation's product or service. The following are some strategies impacting on direct revenue streams.

Cost reduction Purely Web-based businesses that conduct all their transactions over the Internet can experience considerable savings over their 'bricks and mortar' (traditional high-street) competitors. The more a product or service is digitised, the higher the savings will be. For example, selling software, music, books or videos on-line means that, although there are very high initial set-up costs to develop the product, the subsequent variable costs to re-produce and distribute them are near zero if they are downloaded directly from the source via a website. Cost savings include:

- Eliminating storage media such as CD, video tape, floppy disk, external packaging and design of that packaging.
- Holding and controlling inventory – digital products can be stored indefinitely, with no tie-up of capital in physical stock awaiting sale, and can be downloaded at zero variable cost with no need to monitor quantities and initiate re-ordering processes.
- Eliminating postage and packaging costs for the customers and time it takes to carry out this service for the supplier.
- No physical limitations in the numbers and types of goods or services that can be displayed and made available to customers as in a bricks and mortar outlet.
- Producers of these items can sell them direct to the customer without the necessity for middlemen, who would either mark up the cost of the items or take a commission from the supplier. This concept of taking out the middleman is known as disintermediation and will be discussed in more detail in the logistical stream section.

It cost AOL hundreds of millions of dollars to develop its software, hardware, brand and subscriber base, but once the initial amount was spent the monthly relative cost of maintaining each member is negligible.

Reduced transaction costs (identified earlier) have a direct impact on revenue streams because cost of sales will be lower than traditional competitors, and so margins and thus net revenue can be higher. These kinds of cost savings also mean that Web-based businesses have the potential to make prices more competitive, which in turn will attract more customers, increase sales and thus revenue streams. The global nature of the Internet means that the customer base is broadened and the potential volume of sales is increased, thus potentially increasing revenue.

Free offerings of products/services   The theory behind free offerings is that by providing a good or service free of charge, then in the longer term this will create a future source of revenue. The kinds of products or services that are offered free to customers are those that show characteristics of lock-in, which means that customers will be locked in to using the product or service as an integral part of their activity. Once a customer is locked in, then the switching costs are increased because switching to a new product means that users must learn how to use the new one; for example, Microsoft's Windows and UNIX operating systems. Furthermore, Micro-soft's Windows is compatible with other Microsoft applications, which might potentially cause problems if the operating system is changed. Unless the benefits far outweigh the costs of switching to a new product or service, it would be difficult to justify it. Selling complementary products or services that are essential to the full functioning of the free offering will then create future revenue streams.

One example is Adobe Systems, who give away their Adobe Acrobat document Reader software for free. The more users build up a library of Adobe Acrobat documents (.pdf), the higher the switching costs. These switching costs would involve the time-consuming conversion of all Adobe Acrobat documents to another format, and learning a new application. As lock-in is achieved, if users need to edit or create .pdf documents they will need to buy the full version of Adobe Acrobat.

Free offerings are also sometimes used by software developers, as part of the development lifecycle to obtain free feedback to improve the product. This impacts on the revenue stream by reducing lead times and improving quality of products.

Pricing strategies   An important part of profiting from value is to price properly, that is to have an appropriate pricing strategy. Dolan and Moon,[7] leading academics at Harvard University, identify three major pricing mechanisms that can be used for a number of different effects when conducting e-business on the Internet. They believe that different products and different markets require different kinds of pricing mechanisms to maximise revenue streams for organisations in the face of increased product/service price comparison availability, increased quality of information and the overall downward pressure on prices. The following explains each of the three pricing mechanism categories enabled by the Internet and the Web.

Menu pricing or fixed pricing

In menu pricing, the seller sets a price, which the buyer either agrees to pay or not. This is the most common type of pricing mechanism in the retailing sector – there is no negotiation and the seller's attitude is 'either take it or leave it'. In the traditional 'bricks and mortar' world, profits are made because of information asymmetry between buyers and sellers. The transaction costs of extensive comparison shopping from physically going from shop to shop, are too high for the buyer, and so they are prepared to pay the price or not based on very little or no comparative information. There is little opportunity for retailers to frequently change these set prices because it is difficult to detect and act upon changes in customer prefer-ences very quickly and also because it costs time and money to physically change the price labels on products and physical promotional material.

However, on the Internet things are completely different:

- Comparison shopping and the availability of information is high and so buyer transaction costs are low – they no longer have to go from shop to shop or make telephone calls to find out about different prices. An automated electronic search tool ('bot' or 'spider') compares a wide selection of different prices and features of the product or service available on the Web, which enables buyers to make price comparisons easily and quickly, removing any information asymmetry between buyers and sellers. One of these price-comparison websites is Easyvalue.com.
- Sellers can also use comparison shopping to check the prices of their competitors.
- Information about customers can be collected and used immediately and so it is easy for on-line retailers to track the behaviour of on-line visitors. They can see what products or services the visitors are brows-ing; whether they reach the check-out point and abandon the final stage of the transaction; how often they visit; purchasing patterns (how often and which products); payment preferences; and so on. They can also detect the buying or preference patterns of the whole on-line visitor base.
- Web pages can be changed easily, cheaply and immediately to reflect any changes in strategy.

All these features mean that set-menu pricing mechanisms on the Web can take the form of periodic price changes or dynamic price customisation that can have an impact on revenue from direct sales. Figure 5.4 illustrates the different stakeholders in the transaction and shows that the price emanates from the seller to the buyer in one direction only.

Periodic price changes can be made depending on the popularity of a certain product or service. This means that prices can be updated fre-quently with the minimum of cost. This is particularly useful in the travel

Web-Based Pricing Mechanisms

I. Menu pricing (Fixed pricing)

a) Periodic price changes
b) Dynamic price customisation

Figure 5.4 Menu-pricing mechanism

sector where car rental, hotel rooms or airline fares can be changed instantaneously to reflect availability, as in the case of Easyjet. One on-line retailer, eCOST, also update their prices regularly, their website stating that:

> We know that when it really comes down to it, you want the best price . . . When you shop at eCOST.com, you don't have to wonder if you're getting a great value on what you need. We can offer you great pricing because we carefully control our costs and pass the savings directly to you.
>
> To make sure we are offering you the best price at all times, we update our prices at least once per day, and more often as needed. The same goes with our featured products. When you visit eCOST.com, you can be sure you are getting the latest information available.[8]

Dynamic price customisation involves the use of information collected from customers and allows companies to charge different customers different prices. Price customisation includes sellers:

- Offering prices based on the customer's Web-purchase profile, often using personalised e-mail (for example, some clothing retailers).
- Offering different storefronts to different types of customers, as in the case of Dell's Premier Pages, which provide clients with their very own customised Web pages at Dell, enabling on-line and instantaneous price quotations, tools, services and support that are unique to the client.
- Using price comparison sites to develop 'price-matching systems', where customers using a price comparison site will be offered prices

that are automatically adjusted to compare favourably with the competition. In this case, sellers will be maximising the information symmetry of the Internet rather than being afraid of it.

● Monitoring activity of visits on the website and so offering special prices to visitors of Web pages containing less popular items to encourage a sale.

Some of the disadvantages of set or fixed pricing are that customers may be prepared to pay more for the product/service that the seller has asked for or the price is too high for the buyer but the seller might have sold it for less and so a sale is lost. In both cases the seller is losing out. The ultimate aim of menu dynamic pricing is to set a price that matches exactly the buyer's willingness to pay the price, and this is what Web-based set-menu pricing has yet to achieve.

Buyer–seller negotiation

The buyer–seller negotiation pricing mechanism involves the interaction of both the buyer and the seller to achieve agreement on a price, which the buyer is prepared to pay and the seller is prepared to accept (see Figure 5.5). In the bricks and mortar world, this takes place both largely in a market trading environment or business-to-business negotiations for goods or services. Negotiation is also a cultural way of buying mainly in the Far Eastern, Middle Eastern and Asian regions. Some organisations accept negotiation as a way of opening a dialogue and developing a relationship with customers and a route to making a sale. Some of the disadvantages are that it typically takes longer to complete the transaction and so transaction

Web-Based Pricing Mechanisms

II. Buyer–seller negotiation

a) Specified starting point
b) No specified starting point

Figure 5.5 Buyer–seller negotiation pricing mechanisms

costs increase, negotiations must involve parties with the authority to finalise prices and price tends to become the main focus for negotiation rather than added value elements.

The Internet can overcome the disadvantages of negotiation in the 'real world' in a number of ways. For example, some Web stores offer negotiating or 'haggling' facilities where responses can be obtained almost instantaneously, transactions are finalised quickly and the person author-ised to make pricing decisions is contacted directly or the process is automated according to a pre-defined set of criteria. There are two main types of buyer/seller negotiation – specified and no specified starting points.

Specified starting point is where a starting price has been specified somewhere in the negotiation process and so this is the basis on which the negotiations begin to take place.

An example of the specified starting point pricing mechanism is NexTag.com. At NexTag, once a query is submitted, a list of merchants selling the item is returned with the price each is offering. If the price is satisfactory then the sale is completed (this is menu pricing). If the price is not acceptable, then NexTag acts as an intermediary offering the customer the opportunity to counter with a lower price in the hope that the suppliers' circumstances (such as excess stock or the introduction of a newer version) will lead to the customer's price being matched. The suppliers may match the price, or alternatively they may make a counter-offer for a price or refuse to negotiate at all. The responses from the supplier are almost immediate – once the customer offers a price, the list of vendor responses appears immediately.[9] These kinds of sites maintain a relationship with a variety of suppliers who are prepared to take part in the on-line negotiation process.

Itchybid.com also has a similar feature in its 'flea-market' category where buyers can haggle with sellers who mark their items at 'reasonable' prices, which allows a buyer to haggle to get the price lower. If the seller marks their price as non-negotiable, it will be noted and the buyer will know they will not be able to haggle.

CASE STUDY

In their paper, Dolan and Moon cite websites such as MakeUsAnOffer, Adoutlet and Hagglezone as examples of websites enabling buyers and sellers to negotiate on a one-to-one basis. At the time of writing (January 2002) these websites were no longer in operation but there was no detailed information on why they had ceased to operate.

Non-specified starting price is based on the concept of volume buying – different prices are given based on the size of the order. On the Internet, aggregate buying enables individuals wanting the same item to join together and submit a large volume order to manufacturers who offer a price. The higher the volume, the lower the price. This has been done by consumers, for example letsbuyit.com, and also by businesses – usually smaller businesses requiring smaller quantities aggregate with other small businesses to present a large order to the supplier and thus reduce transaction costs. One of the industry sectors that does this is the pharmacy sector. A Web-based organisation called Servall[10] represents the collective power of independent pharmacies to achieve the same kind of service and pricing as larger retailing organisations. Another example where benefits could be seen is in the resource-poor public sector, such as health and education. This would not only enable these public services to aggregate buying power, but it would also enable staff responsible for purchasing to be used more effectively and efficiently elsewhere in the organisation since time taken to undertake direct supplier searches and negotiation would no longer be necessary.

It is debatable whether the first example of buyer seller negotiation mechanism will actually succeed in some Western cultures. Some organisations such as Ford are actually setting up 'haggle-free' websites to counter the stress, uncertainty and distrust of haggling that some customers experience when buying (for example, a car). In order for this mechanism to be successful, a large number of suppliers must be willing to participate to ensure a 'best price' for the customer.

The second type of negotiating mechanism (aggregate buying) actually ties in with the idea of creating a virtual community where value is added and benefit realised for all members of the community.

Horizontal interaction

In both the first and second types of pricing mechanism, the interaction was a one-on-one direct vertical interaction with the buyer and supplier. This pricing mechanism centres on auctions and exchanges where buyers and/or sellers compete against each other in order to finalise a price. Thus, prices can be very volatile and are suitable for certain types of products/ services or organisations. Figure 5.6 shows the three types of pricing mechanism that involve a series of horizontal interactions between buyers and sellers: auctions, reverse buying and exchange.

A classic *auction* is where one or more buyers place a bid for an item (either sealed in an envelope or in open competition with other bidders) and the seller either agrees to sell it at that price or not. The success of auctions is based on getting as many buyers wanting to place a bid to buy the item for sale. The sales price is a reflection of market demand at that particular moment in time. In the bricks and mortar world, one of the problems of auctions is of trying to get together the maximum number of buyers and sellers, and also making sure that the buyers are very interested in the items being sold. Bricks and mortar auction houses tend to focus on specialist or niche items or industries such as antiques and art works or, for instance, the Dutch Fresh Flower Auctions.

As has already been discussed, the Web and the Internet lower transaction costs for: sellers to find a critical mass of buyers in the market;

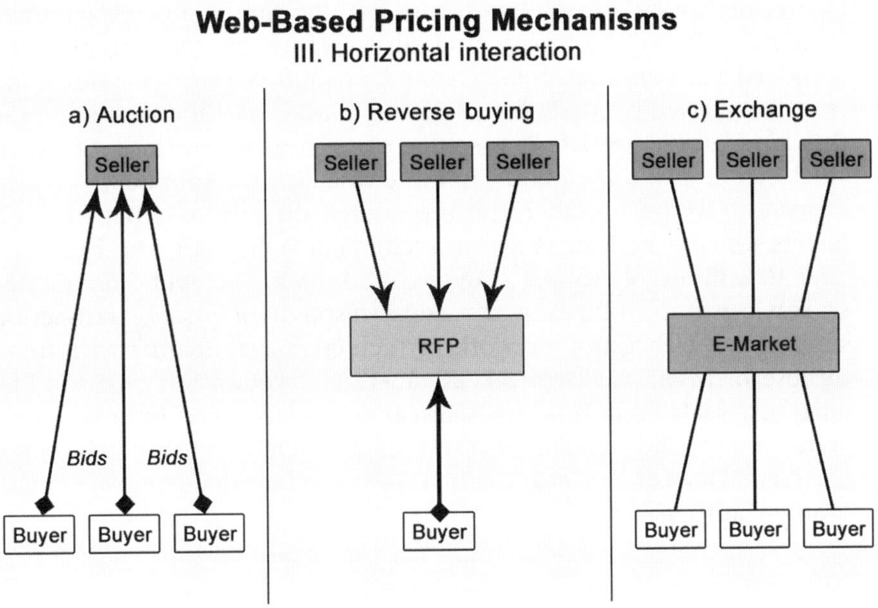

Web-Based Pricing Mechanisms
III. Horizontal interaction

Figure 5.6 Auction- and exchange-based pricing mechanisms

buyers to find even specialist items quickly and cheaply; and the ease and immediacy of the bidding process for all transacting parties. There is a large community of buyers and sellers and a large number of Internet-based auction sites that are catering for them. These sites include:

- *Consumer-to-consumer auctions* – where individuals can sell any item to other individuals. One of the better known on-line auctioneers is eBay. They have a community of over 36 million registered users and in 2000 the value of transactions was over US$5 billion. They offer a wide range of auctioneering services, including eBay Premier, a site on eBay which showcases and guarantees the authenticity of fine art, antiques, fine wines and rare collectibles, and live auctions, enabling traditional auctioneers to extend their sales beyond the auction-house floor and reach millions of potential buyers on-line. A value-added service which develops trust amongst the community of users is a program that allows buyers to rate each other on payment, quality of goods, veracity of descriptions and so on.
- *Business-to-consumers* – where businesses sell directly to consumers. One of the leading auction sites that deals in excess-stock brand-name merchandise is uBid.com. *Internet World Magazine* ranks uBid as the fifth largest e-commerce site by revenue.[11] uBid auctions have a wide selection of product offerings: more than 12,000 branded items which

change daily. uBid have relationships with leading manufacturers such as Sony, HP and Compaq, and also feature products from other approved partners that operate brand or uBid warranties. Sales fulfilment is handled centrally by uBid's distribution facility in the USA. So this kind of auction site is a source of revenue where sales of excess stock can be maximised and capital released for the suppliers.

- *Business-to-business* – where businesses sell directly to other business buyers. One of the leaders in this sector is dovebid.com who have sold over 10 million lots valued at over US$5 billion. Dovebid offer a range of services from valuation of assets, disposal of assets, transaction support and webcasting networks, which enable companies wishing to dispose of assets via live webcast auctions, around-the-clock on-line auctions, sealed-bid Internet sales and private-treaty Internet sales. Some of Dovebid's customers have included AT&T, Boeing, Daimler-Chrysler, Hewlett-Packard, Levi Strauss, Lockheed-Martin, NEC and Warner Brothers.

This type of classic auction is being used by a number of different ISPs, such as AOL, Yahoo.com and Excite, as well as a sales mechanism for some suppliers such as Dell Computers.

Another type of auction is a *reverse auction*. This is where a request for a proposal (RFP) is made by the buyer to the community of relevant suppliers, who decide whether they wish to fulfil the request or not.

In the 'bricks and mortar' world, it is difficult to reach a wide number of suppliers with a request for a proposal or quotation. Often (especially in the public sector) where external bids are required, only regular suppliers could in reality be reached. With smaller organisations, the transaction costs of requesting a proposal were far too high, with the onus on the buyers to find out information about different suppliers before requesting them to make a bid.

On the Web, however, the economic feasibility and cost benefits of reverse auctions are maximised because a single buyer has access to a large number of suppliers. Mondus is a website that enables buyers to place a request for a quotation, which is sent out by e-mail to their database of relevant suppliers. The suppliers then respond with a price and product/service specification, which the buyer either agrees or does not, and Mondus takes a commission of the sale from the supplier, if the sale is finalised.

Using the Priceline model of reverse auction is suitable for perishable commodity goods because it is effective in solving the vendor's short term problem of selling off excess inventory which would otherwise remain unsold and thus perish, leaving the vendor with no return at all. Although this promotes lower prices for the buyers, there could also be an element of uncertainty for the customer, in that the price they have said they are prepared to pay, may not be what they are prepared to pay (but will be obliged to pay), once the details have been matched. So, the lack of customer information and thus power is sacrificed in favour of price, and for the vendor there is an issue of brand name erosion and discontent from full-price customers which must be considered when accepting prices from the customer.

A high-profile variant of reverse auction is Priceline, where customers are asked to 'Just Name Your Own Price[TM]', and our patented technology will make your offer to our world-class partners. We'll tell you the results in 15 minutes or less.'[12]

Priceline allows users to input the price they are willing to pay for airline seats, hotels or car hire, and the respective companies either agree to accept the price or not. However, buyers cannot specify companies they wish to deal with, neither can they specify the time they wish to travel (but they can specify dates). Once the buyer has confirmed the price they are prepared to pay, then they are obliged to pay that price if the details specified are met. The system seems to be attracting a high proportion of repeat customers, with over 60 per cent of nearly 11 million customers being repeat customers in 2001, which grew from 35 per cent in the first quarter of 2000.

CASE STUDY

Exchanges are electronic marketplaces where a group of buyers and a group of sellers interact to trade and set prices for transactions. In the bricks and mortar world, this is relatively difficult because business would have to aggregate together, bringing with them actual, or samples of, products/services they wished to sell. As with auctions, there is a physical limitation in bringing together the maximum number of buyers and sellers together.

On the Internet, as in all the previous discussions, electronic marketplaces are much easier because they enable access to larger numbers of buyers and sellers even for a specialised industry sector; transactions are automated and integrated into business processes, thus improving internal business efficiencies and reducing transaction costs; there are wider choices for buyers across geographical boundaries; and different pricing mechanisms can be used to suit the type of business or industry sector. In fact, the World Wide Web itself can arguably be seen as a huge electronic marketplace where the different websites facilitate interaction and trade between the different stakeholders.

Kaplan and Sawhney[13] developed a framework for classifying the different types of e-marketplaces or e-hubs according to two criteria – how businesses buy and what businesses buy. In this case the way of doing business is particularly relevant (e-marketplaces will be discussed in full later on in the chapter):

- *Systematic sourcing* – where contracts are negotiated with qualified suppliers and tend to be longer-term contracts where relationships develop over time. This kind of buying involves products, which are specialised, where the cost of processing the order is relatively high compared to the cost of the items and where the suppliers are highly fragmented and difficult to find. In this case, an aggregation or catalogue mechanism is in operation and involves bringing a large number of buyers and sellers together and reducing transaction costs by 'one-stop shopping'. Pricing mechanisms used in this kind of market are largely static and involve negotiation between individual buyers and sellers. So facilities provided by the e-hub in this instance would largely centre around a catalogue of products or services offered by a range of suppliers. The e-hub enables the negotiation process to take place quickly and efficiently and at a minimum cost. For example, SciQuest who provide access to and manage a catalogue of complex and specialised products from a range of suppliers to the science research industry. Once a product is found in the catalogue, then the buyer contacts the supplier directly for negotiations using SciQuest facilities.
- *Spot sourcing* – where there is an immediate need that must be filled at the lowest possible cost. Longer-term relationships are not that important in this kind of transaction. The mechanism used here is a matching mechanism where adding a buyer or a supplier to the marketplace benefits both buyers and sellers because it impacts on the overall marketplace dynamics by adding liquidity and increasing competition for either or both parties. The pricing mechanism used in this kind of market is largely dynamic and immediate and involves real-time auction bidding for commodities that can be traded sight unseen, and the buyers and sellers need a level of sophistication to be able to interpret their requirements and deal with the fast changing and dynamic pricing environment where demand and so prices are very volatile, reflecting the troughs and peaks of supply and demand. The trading volumes are very large compared to the relative transaction cost and, as with systematic sourcing, each industry has a particular need.

One of the prime examples is the stock exchange, but others include AltraNet and NTE on-line logistics. In the case of NTE, their exchange works by both shippers and carriers identifying their available shipment or capacity needs and their business requirements. NTE collects shipment orders, computes a market price for each one and matches them to truck routes provided by carriers. The exchange automatically filters their requirements to identify compatible trading partners within a couple of hours. When the delivery of the shipment is confirmed, NTE pays the carrier and bills the shipper.

AltraNet has e-marketplaces for a range of energy resources including gas. Altra eGas provides an exchange for North American and

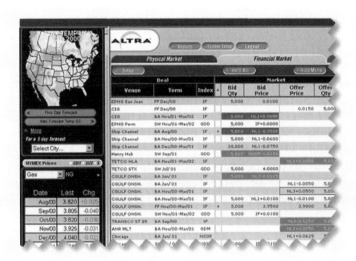

Figure 5.7 Altranet e-marketplace

Source: http://www.altranet.com/browse.php/gas/

Canadian suppliers and buyers of wholesale natural gas (as seen in Figure 5.7). In this exchange, members can view and participate in transactions on-line (using industry-standard trading instruments such as Basis Swaps, Swing Swaps, Fixed Float Swaps and NYMEX); view gas supplies at the specific time; and reduce transaction costs by consolidating all the monthly trading into one primary contract settled at the end of the month's trading. The real-time exchange also enables participants to trade anonymously, where neither buyer nor seller can reveal their identity until the transaction is finalised.

The different kinds of pricing mechanisms already identified above are used in each respective marketplace according to its characteristics. The Internet and Web offer a whole range of pricing mechanisms that not only add value to the stakeholders but also have a direct impact on the revenue stream. This impact takes the form of increasing the volume of sales or maximising the financial return on a product or service, freeing capital and improving cash flow and thus revenue streams. Different products, services and industries can use a whole range of different pricing mechanisms to suit their products and environments.

Indirect revenue streams

The previous section examined the kinds of revenue streams that can arise as a direct result of the business cutting costs, offering free products or services, or using a number of different pricing strategies. However, because of the Internet and the World Wide Web, there are also indirect ways that businesses can improve their revenue streams, for example:

- Internet advertising – placing banner ads or other adverts on the organisation's website for a monthly or annual fee.
- Selling customer information – either actual details or customer pro-files, including surfing habits and other information gathered during the customer's visit to the site.
- Receiving micro-payments by joining affiliate schemes, where payment of a small amount or percentage of a sale is made if a customer is referred from a host site.

In order for any of these programmes to have a real impact on revenue streams, there must be a very high turnover of visitors to the website and businesses must see this as a bonus rather than a strategy to pursue, because the market for Internet advertising and customer databases is very volatile and fluctuates according to economic movements.

WHAT IS A LOGISTIC STREAM?

The logistic stream is the third major area of a business model. It is interconnected with the value stream and revenue stream, both of which have already been discussed. The logistic stream examines the way in which an organisation must re-structure itself to deliver value-added and revenue streams. This includes issues such as organisational culture – ensuring the culture is one that can manage change effectively; ensuring employees and managers have roles in which they can be most effective for pre- and post-restructuring; implementing information, communication and training systems to ensure information flow control; and making sure reward systems are in place to target decision making motivation and development of employees.

The concept of the logistic stream is based on Harvard Professor Michael Porter's theory of the value chain,[14] which examines the con-nected activities and processes within and outside an organisation and how these activities are linked and work together. This process makes it apparent where activities can be re-configured or processes re-engineered in order to create value for the customer or lower costs for the organisation, translating into profit margins or increased revenue streams. It is assumed that the majority of readers will have had some knowledge of the value chain, but the main points are summarised very briefly in this section. Figure 5.8 clearly illustrates the two main categories of a value chain that were identified by Porter:

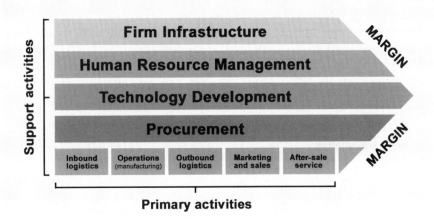

Figure 5.8   The value chain of a firm

Source: Michael E. Porter, *Competitive Advantage of Nations*

- *Primary activities* – all the stages in the creation of a product or service. That is, transforming inputs into outputs. For example, inbound logistics involves the movement of raw materials to the destination for use, operations transforming raw materials into a finished product, outbound logistics, marketing and sales, and after sale service, all of which include customer interface.
- *Secondary or support activities* – cut across the firm and are relevant to the firm's internal activities, such as firm infrastructure, which includes general management and finance, technology development, procurement and human-resource management.

Although the value chain separates customers, suppliers and firms into discrete but interrelated activities, the whole value chain is seen as a system. This system not only incorporates the organisation itself, but involves integration with the value chains of its stakeholders, including suppliers, distributors or retailers, and customers. Linkages not only connect activities inside a company, but also create the interdependencies between a firm and its stakeholders, and these linkages are those that can manage, optimise and coordinate the entire value system to achieve customer added value and cost savings.

Some argue that the value chain does not apply to all industries and is not always a useful metaphor for managers searching for competitive advantage and that it is mainly applicable to manufacturing.[15] I do not subscribe to this view, and will use the concept of the value chain in its broadest sense, that is raw materials are transformed by a process into a finished item which is then promoted and sold to customers – whether this relates to the service sector, the manufacturing sector or any other sector that seems to have intangible elements in it.

Four broad value and revenue streams have been identified previously and can be summarised as: reducing transaction and other costs; exploiting information; value offers; and virtual communities. There are several ways in which an organisation's value systems can be restructured to realise value and revenue streams.

Disintermediation

Disintermediation is the removal of one or more layers in the value chain to increase efficiency, improve responsiveness and reduce costs. Internet and Web-based businesses have been able to shrink the value chain by offering services or products directly from the supplier or producer to the customer. Traditionally, the value chain involves a number of different stakeholders that are involved in the process of producing a good or service.

CASE STUDY

Example 1 (in Figure 5.9) shows the different stakeholders in the traditional value chain. The stakeholders are identified as the suppliers of raw materials, including inbound logistics; the producers or manufacturers of the goods or service that use the raw materials; the distribution channels that include wholesalers, agents and/or retailers; and then finally the buyer. This infrastructure is similar both in business and retail sectors.

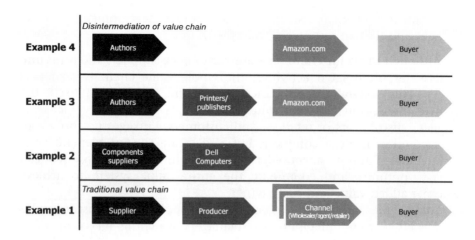

Figure 5.9 Disintermediation in logistics streams

Example 2 (in Figure 5.9) shows disintermediation in Dell Computer Corporation's value chain. In the manufacturing sector, Dell was one of the first companies to sell direct to customers, removing the channel layers (whether agents, wholesalers and/or retailers). Dell have direct links with their component suppliers using valuechain.dell.com, a single portal that provides suppliers with secure personalised access to areas of Dell's intranet, enabling suppliers to look at Dell's manufacturing operations and see how fast their components are moving through Dell's production line. This helps operate the just-in-time system they use to ensure that inventory movement can be monitored, and suppliers can anticipate what components will be needed. This speeds up delivery of components for Dell and also for the suppliers who, by having access to customer-order information, can anticipate needs for latest technology. To improve quality, Dell also have a scorecard system where suppliers are scored against a set of key metrics. These are made available to all suppliers so that they can compare their score with each other, which helps drive quality and reliability at the component level.

By having direct access to customers, and allowing customers to specify machines according to their requirements, this not only improves customer service, but also allows Dell to spot trends that enable them to act quickly and stay ahead of other more traditional customer-push-type competitors.

Example 3 (in Figure 5.9) shows the value chain of Amazon.com, where disinter-mediation allowed them to almost merge the role of wholesaler with retailer selling directly to the public. Amazon.com Inc. is the company that is most closely associated with the e-commerce dot.com phenomenon and is often seen as a template for e-business. Jeff Bezos, the founder of Amazon, wanted first and foremost to develop a totally customer-centric company. By using the Internet he could achieve this:

> In the online world, businesses have the opportunity to develop very deep relationships with customers, both through accepting preferences of customers and then observing their purchase behaviour over time, so that you can get that individualized knowledge of the customer and use that individualized knowledge of the customer to accelerate their discovery process. If we can do that, then the customers are going to feel a deep loyalty to us, because we know them so well.[16]

He introduced '1 Click™', which simplifies the buying process and enables details to be automatically invoked without retyping. The value and revenue streams achieved by disintermediation and dealing directly with the customers is underlined by Bezos himself:

> Bill Gates laid it out in a magazine interview. He said, 'I buy all my books at Amazon.com because I'm busy and it's convenient. They have a big selection, and they've been reliable.' Those are three of our four core value propositions: convenience, selection, service. The only one he left out is price: we are the broadest discounters in the world in any product category. But maybe price isn't so important to Bill Gates.[17]

Disintermediation delivers customer added value, but also reduces costs because of the restructuring of the whole value chain and indirectly the publishing industry.

Amazon reduced book return rates from about 30 per cent to 3 per cent because of the on-line peer book reviews and starring system, thus developing an efficient supply network which processes only saleable books with minimum returns, saving the industry millions of dollars.

The fast turnaround in stock gave the company a positive cash flow and maximized the publisher's credit facilities, giving Amazon about a month of interest free funds:

'Physical bookstores must stock up to 160 days' worth of inventory to provide the kind of in-store selection people want. Yet they must pay distributors and publishers 45 to 90 days after they buy the books – so on average, they carry the costs of those books for up to four months. Amazon, by contrast, carries only 15 days' worth of inventory and is paid immediately by credit card.[18]

Cost savings enables Amazon to sell books at reduced rates of between 20 and 30 per cent less than bricks and mortar outlets.

Example 4 (in Figure 5.9) provides another example of disintermediation in the value chain introduced by Amazon. They allow authors to publish their books directly on-line in the format of e-books or physical books that can be accessed directly by the buyers without any direct investment or cost[19] to themselves.

Disintermediation can shorten the value chain by removing one or more layers. The result of disintermediation is to increase process efficiency and add value to customer relationships while minimising costs.

Re-intermediation

Re-intermediation refers to the reassembly of buyers, sellers and other partners in a traditional value chain in new ways and introducing new stakeholders in the value chain. Again, speaking particularly about Web-enabled business, one of the most influential actors in the business-to-business value chain is the e-marketplace.

Figure 5.10 illustrates two ways in which the value chain is restructured and new stakeholders are introduced.

CASE STUDY

Example 1 shows re-intermediation in the value chain between suppliers and producers via e-marketplaces, e-hubs or exchanges. These bring together a large community of buyers and sellers to minimise transaction costs involved with the purchasing of raw

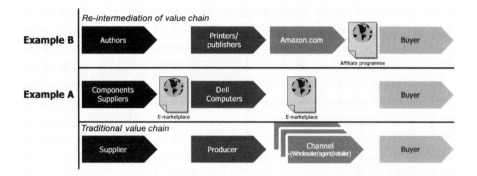

Figure 5.10 Re-intermediation in logistics streams

materials or other kinds of products or services. E-marketplace, e-hubs and exchanges are also introduced to replace the wholesaler/agent/retailer channel, connecting a community of buyers directly to a community of sellers further down the value chain.

Example 2 shows re-intermediation in Amazon.com Inc. via their affiliate programme. Referrals from member websites increases potential revenue streams with minimum capital outlay. The process involves, first, registering with the affiliate programme, and thereafter, a link to the Amazon website will appear on the registered member's website.

Arguably, there is re-intermediation in the process of service and product development and design. The Internet and the Web enable immediate feedback from users or buyers, which can filter back into the product or service development lifecycle. Software developers in particular act upon the feedback from users of beta (trial version) software, which improves any problems in the software. Further value is added by developing a more robust product, with minimum cost and developing a relationship with the users where they feel a part of the organisation and its product. Amazon also uses customer feedback as an integral part of its added value in the book buying process, where users can read independent comments, which has a financial impact by reducing the incidents and cost of returned books.

Infomediation

In the increasingly knowledge-intensive economy that has emerged from the creation of the World Wide Web, there is now an over-abundance of information. There is a need for information to be captured, stored and

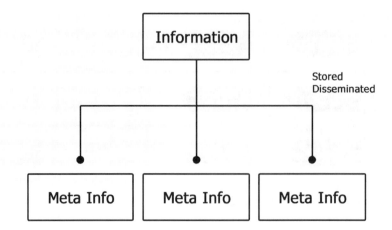

Figure 5.11 Tasks of an infomediary

broken down into smaller fragments of meta information (see Figure 5.11) that is readily accessible and can be used to the benefit of users. The term infomediary was coined by John Hagel in his 1996 article entitled 'The Coming Battle for Customer Information' in the *Harvard Business Review*.[20] Formed from a combination of the words *info*rmation and inter*mediary*, an infomediary gathers and organises large amounts of data and acts as an intermediary between those who want the information and those who supply the information.

Infomediaries can be seen as agents or brokers of information and infomediation is the process of providing this infomediary service. The World Wide Web itself can be seen as a large infomediary storing and disseminating information and adding value by reducing information asymmetry between different groups. An example of an infomediary is an e-marketplace that provides information to buyers or sellers and gives them the facilities to act upon the information they have, such as websites like Autobytel. It offers consumers a place to gather information about specific products and companies before they make purchasing decisions (in this case about cars). The infomediary is largely a neutral entity, a third-party provider of unbiased information. In this instance the information asymmetry between buyers and sellers is minimised and so value is added by making it accessible to users.

This section has identified three ways (disintermediation, re-inter-mediation and infomediation) in which a value chain can be restructured to improve efficiency, add value and lower costs for an organisation. Some have argued that disintermediation can and has led to job losses and business closures because of the removal of completed elements in the value chain. However what is less talked about is re-intermediation and infomediation, the necessity for new layers and skills to be added to the value chain in order to maximise and harness the enormous power, capacity and benefits of the Internet and World Wide Web. No business is static and logistics streams must be flexible enough to incorporate and adapt to any technological changes that undoubtedly will continue to occur.

WHAT KINDS OF BUSINESS MODELS ARE THERE?

The previous section outlined the three main elements that comprise a business model – value stream, revenue stream and logistic stream. These three elements are closely interrelated with changes in any one of the three areas, impacting on one or more of the others. The introduction of the Internet and Web for business saw an explosion in the different kinds of business models that were used and introduced – some describing the way that revenue is generated, some describing the kind of services that are offered, and so on.

Presently, no single, comprehensive and cogent taxonomy of Web-business models has been introduced or is being used. Reading the literature from academics to business media, business models are categorised in many different ways, none of which can be taken as the definitive classification model. This section will introduce some of the business models that have been highlighted by some academics in the e-commerce field.

Michael Rappa

Michael Rappa, one of the pioneers of on-line open courseware and a leading author in the field of Web-based business, identifies a number of generic business models collated from his observations. In his on-line course *Managing the Digital Enterprise*,[21] he describes these business models as:

- *Brokerage* – market makers bringing together buyers and sellers and facilitating transactions. Examples of broker models include *e-market-places* (including exchanges) and auction sites (eBay, auctionet, price-line); *search agents* that retrieve information about, for example, prices (easyvalue, mysimon); and *virtual malls*, such as VirtualMall (UK), hosting a number of on-line retailers.
- *Advertising* – a Web-advertising model and extension of the traditional media broadcasting model where websites provide content and services and advertising messages (usually in the form of banners). This model is

most effective when the volume of traffic to the site is high or very specialised. Examples include portals, whether general (such as yahoo or AOL, where advertisers are prepared to pay for space on a high-volume traffic site) or specialised (such as myAOL or myYahoo where content is customised to suit the individual user), or where visitors are paid for viewing content (such as mypoints).

- *Infomediary* – collecting and disseminating information. This can be sold to organisations for marketing purposes, for example NetZero who provide free Internet access in exchange for user profiles. Another type of infomediary model can also provide consumers with useful information about on-line retailers, for example, epinions.
- *Merchant* – retailers selling goods directly to buyers. There are different kinds of merchants: *virtual merchants* like amazon.com, who only sell on the Web; and *clicks and mortar merchants*, traditional bricks and mortar merchants who also have on-line trading facilities, such as Marks & Spencer and PCWorld.
- *Manufacturer* – similar to the merchant model, this involves manufacturers or producers of a good or service using the Web to reach buyers directly, eliminating wholesalers and retailers, for example Dell Computers.
- *Subscription* – this model involves payment of fees to access information or services. Information providers allow access to high-value reports at a cost or for a subscription fee – such as *Harvard Business Review* or *The Economist.*

This kind of classification model by Rappa is a combination of describing what the business models do and how they make revenue. None of the models that have been observed by Rappa are mutually exclusive, and some are a combination of subscription and advertising models. Rappa himself admits that his taxonomy is neither exhaustive nor definitive, and indeed it is not.

Paul Timmers

Paul Timmers, head of the sector in the European Commission in charge of IT research and development programmes for e-commerce, has also developed a framework for the analysis and classification of business models. He suggests that the classification of business models can be achieved through 'value chain reconstruction and de-construction . . . and identifying possible ways of integrating information along the chain'.[22] By using this technique, he identifies 11 different business models (compared to Rappa's nine models) that are illustrated in Figure 5.12. Each model is classified according to the different elements of the value chain once it is deconstructed, the interaction patterns (whether 1–to–1, 1–to-many or many-to–

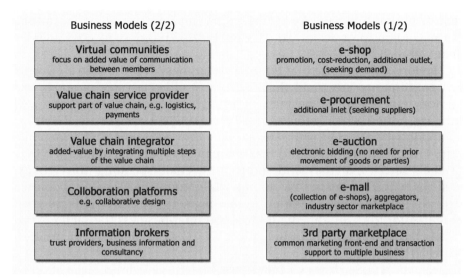

Figure 5.12   Timmers's classification of business models

1) and identifying where information processing can be integrated into the reconstructed value chain.

The two dimensions of analysing the business models are:

- Degree of innovation, which ranges from an electronic version of a traditional way of doing business (for example e-shops), to more innovative ways of doing business by, for instance, offering products or functions that did not exist before.
- The extent to which these new functions are integrated within the business model, ranging from single function (such as e-shops that provide only marketing functions over the Internet) to those fully integrated within the value chain (for example, e-marketplaces that offer a whole range of products and services, such as logistics and tracking).

For more details, read Timmers's book *Electronic Commerce: Strategies and Models for Business to Business Trading.*[23]

E-marketplaces

The e-marketplace is a business model about which much has been written. Reports from commercial research and consultancy organisations, such as Gartner Group and Boston Consulting Group, continue to indicate that although the volume of business-to-consumer transactions is higher than that of business-to-business, the total value of the transactions in the business-to-business sector far exceeds that of business to consumer by about 10-to-1.

Reports also indicate that business-to-business over the Web is growing and continues to grow and that the total worldwide value of goods and services purchased by businesses through e-commerce solutions will increase from US$282 billion in 2000 to US$4.3 trillion by 2005 – a compounded annual growth rate of 73 per cent according to International Data Corp.[24] The report found that companies expect to conduct the bulk of their direct materials and indirect materials spending through exchanges within 3 years: 'We found while companies are disappointed with the benefits they've gotten from e-marketplaces, they still see great potential for these intermediaries to make inter-business transactions and collaboration easier and more effective' (Giga Vice-President Andrew Bartels).[25]

Kaplan and Sawhney's[26] framework, mentioned earlier in relation to exchanges (see p. 169), classified the different types of e-marketplaces or e-hubs according to how businesses buy and what businesses buy (summarised in Figure 5.13). What businesses buy are:

- *Manufacturing inputs* – where the products or services bought are specific to the creation of a particular good or service, for example raw materials. The items bought are specific and different for each industry sector. For example, an advertising agency does not buy raw steel in order to produce its service.
- *Operating inputs* – where items bought are not part of the finished product or service but are more related to maintenance, repair and operating goods. The items bought are not specific to certain industries but are general and relevant to all – for example, office supplies and air tickets are necessary across all industries.

In their matrix, Kaplan and Sawhney specify the type of e-marketplace which can be classified according to their two main criteria. These are:

- *Maintenance, repairs and operations (MRO)* deal with low-value operating inputs that have relatively high transaction costs. The MRO hubs increase efficiency in the purchasing process and lower transaction costs by aggregating a large number of suppliers in one location.
- *Yield manager* provide liquid markets for buying and selling operating resources where suppliers of fixed cost assets or services can sell their excess capacity easily and immediately. There is a high price and demand volatility in this quartile because of the flexibility and dynamic supply and demand that happens at short notice. For example, the

Figure 5.13 How e-hubs work

Source: S. Kaplan and M. Sawhney, 'E-hubs the new B2B marketplaces', *Harvard Business Review*, May–June 2000

need for manufacturing capacity, advertising space, labour or any of the utilities at short notice and for a short period of time.
- *Exchanges* – similar to commodity exchanges, enable the fast exchange of commodities for production without problems of negotiating contracts. It is usual that the participants in the transaction remain anonymous until it is finalised.
- *Catalogue* – the non-commodity manufacturing input which is industry specific and with specific buyer or seller focus. Automated sourcing means that transaction costs are lowered, but because of the specialised nature of the product or service, special logistics requirements are needed and participants must work closely with distributors.

This model is a useful framework for understanding business models, but it must be used in its broadest sense. E-marketplaces are diversifying, developing and changing constantly to keep up with demands of customers and changes in the technology and Web-based business environment. Not only do they offer transaction facilities but the majority of them also provide technical solutions to improve the procurement cycle and make more efficient the value chain. They sell and support complete hardware, software and support solutions for businesses as well as e-marketplace trading facilities.

According to Forrester Research (an Internet consulting firm), by 2004 a shakeout in the business-to-business e-marketplace sector will leave only 180 out of the present 1,000+ companies surviving.[27] They feel that e-marketplaces must develop their service offerings even more and include quality, service, stability of the brand and warranties. According to a recent report by Gartner's GartnerG2, a business strategy research firm, e-market-places will broaden their offerings even further to include supply-chain collaboration and demand forecasting.

'Companies like Ford Motor and BHP, the Australian miner, . . . told us in their own way that enabling a transaction online is interesting, but insufficient, and that we had to do more than that for them to become clients' (Michael S. Levin, e-Steel's chief executive).[28] E-steel have since developed software that their clients use to help integrate their manu-facturing processes with those of their suppliers, using the Web. For example their software enables Ford to perform a whole range of manage-ment tasks, including tracking and managing the manufacturing steps that begin when it orders steel from a supplier; moving the steel to plants for processing, while accounting for the different specifications for rolling the steel; stamping it; and moving it to various processors and assembly plants. The software costs each customer millions of dollars a year and requires multi-year contracts. E-steel's marketplace still has value, 'but only as part of a much more powerful set of tools'[29] and for serving as a place for attracting prospective software clients.

EGovernment

EGovernment is not a business model *per se*, but many national and international governments are pursuing a policy of eGovernment, ena-bling electronic access to a whole range of information and services both to individual citizens and to businesses.

> eGovernment is not about new technologies, it is about how governments can make life easier for citizens and companies by serving them better. We should always remember that in delivering its services, the role of a govern-ment is special. Because a government does not choose its clients, it must be ensured that all citizens have access to the improved services. No one must be excluded. (Erkki Liikanen, EU Commissioner for Enterprise and the Informa-tion Society)[30]

In the UK, on 31 March 1999 the government set a target of making 25 per cent of government services accessible electronically by 2002, 50 per cent by 2005 and 100 per cent by 2008. However, the government found that e-commerce uptake was progressing at such a rate in the UK that in March 2000 the Prime Minister tightened the target for electronic delivery of services to ensure that all key services will be electronically available by 2005. The government's report[31] tracking progress to date (March 2001) found that:

> The Department [of Trade and Industry] remains on track to meet this target and is working with a number of other departments and bodies and contributing to central initiatives such as the UK Online programme. The Department has identified 62 key services of which 16 are now available electronically. By 2002, 43 of these key services should be available, and the remaining 19 by 2005. Examples of progress include: the launch of UK online for business in September 2000 (31); . . . British Trade International which will be investing £20 million over 2001–04 in information and communication technology to enable it to deliver its services world wide (33). The Department's Export Control Organisation (ECO) is planning to introduce acceptance of export licence applications over the Internet by 2002. Further information . . . can be found at the Internet site for the E-Envoy (34).[32]

At an eGovernment conference in November 2001,[33] the key themes of the EU's eEurope Action Plan 2002 was implementation of eGovernment quickly and effectively to promote growth, employment and quality of life for citizens in Europe. These plans are still in the stages of development and as yet there is no comprehensive model of what an eGovernment should look like. However, a number of key principles were agreed for the development and implementation of e-government in Europe, and this provides a useful draft template for anticipating the similarities that might emerge across European eGovernments:

- The technology should be used to encourage participation and strengthen democracy by raising awareness and facilitating participation in elections, especially European elections in 2004.
- All individual citizens and businesses must be able to access on-line services but still have a choice of service-delivery channels, especially human interface.
- Change is needed within the government infrastructure to include new administrative responsibilities, training, skills, employment contracts, and so on.
- The importance of trust and security is paramount and so coordination across Europe must be strengthened to ensure the security of networks guarantee safe access to eGovernment services and encourage the large-scale and compatible use of electronic signatures wherever appropriate.

- With the need for coordination of EU eGovernment initiatives, there is a necessity to establish a common view on which key services should be made available on-line consistently across Europe.

As already indicated, plans for developing a common model for European eGovernment are still at the development stage and plans for progress reports are scheduled for 2003. A study ('eGovernment from Policy to Practice'[34]) of on-line public services across all Member States was commissioned by the European Commission[35] in November 2001. It measured the degree to which e-Government services are provided on-line, by allocating percentages for different stages of development, from simple one-way interaction to full electronic case handling.[36] The performance of each Member State was analysed for benchmarking purposes. The study was useful in revealing the types of services that are being offered across Europe. These can be categorised into four major areas:

- *'Income-generating services'* include financial transactions and flow of funds between individual citizens, businesses and government such as income tax, VAT and other contributions. This was the most developed group of services, with an average of 62 per cent of sophisticated implementation. Income-tax payment was the most widely implemented on-line service. Some 9 out of the 16 Member States (including the UK, Spain and France) scored top marks for degree of sophistication for on-line payment of income tax and VAT (meaning that decision, notification, delivery and payment facilities were all available), with Germany and Ireland amongst those with relatively less sophistication.
- *'Registration services'* involved the recording of details, for example marriages, deaths, births, car registration and company registration. This group of services was relatively underdeveloped with only 44 per cent of respondents offering the range of services, but registration of companies was the most widely available on-line registration service offered by over half of the Member States.
- *'Returns'* is the provision of services by the government, for example social security benefits, job search, public-library services and health-related services. This was also relatively underdeveloped, scoring 40 per cent on the degree of sophistication, but the job-search facilities were very highly developed across all Member States.
- *'Permits and licences'* include official documentation delivery services, for example driving licences, passports and planning permission. This was found to be the least developed set of on-line services, scoring only 33 per cent in terms of sophisticated implementation.

Overall, electronic services for businesses are significantly more sophisticated (52 per cent) than services for citizens (39 per cent), with the exception of the Benelux countries where citizens' services are more advanced. The report also found that public services, which were centrally controlled and required simple administrative procedures (for example, job searches, income tax, VAT, corporate tax and customs declarations), were most suitable to be put on-line. More complex operations requiring a number of different bodies and organisations, such as environment-related permits or planning permissions, involved a whole set of procedures that needed coordination by local service providers and, in order to get integration of technology, needed back-office reorganisation. As with all business models, the eGovernment model is also still in the early stages of being developed and refined.

Peer-to-peer (P2P) networking model

Technically speaking, peer-to-peer networking is a communications model describing the method of connecting computers in a way so that each computer acts as a server to all the others on a network. In contrast to a client/server network, each computer can communicate directly with other computers without having to go through a central server. With peer-to-peer, each party with similar and compatible hardware and software can initiate a communication session. More recently, peer-to-peer has come to describe applications in which users can use the Internet to exchange files with each other directly or through a mediating server:

> P2P is a class of applications that takes advantage of resources – storage, cycles, content, human presence – available at the edges of the internet, . . . Because accessing these decentralised resources means operating in an environment of unstable connectivity and unpredictable IP addresses, P2P nodes must operate outside the DNS [domain name] system and have significant or total autonomy from central servers. (Clay Shirky, American analyst and expert on P2P networks).[37]

According to Shirky et al.,[38] the press coverage of P2P is based on an erroneous premise that P2P is totally decentralised, with all peers being the same and having no central guiding intelligence. He maintains that P2P does not present a choice between centralisation and decentralisation, but that most P2P systems are in fact 'impure,' or 'hybrid', relying on a central server or one or more 'super peers' to boost and support connectivity or resource identification. For example, Napster required the user first to connect to a main control server, which indexed and managed distributed data resources on the network, holding a directory of where all available files were stored. 'Pure P2P' refers to a model, such as Freenet, where all participating computers are peers. No central server is used to control, coordinate or manage the exchanges among the peers.

On the Internet, peer-to-peer networking can be seen as a type of dynamic and fleeting specialised Internet network within the wider global Internet. Some have even called peer-to-peer computing the third generation of the Internet.[39] The first generation Internet was vital for users within the research community and other early adopters, but irrelevant to the rest of the world. The second generation was the Web, which introduced the Internet to the masses. This third generation makes new services available to end users cheaply and quickly by making use of their PCs as active participants in computing processes rather than as just clients and users.

Shirky *et al.* introduced the concept of Presence, Identity and Edge Resources (PIE) which underlines P2P networking. They describe this as: 'Working backward, Edge Resources include content, storage, cycles, bandwidth and even human attention, accessible at the edges of the network, which is to say resources accessible on individual PCs. Identity is simply a name for one of those resources – a machine, a document or a person. Presence is the ability to detect whether that resource is accessible in real time'.[40]

Pat Gelsinger, Intel's chief technology officer, in his Intel Developer Forum keynote speech,[41] outlined a few possible applications of peer-to-peer networking for businesses:

File sharing   The legacy of Napster (see 'The Story of Napster' below, pp. 191–94) has laid the foundation for the future of consumer file-sharing services. Napster has shown that a fully decentralised service has a better chance of surviving legal attacks than centrally managed services. In fact the business model for consumer file sharing can only be one of a licensed, subscription-based service offered by a third party content provider or directly by the content producers. In the short term, however, the only realistic business model is intra-organisational or business-to-business. Organisations are currently exploring the advantages of using P2P as a way to minimise networking costs by removing the need for a centralised server. This allows employees to share files, and is also a cost effective way for business partners to exchange information with each other directly without the additional costs and problems of setting up a complex extranet. 'You don't necessarily share everything on your machine, . . . instead, a consumer or a corporate IT department might partition part of the hard drive on a PC to be used for shared space'.[42]

Distributed computing   This is where multiple computers remote from each other have a role in a computational problem or information processing to maximise the efficiency of the network and other resources. Organisations are also looking at ways of harnessing the idle computing power and resources of millions of computers on the peer-to-peer network. A wide

range of enterprises will find significant cost savings and process accelera-
tion using P2P distributing computing. For example, Gelsinger maintains
that Intel saved US$500 million in costs over ten years by using distributed
computing facilitated by Intel's own internal processor development tool,
Netbatch. This allowed engineers to take advantage of unused processing
power on some 10,000 workstations across 25 worldwide Intel locations to
run computer simulations for chip designs.

According to Intel,[43] their peer-to-peer program, using 6 million PCs
running only 20 per cent of the time, can generate greater than 300
teraflops of computing power. (The world's fastest supercomputers can
perform at about 10 teraflops during its peak operation, which can costs
US$100 million to build and more than US$15 million a year to
maintain.)

CASE STUDY

Applications, which are using peer-to-peer distributed computing power, are large
scientific research projects where individual computer users on the P2P network allow
some of their computer's processing capacity to be used by usually socially beneficial
projects such as the SETI@home (Search for Extraterrestrial Intelligence) project. This
project used the computing power of over 2.6 million P2P users, donating the
equivalent of over 500,000 years of processor time to run an application, which
downloads and searches radio telescope data for patterns indicating extraterrestrial
intelligence.[44] The National Foundation for Cancer Research (NFCR) Centre for Drug
Discovery at the University of Oxford, England, is working with United Devices (ud.com)
and others to access greater computational power from hundreds of thousands of P2P
network users. This extra computational power will enable researchers to run applications that screen for proteins or model molecular data sets in the search for new drugs
to treat cancer.

Instant messaging (IM or IMing) This enables users to locate other users,
establish an independent chat session with another user, exchange comments in real time, and share files and applications. Once connected and
using the same kind of software, IM users must be on the P2P network at
the same time and the intended recipient must be willing to accept the
messages (it is possible to reject messages). Unlike e-mail, messaging is
immediate where the delay is rarely more than a second or two and it is
direct to the user without having to go through POP3 and SMTP mail
servers. With IM, anonymous users gain identity and transient connectivity yields to presence, which indicates whether users are off-line or on-line
(the PI of Shirky's PIE).

IM software is largely proprietary and was first released and pop-
ularised by America Online (AOL), which bought the Mirabilis/ICQ company in 1998. Due to its popularity, other ISPs implemented proprietary
messaging functions for their users. AOL is currently the most popular IM

software but both Microsoft and France Telecom's open source Jabber software could potentially destroy AOL's market lead, mainly because of the platform capabilities and services provided by Microsoft, and also the source code of Jabber is freely distributed and re-distributed and so can be used and modified to integrate with other applications without infringement of copyright.

Many organisations have experimented with migrating IM applications to their office systems; however, this still remains controversial.[45] The advantages are that the software provides a boost to productivity by enabling quick answers from suppliers and co-workers without the delays of voice mail and e-mail. It is also less expensive. The disadvantages, raised mainly by IT managers, are that IM software breaches security, unauthorised IM applications create support problems and there are worries that IM conversations can serve as a distraction rather than a productivity tool.

Edge services   These are based on the concept of distributed computing, using facilities on the 'edge' of the core network (the path between client and server where content processing or storage is requested)[46] to provide improved services. Edge services can include:

- Providing backups, or excess storage capacity for the increasing volumes of data being accumulated.
- Caching content on computers on the 'edge' of the network to enable multiple users to download content from the cached source without having to go through a central server requesting the information.
- Mirroring file servers to provide faster connection times for a larger number of users.
- Distribution of content closer to the users.
- Delivery of broadcast, multicast or streaming data.
- Reformatting of pages for wireless browsers.

The aims and objectives of these services are to improve performance and response times as multiple users vie for access to critical data, facilities and resources at the same time. By using edge services, the capacity for increased bandwidth can be minimised; more multi-media facilities can be used to a higher quality for training and videoconferencing, amongst other uses; network bottlenecks can be avoided, reducing the time it take for a request for content to be received and fulfilled; and spare storage capacity can be harnessed and information can be broken up, encrypted and stored on peer computers in the network. This maintains a high level of improved service and reduced loss in productivity because of network performance problems.

One example is content delivery networks (CDN). In 2002 this is still a very new area and involves 'using a new level of intelligence now available in IP network components to efficiently deliver customized content in the format of a user's client device'.[47] Organisations can improve the performance of the Internet by utilising local delivery mechanisms using non-centralised computers on the network where content can be cached (saved in local and temporary memory) or stored and get content as close to users as possible.

Gelsinger[48] demonstrated so-called edge services, which Intel uses for employee training. Using edge services, a document can be downloaded by a PC user to a local site via a wide area network connection. That PC then becomes the local server for that document.

Peer-to-peer networking is a truly socialist model for using the Internet and it is what the inventors had in mind when they were developing it. There is total autonomy from centralised resources and each computer on the network is equal. Although this model is still in its infancy relative even to other Internet models that have been introduced, it has attracted much interest and investment. Despite the financial fall-out as a result of the deflation of the dot com bubble in 2000/2001, and the reluctance for further investment in technology, corporate investment has been particularly brisk in P2P with over US$165 million invested in 2001. The pattern of business application of the P2P model, according to a survey by Shirkey *et al.*, is mainly collaboration and file sharing and, to a lesser extent, distributed computing, which hints at the developing methods of working in companies.

There is no single definitive taxonomy for Internet business models. Each business model is unique in its own way and each can be implemented in a variety of ways. Any given firm may combine different models as part of its Web-business strategy to yield an overall plan that is profitable. Business models on the Web are continuing to evolve and develop with new and interesting variations emerging, a trend expected to continue in future as technology also develops.

Unlike the UK, business models are patentable in the USA. Already companies such as Priceline (reverse auction method), Amazon (one click way of purchasing), Doubleclick (methods of on-line advertising and measurments) and Pointcast (information advertising and distribution system) have patented their business models in the USA. This adds an extra dimension to the future evolution and development of business models – the impact of which has yet to be determined.

The Story of Napster

With the advent of e-commerce came the process of digitisation and the creation of MP3, a standard technology and format for compressing sound into a very small file (.mp3), while preserving the original quality. This fuelled the use and development of

CASE STUDY

music file-sharing applications. Napster, created by Shawn Fanning in January 1999, while still an undergraduate at Northeastern University in the USA, became the world's leading file-sharing software application. Fanning combined his interest in music and computing by developing an application that allowed a community of users to share personal music files (MP3).

Napster was essentially an index site. The company compiled a list of Napster software users and the files stored on their hard drives and made that list available to other users when they installed the Napster software. A user simply searched for the file they wanted and downloaded it directly from the hard drive of the computer on which it was located. The search and download were free to the user, and Napster was not involved in the download process. Because Napster searched individual hard drives, the number and variety of MP3 files varied. Not all Napster users were on-line at the same time, and so the variety and quality of files was in a state of constant flux.

Figure 5.14 shows the impact of the original early Napster model on the music industry. The artist could make their music available to Napster users directly or alternatively one buyer could make a single .mp3 file available to the whole community of users, eliminating the necessity for users to buy directly from the music retailers and totally destroying the traditional music value chain.

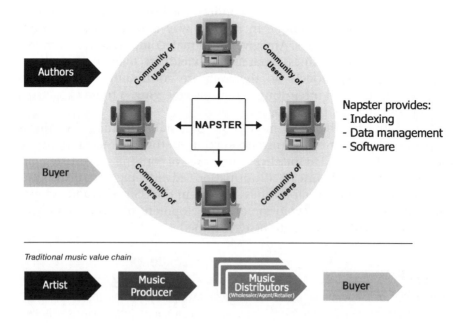

Figure 5.14 The impact of Napster on the traditional music industry value chain

When the beta version of Fanning's Napster software received over 300,000 hits in the early days of its release, this led to a lot of interest from the commercial sector, attracting investment from major venture capitalists and resulting in the growth of the company to 50 employees.

Napster also received a lot of interest from another quarter, which was much less positive – the music industry. Napster has since been under constant pressure from the recording Industry Association of America (RIAA), who interpreted Napster as copyright-infringement software: 'With Napster, every song by every artist is available for download at no cost, and, of course, with no payment to the artist, the song writer or the copyright holder. . . . If you're not fortunate enough to own a computer, there is only one way to assemble a music collection the equivalent of a Napster user: Theft' (Lars Ulrich, drummer of the rock group Metallica).[49] But because the MP3 files did not reside on Napster's servers, and Napster did not charge a fee for the service, critics felt the RIAA had a weak legal case. Napster simply allowed individuals to share music, as do tape recorders and CD burners. However, in March 2001, due to a court order, Napster blocked the trading of over 100,000 files of copyrighted songs. The court ruled that Napster's technology was an infringement on the copyrights of published music. On 6 March 2001, a court order banned Napster from allowing its users to download copyrighted music from other users located using its website and its software. Napster was given 72 hours from the time it received a list of the songs to ban them. The record industry claimed that Napster had not made enough effort to comply with the court order and Napster countered with an argument stating that the lists of songs provided by the record companies were not accurate enough and did not contain details telling Napster where the songs were listed.

The record industry continued to battle against Napster for months, because of fears that the popularity of the system was cutting the number of CDs sold, and thus their profits. Napster introduced new software to filter out banned songs, thus blocking the swapping of copyrighted music. Napster saw its 60 million users fall by 65 per cent,[50] losing them to other sites providing free music download facilities. Legal battles continued, with the music industry accusing Napster's efforts of being inadequate: 'Calling this type of filter effective is like calling an umbrella full of holes a hurricane shelter' (RIAA president Hilary Rosen).[51]

On 2 July 2001, the court awarded an injunction ordering Napster to remove all copyrighted music from its site. This led to the final closure of Napster's file sharing website. Napster planned to come back on-line with a subscription-based service offering 'legally endorsed content' in early 2002.[52] By September 2002, Napster had filed for bankruptcy and its assets were in the process of being sold.

The story of Napster had revolutionised the music industry and has spawned a whole new range of successors that have changed their models. For example, Grokster.com, Kazaa and Music City swap not only music but also video files; in some cases, cinema films were downloadable from the website at the same time as the films were being released in the cinema. The 'entertainment industry' is continuing their campaign and 30 companies, including Disney, Paramount and Sony, have filed a lawsuit against the three Internet sites: 'The suit states: "Defendants have created a 21st Century piratical bazaar where the unlawful exchange of protected materials takes place across the vast expanses of the Internet."'[53]

However, unlike Napster, the three sites do not require a central company to create the downloadable files because they are swapped between users. Other sites such as Gnutella have a totally decentralised system allowing users to exchange all types of files over the Internet directly, without going through a website. After launching the program, the user enters the IP address of another computer belonging to the network. Once the computer finds another network member on-line, it will connect to that user's connection (who got their IP address from another user's connection and so on). Users can choose how many member connections to seek at one time and determine which files they wish to share or password protect. So, after installing and launching Gnutella, a user's computer (node) becomes both a client and a server in the network, which allows individuals to exchange information with each other directly without the supervision and restrictions of brokering websites or other third parties. In effect, each individual in the peer-to-peer community becomes responsible for the content of their own machines.

HOW CAN A BUSINESS MODEL'S VIABILITY BE ASSESSED?

Timmers maintains that the commercial viability of a business model can mainly be assessed by looking at the marketing strategy – for example, what competitive advantage is being built, market positioning, marketing mix, product–market strategies. His focus is largely on marketing.

Affuah and Tucci[54] introduce a framework for the analysis of business models developed to exploit technological change based on two major criteria:

- *Imitability* – the extent to which the technology can be copied, substituted or leapfrogged by competitors.
- *Complementary assets* – control, strength and importance of all other capabilities that are needed to exploit the technology (apart from those that underpin the technology or invention itself). For example: brand image and reputation; manufacturing; distribution channels; customer service; relationships with suppliers and customers.

Affuah and Tucci give examples of the different kinds of businesses that are likely to profit from innovation by using this framework. For example:

- When technology/invention is easy to imitate and complementary assets are freely available or unimportant then it is difficult to make money and organisations must continue to innovate to ensure that they remain ahead of the competition. The majority of Internet start-ups fall into this category.

- When technology/invention is easy to imitate but complementary assets are tightly controlled and important then the controller of the complementary assets makes money. Affuah and Tucci cite the example of RC Cola who invented diet and caffeine-free cola but both Pepsi and Coca-Cola profited from RC Cola's invention because it was easy to imitate and they had the superior brand name, reputation, distribution channels and marketing infrastructure to exploit it. In order to achieve profitability, complementary assets must be developed in-house or acquired through alliances, joint ventures or acquisitions.

- When technology/invention is difficult to imitate but complementary assets are unimportant then it is the inventor that profits from the invention. This is particularly the case with rare *objets d'art* and branded luxury goods – for example, the Stradivarius violin. In order to maintain profitability, copyrights and patents can be applied to prevent unauthorised copying. In an age where technological inventions are moving so quickly into obsolescence, this is not a long-term strategy for inventors of technology.

- When the technology/invention is hard to imitate and the complementary assets are tightly held and important then both the inventor and the holder of the complementary assets profit. If they are separate entities then the one with the most negotiating power will manage to gain more of the profit. An example of this is the music and film industry. The artists are the inventors and the music and film distribution companies such as Sony, Virgin and Disney hold the complementary assets. Usually, in the early days of an artist's career before the onset of success, it is the distribution companies that have the upper hand. However with popular success, the negotiating power of the inventors increases and so does their share of the profits.

Other measures of a business model's viability are the traditional measures used by all business, which were briefly forgotten in the 'dot com' frenzy (discussed in the next chapter). These include:

- *Financial measures* – since the aim of a business model is to plan for a sustainable business, the financial measures, such as cash flow, earnings, profit margins, market share and operating costs are crucial in determining its viability.
- *Competitor benchmarking* – identifying the organisation's main competitors and comparing the range of products, services, prices, customer service, financial performance and a range of other measures to determine the organisation's own performance in the context of its competitors.

- *Market analysis* – understanding the market and how it works and the impact of new technology on the industry sector. Market analysis also involves identifying the major players in the market and market share, and how share can be built.

When considering these measures it is crucial to take into account the characteristics of the Internet, such as its relative low cost; ubiquity; global nature of networks, markets and reach; 24/7 availability; digitisation of data, transmission and processes; multi-media capabilities; and network externalities (discussed in detail in Chapter 8). The nature of the Internet and World Wide Web has spawned a knowledge-based economy where knowledge-based products have very high set-up costs relative to the variable costs of producing and offering each subsequent unit. For example, software development set-up costs are huge but once it is developed and posted on the Internet, the cost of duplicating the product selling it to customers (by download) is almost zero. With AOL it cost hundreds of millions of dollars to develop its software, hardware brand and subscriber base, but once the initial amount is spent the monthly relative cost of maintaining each member is negligible. This underlines the importance of gaining market share as a crucial strategy for high fixed cost, low variable cost products. In order to attract market share, it is essential to develop a brand name and reputation, and so the spending on advertising and promotion is very high. Some of the other strategies have already been discussed earlier in the chapter and include:

- Giving away a product and charging for later versions (creating lock-in and raising switching costs).
- Giving away a product X and charging for complementary product Y – for example, in the computer games sector some of the games machines are sold at considerable losses in order to gain market share, but the shortfall is recouped many times over with the volume and price of the games that are sold.
- Pricing low to penetrate the market and gain market share.

The whole concept of business models and their viability is simple. A company produces a good or service and sells it to customers. If the revenues from sales exceed the cost of operation then the company makes a profit. The perceived difficulty seems to be coming from a lack of understanding of the technology and its characteristics, where business models become more intricately woven and the inclusion of other 'network' factors makes the assessment of who makes money and how much is not always clear at the outset.

E-commerce and technology will continue to give rise to new kinds of business models. But the Web is also likely to reinvent tried-and-tested models. The history of radio and television broadcasting can put this difficulty in perspective. Radio and television programming has been broadcast over the airwaves free to anyone with a receiver for much of the past century. The broadcaster is part of a complex network of distributors, content creators, advertisers (and their agencies), and listeners or viewers. By looking at the broadcasting industry today, this may give an indication of how e-commerce and e-business may develop in the future.

SO WHAT DOES THIS MEAN?

Business models are not a new concept. Figure 5.15 takes six major areas of a business and compares the different foci of traditional and Internet-based businesses to illustrate the kinds of changes that have occurred. With *production*, the traditional business models incorporated mass production and manufacturer push, a culture encapsulated in the utterance of Henry Ford, one of the earliest mass-producing car manufacturers, who said that customers could 'have any colour so long as it was black'. The Internet has enabled customers to communicate directly with manufacturers, specifying and receiving the kind of products and services they required. The idea

	Traditional Business Models	New Business Models
Production	Mass Manufacturer push	Personalised Customer pull
Distribution	Middleman	Direct
Communications	Hierarchical Closed	Networked Open
Finance	Slow Difficult	Faster Easier
Markets	Local Mass	Global Niche
Assets	Tangible Physical	Intangible Virtual

Figure 5.15 The creative destruction of business models

of disintermediation and re-organising the *distribution* channels is one of the premises of the new Internet-based business model.

Since the Internet is the tool for communications in e-commerce, it has enabled networked and open communication with a whole range of stakeholders directly, which has flattened and opened up organisations, making them less hierarchical and more interconnected. The open and wide-ranging communications facilities also opened up international and global markets. Where traditionally markets were mainly local and mass markets, with distributors being used to expand to wider geographical markets, the Internet enabled business to access global markets and target customer niches easily and cost-effectively. In an environment dominated by the electronic and digital, assets are no longer physical but are also virtual and intangible, and include ideas, knowledge and information: all are the basis on which new business models function. The financing of business models has traditionally been lower amounts, where returns are expected over a longer period of time and the process of attracting finance has been a difficult process. With Internet-based business models, financing was in the early stages extremely easy to attract, as venture capitalists and investors were keen to get involved in the new and attractive business revolution. This is no longer the case, but infrastructures still remain, which make attracting financing much easier than previously. This is discussed in more detail in the next chapter.

SUMMARY

Business models are not a new concept. A business model is simply a method of doing business whereby an organisation can sustain itself in the short term and develop and grow in the medium to longer term. A well-planned and successful business model will in the longer term give the business a competitive advantage in its industry, enabling it to earn more profits than its competitors.

The main elements of a business model are revenue streams, value streams and logistics streams. None of these streams are mutually exclusive and all work together to add value to stakeholders of the company, which manifests itself in increased revenue and the need to re-engineer business processes and value chains for successful implementation. Internet technology has enabled a wide range of business models and has impacted on value, revenue and logistics streams both indirectly and directly. However, the capability of technology is just one criterion in model selection.

There are many business models that have been created and implemented, but these are still in the early stages of development and 'the' business model suitable for Internet business has yet to be commercially and empirically proven over a sustained period of time. Assessing the viability of business models is not and can never be an exact science. Because e-commerce is still in the relatively early stages of its lifecycle, there are only a few frameworks that can be used to analyse the viability of the business model. Using these analytical frameworks will, at the very least, increase the probability that the business models are based on sound and realistic principles. E-commerce businesses combine a number of different business models; each one is not mutually exclusive.

The next chapter will illustrate how badly business models can be put together and the impact of this on the business itself and the economy as a whole.

DISCUSSION QUESTIONS

1 What is a business model and why is it used?
2 Explain how Internet-based businesses can create value streams, revenue streams and logistics streams.
3 Identify the different kinds of dynamic pricing strategies and explain the benefits and limitations of each.
4 Identify five different business models and classify them.
5 What are the advantages and limitations of using Affuah and Tucci's framework for analysing a business model's viability?
6 Suggest a framework which you believe would analyse the viability of an Internet business model.

REFERENCES

1 A. Affuah and C.L. Tucci, *Internet Business Models and Strategies: Text and Cases,* International Edition, McGraw-Hill, 2001.
2 B. Mahadevan, 'Business models for Internet-based e-commerce: An anatomy', *California Management Review,* Berkeley, Summer 2000.
3 R. Coase, 'The Problem of Social Cost': http://www.sjsu.edu/faculty/watkins/coase.htm (accessed October 2001).
4 R. Jacobso, 'E-marketplaces – The next revolution – CIO-Asia – Analyst corner November 2001': http://www.cio-asia.com/dev/idgcio.nsf/CIOList/FCBD5B7602EBB50048256AF5000B528A!opendocument (accessed December 2001).
5 http://www.amazon.co.uk/exec/obidos/subst/associates/join/associates.html/026–2237253–1791610
6 http://www.hmce.gov.uk/business/electronic/evr-getting.htm
7 R.J. Dolan and Y. Moon, 'Pricing and market making on the Internet', *Harvard Business Review,* 9/11/2000, HBS Publishing (Product Number 500065).
8 E-Cost website: www.ecost.com
9 'Working the Web bazaar', from May 2000 edition of *PC World*: http://www.pcworld.com/resource/article/0,aid,15823,pg,4,00.asp

10 www.servall.com

11 About Ubid – Website: www.ubid.com

12 Pricelinewebsite: www.priceline.co.uk

13 S. Kaplan and M. Sawhney, 'E-Hubs the New B2B Marketplaces', *Harvard Business Review*, May–June 2001.

14 M.E. Porter, *Competitive Advantage of Nations*, Palgrave Macmillan, 1998.

15 A. Affuah and C.L. Tucci, *Internet Business Models and Strategies: Text and Cases*, International Edition, McGraw-Hill, 2001.

16 Speech by Jeff Bezos, The CommonWealth Club of California: http://www.commonwealthclub.org/98–07bezos-q&a.html (accessed December 2001).

17 W.C. Taylor, 'Who's writing the book on Web business', *Fast Company*, Issue 5, p. 132, October 1996: http://pf.fastcompany.com/online/05/starwave2.html (accessed January 2002).

18 R.D. Hof, E. Neuborne and H. Green, 'Amazon.com the wild world of e-commerce', bureau reports from *Business Week*, 3 December 1998: http://www.businessweek.com/1998/50/b3608001.htm (accessed January 2001).

19 Amazon.com case study: http://www.isss-awareness.cenorm.be/Case_Studies/amazoncom_case_study.htm (accessed January 2001).

20 Definition of infomediation from Webopedia: http://www.webopedia.com/TERM/I/infomediary.html

21 http://digitalenterprise.org/models/models.html

22 P. Timmers, 'Business models for electronic markets. Focus theme EM', *Electronic Markets*, Volume 8, No. 2, 1998: http://www.electronicmarkets.org/netacademy/publications.nsf/all_pk/949/$file/v8n2_timmers.pdf?OpenElement&id=949

23 P. Timmers, *Electronic Commerce: Strategies and Models for Business to Business Trading*, John Wiley and Sons Ltd, 1999.

24 'B2B e-commerce will survive growing pains', *CyberAtlas*, November 2001: http://cyberatlas.internet.com/markets/b2b/article/0,,10091_930251,00.html (accessed December 2001).

25 'B2B e-commerce will survive growing pains', *CyberAtlas*, November 2001: http://cyberatlas.internet.com/markets/b2b/article/0,,10091_930251,00.html (accessed December 2001).

26 S. Kaplan and M. Sawhney, 'E-hubs the new B2B marketplaces', *Harvard Business Review*, May–June 2001.

27 B. Tedeschi, 'Some business-to-business marketplaces showing staying power', *New York Times* on the Web, 16 July 2001: http://www.newview.com/news/pressroom/inthenews/2001/jul/nyt_ecommerce_esteel.shtml (accessed December 2001).

28 B. Tedeschi, 'Some business-to-business marketplaces showing staying power', *New York Times* on the Web, 16 July 2001: http://www.newview.com/news/pressroom/inthenews/2001/jul/nyt_ecommerce_esteel.shtml (accessed December 2001).

29 B. Tedeschi, 'Some business-to-business marketplaces showing staying power', *New York Times* on the Web, 16 July 2001: http://www.newview.com/news/pressroom/inthenews/2001/jul/nyt_ecommerce_esteel.shtml (accessed December 2001).

30 'EU Ireland Commission publishes first survey of e-government in Europe', 30/11/2001: http://www.euireland.ie/news/infosoc/1101/egovsurvey.htm (accessed December 2001).

31 'Figure 1.2 performance against departmental operations and CSR PSA
   productivity targets', *Government's Expenditure Plans for 2001–2002*, DTI Report
   (published in March 2001): http://www.dti.gov.uk/expenditureplan/
   expenditure2001/intro_chap1/chap1/section3.htm (accessed December 2001).
32 'Chapter 1 – information age government 1.25', *Government's Expenditure Plans
   for 2001–2002*, DTI Report (published in March 2001): http://www.dti.gov.uk/
   expenditureplan/expenditure2001/intro_chap1/chap1/section4.htm (accessed
   December 2001).
33 'Ministerial declaration: eGovernment – a priority for Europe', *EU Ireland*,
   30/11/2001: http://www.euireland.ie/news/infosoc/1101/egovdeclaration.htm
   (accessed December 2001).
34 http://europa.eu.int/information_society/eeurope/egovconf/documents/
   CGEY%20Final%20Summary%20Report2611011%20with%20disclaimer.doc
35 'Commission publishes first survey on eGovernment services in Europe', *EU
   Ireland*, 30/11/2001: http://www.euireland.ie/news/infosoc/
   1101/egovsurvey.htm (accessed December 2001).
36

Stage	Intervals		Definition
	Score	Percentages	
0	0–0.99	0–24	No publicly accessible website(s) or the website(s) do not qualify for any of the criteria for the stages 1 to 4.
1	1–1.99	25–49	**Information** necessary to start the procedure to obtain the service available on the website(s).
2	2–2.99	50–74	**Interaction:** downloadable or printable form to start the procedure to obtain the service on the website(s).
3	3–3.99	75–99	**Two-way interaction:** electronic forms to start the procedure to obtain the service on the website(s).
4	4	100	**Transaction:** full electronic case handling of the procedure by the service provider (including decision, notification, delivery and payment if necessary).

'Summary report – Web-based survey on electronic public services', October
2001, by Cap Gemini for the European Commission: http://europa.eu.int/
information_society/eeurope/egovconf/documents/CGEY%20Final%20
Summary%20Report2611011%20with%20disclaimer.doc (accessed December
2001).
37 K. Lillington, 'Power to the people', *Guardian*, 22/2/2001: http:/
   /www.guardian.co.uk/Archive/Article/0,4273,4139668,00.html (accessed
   January 2002).
38 C. Shirky, K. Truelov and L. Gonze, 'P2P networking overview: The emergent
   P2P platform of presence, identity, and edge resources', O'Reilley Research,
   September 2001 (est.): http://www.oreilly.com/catalog/p2presearch/summary/
   index.html (accessed December 2001).
39 C. Shirky, K. Truelov and L. Gonze, 'P2P networking overview: The emergent
   P2P platform of presence, identity, and edge resources', O'Reilley Research,
   October 2001: http://www.oreilly.com/catalog/p2presearch/summary/
   index.html (accessed December 2001).

40 C. Shirky, K. Truelov and L. Gonze, 'P2P networking overview: The emergent P2P platform of presence, identity, and edge resources', O'Reilley Research, October 2001: http://www.oreilly.com/catalog/p2presearch/summary/index.html (accessed December 2001).

41 J.G. Spooner, 'Intel: The future is peer', ZDNet News, 24/8/2000: http://www.zdnet.com/zdnn/stories/news/0,4586,2619470,00.html (accessed December 2001).

42 J.G. Spooner, 'Intel: The future is peer', ZDNet News, 24/8/2000: http://www.zdnet.com/zdnn/stories/news/0,4586,2619470,00.html (accessed December 2001).

43 'Peer-to-peer computing for bio-informatics': http://cedar.intel.com/cgi-bin/ids.dll/content/content.jsp?cntKey = Generic+Editorial%3a%3ap2p_cure&cntType = IDS_EDITORIAL

44 D. Barkai, 'Initiatives and technology – an introduction to peer-to-peer computing', Intel® Developer Update, February 2001 issue: http://cedar.intel.com/cgi-bin/ids.dll/content/content.jsp?cntKey = Generic+Editorial%3a%3ap2p_barkai&cntType = IDS_EDITORIAL&title = Overview&path = 1 (accessed December 2001).

45 D. Delmonico and G. Williams, 'Instant messaging overview', Internet.com Serverwatch, 15/1/2002: http://serverwatch.internet.com/articles/imservers/index.html (accessed January 2002).

46 CDN white paper, 'Content networking and edge services: Leveraging the Internet for profit: A technology backgrounder', Stardust.com, Inc., 19 September 2001, p. 18: http://www.spegadmin.com/Uploads/6/pdfs/CDN_whitepaper.PDF (accessed December 2001).

47 CDN white paper, 'Content networking and edge services: Leveraging the Internet for profit: A technology backgrounder', Stardust.com, Inc., 19 September 2001, p. 18: http://www.spegadmin.com/Uploads/6/pdfs/CDN_whitepaper.PDF (accessed December 2001).

48 J.G. Spooner, 'Intel: The future is peer' (quotation from Intel's Gelsinger), ZDNet News, 24/8/2000: http://www.zdnet.com/zdnn/stories/news/0,4586,2619470,00.html (accessed December 2001).

49 'Napster expelled by universities', 26/9/2000: http://news.bbc.co.uk/hi/english/business/newsid_942000/942090.stm (accessed December 2001).

50 'Napster use slumps by 65%', 20/7/2001: http://news.bbc.co.uk/hi/english/business/newsid_1449000/1449127.stm (accessed December 2001).

51 'Napster faces new court battle', 9/4/2001: http://news.bbc.co.uk/hi/english/business/newsid_1269000/1269608.stm (accessed December 2001).

52 'Napster to relaunch in 2002', 30/10/2001: http://news.bbc.co.uk/hi/english/entertainment/new_media/newsid_1627000/1627438.stm (accessed December 2001).

53 'Post-Napster sites face industry wrath', 4/10/2001: http://news.bbc.co.uk/hi/english/entertainment/new_media/newsid_1578000/1578616.stm

54 A. Affuah and C.L. Tucci, *Internet Business Models and Strategies: Text and Cases*, International Edition, McGraw-Hill, 2001.

From dot com to dot bomb

LEARNING OBJECTIVES

- To understand the 'dot com' phenomenon.
- To identify the reasons for the rise and fall of the dot coms.
- To be able to summarise the lessons learnt.

INTRODUCTION

This chapter is an epilogue to Chapter 5. We will investigate the dot com phenomenon, and identify the catalysts of its rise and fall and the lessons that can be learned.

'THERE'S GOLD IN THEM THERE DOT COMS'

In 1997/8 the dot com gold rush began in the USA, followed by Europe 12–18 months later. The received wisdom at the time was that businesses either went 'on-line' or went out of business. There was a frenzy as companies and individuals rushed to get involved with Internet businesses. The Chairman of Intel, Andy Grove, was 'widely quoted as saying that in five years' time all companies will be Internet companies or they won't be companies at all'.[1] In the UK, the Prime Minister, Tony Blair, was also 'vigorously urging business to embrace the Internet or risk bankruptcy'.[2] And so the dot com gold rush came to the UK.

Forecasts and predictions for the growth of e-commerce were of lofty proportions. Although there was no common agreement by researchers on

Figure 6.1 The early dot com phenomenon

the exact figures for the total revenue worth of e-commerce, there was agreement that there would be exponential rates of growth, with some anticipating ten–fold annual compounded growth year on year. Surveys were forecasting the growth of e-commerce for home shopping, banking and other services in Western Europe to grow to around US$223bn by 2002 from its estimated US$19bn in 1999, with the US e-commerce market rising to US$843bn (nearly 10 per cent of its gross domestic product [GDP]) from US$109bn in 1999. Management consultants Datamonitor estimated worldwide revenues of more than US$1,000 billion by 2003, while other studies by US IT research consultancy Forrester and accountants KPMG suggested even higher figures. Research carried out by the Henley Centre for Forecasting suggested shopping in cyberspace was growing six-fold every month.[3]

For the UK, estimates of consumer spending on the Internet soared to similar lofty heights with Verdict Research[4] estimating consumer spending on the Internet rising to £7.3 billion in 2004 from its estimated £581 million in 1999 (see Table 6.1). Predictions and forecasts for the potential revenue opportunity of e-commerce were coming from all quarters, Robert Conway of PricewaterhouseCoopers stated that 'E-business will be mega for the next five years',[5] while Intel's executive Craig Barrett, addressing the *Wall Street Journal Europe*'s conference on converging technologies in 1999, said: 'I think all of the forecasts are underestimates. (E-commerce) is going to be a bigger phenomenon than any of us estimate'.[6]

Growth in the number of Internet users gave fuel to the predictions of the growth in e-commerce and raised the profile of dot coms. The number of users was growing exponentially mainly due to the growth of 'free'

TABLE 6.1 Projected Internet shopping in the UK by 2004

UK Internet Shopping for	1999 £ million	2004 £ million
Groceries	165	2395
Clothing	5	1210
Computer software	122	934
Music	85	575
Books	106	430

Source: Verdict Research

Internet access pioneered by the British ISP Freeserve, where only costs of the Internet calls were charged. During 1999, net use was estimated to have risen by almost a third in Europe, compared with less than one-tenth in the USA. However, in the USA they had a good two or three years head start and so had achieved a critical mass of users. In the UK, an ICM poll for the *Guardian* newspaper found that 37 per cent of adults used the Internet either at home or at work, and that almost half the adult population – 21 million people – are 'likely to be online by the end of next year (2001)'.[7] With the growing number of on-line users, a survey by Datamonitor[8] in 1999, found that shopping and financial services were the most popular uses. More than one in five consumers with access to the Internet ordered products on-line and 8 per cent used it to monitor their finances.

Development of improved technology (broadband) meant higher bandwidth would be introduced, enabling higher-quality and faster Internet access. This, coupled with competing telecommunications companies offering unmetered single monthly fees for accessing the Internet, meant that the growth in the number of Internet users forecasted would become a reality. 'If 1999 was the year of the online retail explosion, 2000 will be the year of the online media explosion' (Toby Strauss, Internet analyst at mortgage brokers John Charcol).[9]

Established high-profile companies were publicly sharing experiences of their e-commerce success, giving credence and legitimacy to the 'power' and attraction of e-commerce. Intel, the world's biggest computer chip maker, at the Wall Street Journal Europe's conference in 1999, revealed that it expected its e-commerce related revenue to generate about half of its total sales (around US$15 billion); having started from zero nearly a year ago, they expected e-commerce transactions to represent 90 per cent of their total revenue by 2001/2002. 'Essentially all of our businesses will be conducted in this fashion',[10] claimed Intel's Chief Executive.

Sun MicroSystems introduced the concept of the on-line three A's 'Anything, Anywhere, Anytime'[11] explaining how Sun had created 'MySunCentres', which personalised websites for customers and partners, giving them access to rich and dynamically changing information to match each visitor's profile. This was a way of improving stakeholder relationships, which improved the efficiency of the organisations and impacted on its revenue stream.

Leading consultancy firms were directly helping the start-ups and indirectly contributing to the hype with more forecasts and reports. Many of the top consultancies believed they could cash in on the potentially lucrative innovative ideas emerging from on-line start-ups. Many were offering a range of expert financial services, management skills and even premises for a fee or an equity stake in the new dot com companies. One of the global consultancies, Bain & Company, launched Bainlab, a subsidiary devoted to developing and funding Internet projects. Many of the top consultants were tempted away from their lucrative and 'safe' jobs to become CEOs and sit on the board of directors of some of the new start-ups. One the executives from Andersen Consulting left his position to join on-line grocer WebVan.

Expectations of high profitability from the dot coms were based on the number of site visitors, operating costs and the growth of advertising revenue. In 1999, these profit expectations fuelled a demand for shares in Internet companies that could not be met. Demand exceeded supply of shares and so many Internet companies were overvalued even though they were making a loss. With few Internet companies actually making money, it was hard for analysts to work out how to value them except by looking at the long-term growth potential. The numbers on the Web continued to increase rapidly, building strong brands and unique products.

CASE STUDY

Jelly Works, a UK Internet investment company, was floated on London's Alternative Investment Market, offering 10 per cent of the company within two months of its incorporation. Jelly Works's website has an on-line process for entrepreneurs to make their bid for cash to help their start-up or expansion. Its shares rose 2000 per cent within three days of floating from an initial 5p, to 99.5p per share, increasing the company's valuation from £10 million to £200 million. That company had a host of well-known business figures on its board, including Jonathan Rowland, founder of and investor in a number of Internet firms, such as 365 Corp and Demon Internet.

Flightbookers, the long-established London-based bricks and mortar travel business with annual sales of about US$50 million,[12] launched Ebookers, the on-line spin-off. Ebookers offers travel products and services on-line, including negotiated discount airfares, hotel and car rental bookings. The on-line business had sales of about £10 million a year and reported a loss in the first six months of 1999, but floated on the New York Stock Exchange at a price of US$18 per share, which had risen to US$43 before finally closing at US$26.5 per share by the end of the first day's trading.

In September 1999 the rival UK on-line travel agency, Lastminute.com, announced it was considering a flotation.

In the USA the phenomenon was even more pronounced. One of the first dot coms, and often seen as the blueprint for the 'dotconomy', Amazon.com was making losses despite its 4 million customers and sales approaching US$1 billion a year. However, at the time (January 1999), its shares could virtually double in a week because of news of a share split and an announcement of a new warehouse to speed distribution. Amazon shares rose from US$14 to US$187 a share within 6 months[13] and the market valuation of the company reached US$30 billion – more than leading US retailer Sears Roebuck. However, Jeff Bezos, the owner of Amazon.com, whose personal stake was worth US$15bn, had the sense (lacking in some investors) to cash in more than US$60m in stock along with his fellow Amazon.com directors at the height of the frenzied prices.

Headhunting was rife in an environment where there was a severe shortage of personnel who could understand and use the technology. Coupled with shortages came high salaries. Some companies would offer a bounty of up to £5,000 for finding and recruiting an employee in their organisation. Traditional bricks and mortar companies with old-fashioned pay scales were unable to compete with the 'sexy young dot com scene' which offered high salaries and a stake in the company through stock options. The pull of the stock market flotations, with millions of pounds available and the promise to 'make a million', attracted many high-flying employees away from their relatively lucrative and 'safe' jobs. As in the case of 30–year-old Michael Ross, who quit his £100,000–a-year job at McKinsey management consultants to head up Easyshop, an on-line retailer selling lingerie.

There was also growing resentment amongst the old staff because new staff were often rewarded with higher salaries and allowed to work in a separate and more modern environment than their traditional co-workers. However, the argument was that these talented people made things happen and so they would have to compete. One executive put it bluntly, 'Fuck the pay scales and pay the market rate.'[14] Other companies offered stock options in the parent company. Others were thinking of spinning off their Internet businesses, to create 'valuation currency' in which key staff could share. One Wall Street analyst with the reputation of being a dot com guru was supposedly enticed to change companies with a deal worth about US$7.5 million.[15] In the fast moving environment, loyalty was rare and incentives were in abundance to try and buy that loyalty.

A groundswell of contemporary folklore, legend and hype was created about teenagers, school dropouts or ex-corporate high fliers emerging from the chrysalis of garages, bedrooms, squats or cramped offices in Manchester, Birmingham and London, having come up with a simple idea, designed a Web page and attracted investors, to become the dot com millionaire butterflies taking the stock exchange by storm. An *Observer* study[16] of Britain's new rich in 1999 revealed that there are 90 British multimillionaires aged 30 or under, most having made their money in the new cyber economy of the Internet, telecommunications and computers, overtaking more established industries.

CASE STUDY

Jason Drummond created a business registering names on the Internet and estimated to be worth £24m. Adam Twiss and Damien Reeves, Cambridge University graduates, started Zeus Technology, a company that develops Internet software, valued at £30m. Adam Laird, 27, left Boston Consulting to run Magicalia, after lining up £1m of venture capital to back its string of hobby-focused websites. Tim Jackson's on-line auction house, QXL, was about to float for an estimated £400m. This, however, was only small fare compared to their US counterparts – 29-year-old Jerry Yang, founder of Yahoo!, was reckoned to be worth nearly US$1bn and Jeff Bezos, founder of the on-line bookseller Amazon.com, was worth US$7bn. 'Everyone's looking to do something on the Internet and make money. It's a combination of the gold rush and the Wild West. It is nice to be in a room where everyone thinks they are going to be millionaires'[17] (Nick Denton, First Tuesday,[18] a business networking and matchmaking company).

The Internet stock surge was being led by people who traded shares on the Web. The growth of e-commerce was a catalyst for the growth of on-line financial services such as stock brokering and banking. Stock trading service companies like E*trade and Charles Schwab set up low commission and simple on-line trading facilities, enabling anybody to become a day trader trading in and out of shares several times a day. Many people signed up to the notion of becoming shareholders at the click of a button and were investing in shares in the very short term. It was estimated that the average investor in Internet stocks only held that company for less than a week.[19]

CASE STUDY

Nicholas Birbas, a 25-year-old former waiter, gave up his day job making US$500–600 dollars a week and is now making around US$50,000 a month trading on the Internet. He epitomised the day traders who knew nothing about the companies in which they invested, did not examine balance sheets or financial statements but spent all day in internet chat rooms like Tokyojoe or Silicon Investor swapping tips and gossip. They then traded stocks hour by hour, watching for every small movement in the price. '"I just play on momentum . . . When I see the volume taking off, fundamentals don't mean anything at that point. I get in and get out and just keep doing that," Birbas says. His ideal trade is around 2000 shares at $20 (for an investment of $40,000) then he waits for the stock to rise $3 or $4 and sells: An instant profit of around $8000.'[20]

E-trading contributed to the overall volatility and inflation of dot com stock. The increased numbers of 'day' traders led to a shortage of some shares, such as E-bay, and fuelled the inflated stock prices since supply could not meet demand.

Trading on the Internet also meant that rumours and speculation spread more quickly, through the use of the Internet and the numerous press releases or news stories about companies. A tip posted on a popular bulletin board, or broadcast by a particular analyst with little or no justification, was sending share price rocketing or plummeting. In the UK, a Channel 4 gameshow, *Show Me the Money*, had analysts making stock tips on the programme, leading to a number of companies experiencing a rise in their shares following the tips.[21]

In a couple of incidents, companies inadvertently benefited from the dot com fever rumour mill. Osprey communications, a London-based advertising and marketing company, experienced a rise in their share price (which had been stable for the past month) from 7p to 15p owing to mistaken identity, leading to the valuation of the company to almost twice what it was only a week previously. The Chief Executive of Osprey explained:

> We hear someone was looking down a newspaper listing of media stocks, misread Osprey Comms as Osprey.com, assumed it was an internet stock and took a punt without really thinking why . . . It is very nice to see the jump in the company's share price but it is nothing to do with us. We do have an e-commerce division that is performing very well but nothing has changed at the company to explain the movement in the share price.[22]

Similarly a company called Rodime, a floppy-disk-making company based in Edinburgh, which was suffering losses, saw its shares double rising from 6.5p to 12.75p on the mistaken assumption that it was being merged or taken over by an Internet company. The same thing happened with a company called Ultima Networks, which enjoyed a 36 per cent rise in shares because of rumours of mergers/acquisitions.

An environment of information symmetry was created by the growth in the number of sources of financial information that was available to both professional and home shares traders. With the growth of the Internet came the growth of cable, digital and satellite television, which began broadcasting 24-hour programming. A variety of national and international television stations were broadcasting special programmes where financial information was available 24 hours a day and covered all the financial and business markets and economies of the world. Traders could instantly access a whole range of information delivered through the mass availability of financial information websites, television and radio, and make a decision to buy or sell and complete the transaction within seconds and at the click of a button.

And so the late 1990s witnessed this dot com frenzy on both sides of the Atlantic. The prediction for the new millennium was that it would continue. Ivo Philipps of Screentrade, the on-line stock brokers, predicted that 'There will be numerous internet launches and flotations in the first quarter of 2000, with further "phenomenal" growth over the next two years'.[23] But Nancy Smith, the head of investor education and the US Stock Exchange Commission, warned: 'What is happening is that investors are pouring their money into anything that has "dot com" after it. Nobody knows where it is going to end, who is going to be standing at the end of the day'[24]

'ALL THAT DOT COM GLITTERS IS NOT GOLD'

There is no doubt that the advancement of electronic commerce, and the birth of the dot coms that ensued, was a phenomenon that characterised the revolution in technology and the reaction of business and society to it. As with all revolutions there is a period of euphoria and optimism that drives the revolution onwards into the mainstream. With this move into the mainstream, reality reasserts itself, and where previously ignorance, naiveté, innovation, novelty and enthusiasm obscured the facts, a time for consolidation, reflection and analysis replaces the initial frenzy of euphoria. And so this was the case with the dot com boom. The following section will examine some of the high-profile dot coms that 'bombed' as a result of investors returning to sanity and sound practices of business analysis.

In mid-2000, the demise or takeover of a number of high-profile sites signalled the beginning of the dot com shakeout. Forrester Research published a report by David Cooperstein, 'The Demise of Dot Com Retailers',[25] predicting that the shakeout would be dramatic and bloody. The report predicted that of the hundreds of e-tailers in some market segments, at most only three would be left in each niche after the shakeout. It also predicted that a similar shakeout would occur in the business-to-business sector. Already B2B stock values have fallen dramatically (the share price of Freemarkets fell by 89 per cent) a trend which others are following. Forrester predicted that low profit margins, competition from established traditional businesses and lack of investor capital would drive most of the dot coms out of business by 2001.

PriceWaterhouseCoopers commissioned a report[26] to examine the 'burn rate'[27] (the length of time a company can continue to operate before needing to raise additional cash) of 28 Internet companies listed on the Stock Exchange (including techMARK)[28] and AIM.[29] The report's findings revealed that 25 of the 28 companies had short burn rates – the average being 15 months – but ten of the companies had a burn rate of less than

12 months and one in four had a cash burn rate of six months. This meant that 25 companies would have spent their cash reserves by August 2001, well before they could break even. They identified marketing and technology costs as being responsible for the fast rate of 'cash burn'. It also said business-to-business companies were far more likely to get extra funding than business-to-consumer companies.

Since 2000, there have been some very high-profile closures of dot coms resulting from cash burn out, fraud, overspending, inability to attract more funding and a range of other reasons. For example, Clickmango.com attracted £3 million investment, including investment from the English actress Joanna Lumley. The site sold natural healthcare and beauty products on-line and employed 18 people, but closed five months after its launch having only achieved £100,000 of sales. Other closures include Furniture.com and etoys (later bought for some US$3 million and revived by bricks and mortar company KoB Toys, with an 80–year history of selling toys in the USA). So what is the reality of the dot bombs? Table 6.2 has been compiled to give a flavour of the kinds of Internet companies that have closed down and the reasons for it.

Boo.com to Boo.bomb within six months

CASE STUDY

One of the earliest high-profile and often-quoted examples of a failed dot com is Boo.com. Boo.com, a European on-line clothing retailer, was finally launched on 3 November 1999 to a loud fanfare of publicity after overcoming five months of technical delays. The Swedish founders were Patrik Hedelin, a corporate financier, Ernst Malmsten, a poetry critic who dropped out of studying history, and Kajsa Leander, a former Vogue model. The trio originally came together to launch a Swedish on-line bookstore (bookus.com), which they sold to fund Boo.[30] Their ambitious aim was to be the first truly global shop selling a selection of branded sports and fashion goods in seven different languages and several currencies, using a virtual shop assistant (Miss Boo) to guide customers through the whole shopping and buying process. *Fortune* magazine featured it as one of the 'coolest' companies of the year.[31] Investors and shareholders in Boo included the French billionaire owner of the LVMH (Louis Vuitton Moet Hennessy) luxury goods group Bernard Arnault; the Italian clothing family Benetton; and US investment banks Goldman Sachs and JP Morgan. Investing an estimated £80 million, the company had offices in London, Stockholm, Paris, New York and Munich employing some 400 people.

Sales for the Christmas period were valued at over US$100,000[32] when a report from investment bank CSFB ranked it as the number one retail site in the USA in overall e-commerce terms.[33] But this was not enough to save 100 jobs, which were axed in January 2000. It was later revealed that despite the five-month delay in the launch of the website, the management had ordered a whole season's worth of high-fashion sportswear, which it later had to sell at a discount as outdated stock. When the website was

TABLE 6.2 A selection of dot coms to dot bombs

Name of site	Details	Date of closure
DrKoop.com.	A website based on the vision of Dr C. Everett Koop, the former US Surgeon General, who believed that people should be empowered to better manage their personal health with comprehensive, trusted information. drkoop.com provided users with comprehensive healthcare information, access to medical databases, real-time medical news, interactive communities and opportunities to purchase healthcare-related products and services on-line. Investors put in over US$100 million.	17/12/2001 filed Chapter 7[a] bankruptcy and is shutting down.
iPublish.com	Electronic book publisher part of Time Warner, selling electronic reprints of books and original e-books from new authors. At its demise, it had US$10 million losses and axed 29 employees.	5/12/2001
Net2000 Communications Inc	Telecommunications company offering telecommunications services, videoconferencing and a range of other services. At their peak their market capitalisation was US$1.5 billion and offered BMW cars to employees for signing on. They had already gone through consolidation processes by selling off different parts of the organisations and paring down the 900 employees to 200. The company is US$115 million in debt.	20/11/2001 filed for Chapter 11 bankruptcy[b] and was selling off its assets. Ten of its affiliates also filed for Chapter 11.
allmybills.com.au	A major Australian dot com start-up received initial seed capital of US$2.5 million and offered consumers a consolidated on-line bill-payment service. Six months later it closed, losing its 25 staff whom they still owed some US$100,000 and owing creditors US$1.2 million. No other funding was forthcoming.[c]	7/17/2000
Pixelon.com	The founder and CEO of Pixelon, Michael Adam Fenne, a computer programmer, was really David Stanley, an ex-con running from the law. He claimed to have invented a new way to broadcast video on the Internet, and was reported in the media to have 'developed the industry's most advanced proprietary system for compressing analogue media sources into digital multimedia files viewable by personal computers worldwide. The company holds eight patents surrounding its technology, and has an array of specialised delivery systems for its clients in the entertainment, advertising, sports, corporate and live broadcast industries'.[d] He raised around US$30 million but this information was untrue. It was	27/6/2000

TABLE 6.2 Continued

Name of site	Details	Date of closure
	reported that he spent the money lavishly and even spent US$16 million on a launch party which featured a performance by Kiss and The Who (in a very rare reunion gig) in Las Vegas.	
giftemporia.com	This high-end shopping destination had the backing of former President Bush (senior). Nine months later the site ceased to exist.	28/6/2000
somerfield.co.uk	British supermarket chain Somerfield announced it was shutting down its 9-month-old on-line shopping service on 25 June. 228 jobs will be 'affected'. This, however, was revived in 2001.	19/6/2000
PlanetAll.com	A Web-based address book/community site, which was acquired by Amazon. The Web page's excuse was that Amazon has 'succeeded' in integrating its services into Amazon.com.	20/6/2000
Flake.com	A portal for breakfast cereal. 'I'm discouraged, and I'm essentially broke', says the founder	16/6/2000
Surfbuzz.com	The on-line auction site informed its customers that it 'will no longer be operational nor continue to exist'. After burning through its cash.	7/6/2000
Toysmart.com	The Disney-owned retailer said it was going out of business after burning through most of its cash and being unable to raise more. Walt Disney Co. bought majority interest in 1999, six months before it went bankrupt. It had 170 employees at shutdown.	29/5/2000
Digital Entertainment Network (DEN)	Provided original Web videos for young people. More than 300 workers were laid off. DEN raised more than US$68 million from Dell, Microsoft and others.	May 2002

Sources: This table has been compiled from a number of websites that have logged the failed dot coms, giving irreverent and sometimes obscene views of their failure[e]

Notes:

[a] Liquidation bankruptcy

[b] Under the bankruptcy code, a Chapter 11 filing allows a company to continue operating while it works with creditors to reorganise and develop a plan to keep the company in business.

[c] K. Nicholas, 'Allmybills runs out of Cash', Biz.com: www.smh.com.au/news/0007/14/bizcom/bizcom03.html

[d] 'Actual Results May Vary . . .', The Industry Standard, 26/6/2000: http://www.thestandard.com/article/0,1902,16361,00.html

[e] Such as: 'dot com graveyard', Washington Post Online: http://www.washtech.com/news/dotcom/6547-1.html; 'Dot com doom', News headlines from Moreover: http://www.moreover.com/cgi-local/page?o = portal&c = Dot%20com%20doom%20news. Also, the archives of f***kedcompany.com (the *** indicate the letters 'uck'), but be warned this website contains obscene and sometimes libellous material. Another site, which actually preserves the home page of the now defunct websites, is http:/ /www.disobey.com/ghostsites/ (compiled by Steve Baldwin, who keeps a museum of e-failures).

launched, it was too technically demanding for the target audience who were either unable to load it because it 'crashed' their PCs or because it took over an hour to place an order. Apple Macintosh users were totally unable to use the site, and complaints from potential customers were either ignored, or received a response that the site only catered for people with fast connections and the right equipment.[34] Despite website improvements that enabled an easier and faster ordering process and access for Apple Mac users, prices more competitive than high-street competitors and an increase in revenues to US$657,000 for the month of February compared to US$680,000 for the three months from November 1999, it seemed disaster was imminent.

In February 2000, Patrik Hedelin (aged 30) decided to return to Sweden to 'spend more time with his family' and took a non-executive role at Boo. He was replaced by the new finance director Dean Hawkins who used to be second in command at Adidas.[35] Hedelin stated that he may pursue other Internet opportunities as long as they did not conflict with his commitments to Boo, but denied there were any problems with the company, stating that it was normal for a start-up to have teething troubles in its early life. Hawkins and the technology manager (recruited from BSkyB) left to join other Internet firms very soon after. Rumours were rife that Boo were burning cash at a faster rate than expected and were attempting to raise an additional £20 million to keep afloat.

Pressure from their investors and shareholders finally led to the directors at Boo.com calling in liquidators from the accountancy firm KPMG after existing investors refused to add to the estimated £80 million and no other source of funding to keep the company afloat was forthcoming. Although those losing their jobs 'were obviously very angry', it was reported that recruitment agents were seen handing out cards to staff leaving the building. KPMG received 30 offers for the company within days of the announcement and expected to sell it within one week. The Boo.com era – associated with high prices; luxury expenses (including Concorde flights, entertaining at top restaurants and a champagne lifestyle); being dubbed 'the most expensive call centre in the world' by one analyst for employing 80 people in London's fashion centre, Carnaby Street, instead of the more typical call centres sited in industrial estates on the edge of medium-sized towns[36]; and a burn rate of nearly US$20 million for each of the six months it traded – had come to an end.

Boo.com was sold to the US fashion Internet portal fashionmall.com for an estimated £250,000. This was mainly for the brand, the logo and the right to use the domain name that was established by Boo. The CEO of the company admitted to feeling fortunate that the original Boo team spent so much money on marketing. It expects to spend a maximum of US$1m on marketing, compared to the US$40m the original Boo spent. However, the high level of awareness they created is now helping her cause: 'Retaining the name Boo uses this awareness of the name to bring people to our site so they can see how great our product is . . . We have the same sort of irreverent sense of humour as our predecessors.'[37]

The new Boo is very different from its predecessor. They believe they have learnt many lessons from the original Boo. The new company has only nine employees compared to original Boo's four hundred, and is also financially secure with about US$27m in the bank, which is estimated to last ten years based on the current burn rate. The new Boo also has a different business model, which the CEO explained:

> We do not own and sell our own inventory, what we do is connect people to great e-tail sites and product. So our value to the visitor is about connecting them to interesting places through Boo . . . We have a very long-term view about this. We're not trying to take over the world in a year, we're trying to take over the world in a series of years.
>
> We will have some of the same brands the original Boo had but when they are on our site it is not because of the brand, it is because the product is really cool.
>
> It will work because we are applying the lessons of the original Boo to a new business model and retaining all of the positive elements of the Boo brand.[38]

Fashionmall.com focuses on the 18–30 American and British markets, and specialises in beauty products, clothes, gifts and toys – from hi-tech gadgets to motorcycles. There is also a community aspect to the site: users can talk to each other in the party section. The new Boo.com plans to make money through advertising and sponsorship on the website and is also developing a database that can be sold to companies that want to know about and target the people Boo.com attracts. Expectations were that the company would achieve profits within two years. In fact, the company broke even in the second quarter of 2001 and began to make a small profit (after reducing its staff to 3) in the third quarter of 2001.

In an epilogue to the Boo.com story, the founders were interviewed by the *Guardian*[39] 18 months later (October 2001) and answered charges of extravagance and inexperience, which they were in the process of reflecting upon in a book they were writing of their experience:

> We made mistakes. I'm not denying that but a lot of the time I felt very isolated. I was left by myself and should have had a strong chairman who had been there before and could tell me 'Ernst, you can't do that, do this instead'.
>
> I was quite young and inexperienced. I was only 28. The company was too ambitious. We tried to do everything in too many areas and too quickly and it was just unrealistic.
>
> The structure was so complex that sometimes neither us nor the investors knew which of the holding companies we were supposed to be putting money into.
>
> Everyone got caught up in the hype. It's easy to forget what people were saying at the time.

In response to the stories of their Concorde travelling (where tickets are around £5,000–£10,000 each), caviar eating and champagne quaffing extravagances that were part of the process of cash burn, Ms Leander said:

> I only flew Concorde three times and they were all special offers . . . Some people might think it's glamorous to fly to New York every other week and have dinners with investors but I have a young child I hardly ever saw and I'd have rather been at home with her.

And that stuff about the free coffee and fruit. I mean doesn't every office have free coffee and fruit?

We only had two [parties] and they weren't as extravagant as people said.

Mr Malmsten adds:

We went out a lot because it was a new company with a good spirit but it wasn't charged to boo. Yes, I went to Nobu for dinners and yes it was glamorous but fashion is a glamorous business.

When boo closed it was the worst day of my life. It was so sad seeing all those people lose their jobs. A lot of them had become very good friends. I cried a lot.

If I do something else I need a mentor, someone who is a wise person who can in some way look after me. I felt quite alone at boo.

As well as the book being written by co-founders Ernst Malmsten and Kajsa Leander, the third partner, Patrick Hedelin, also wrote a book about the time at Boo.com which the other two refute as being in some instances exaggerated and untrue. A film production company has an option on the rights to the book *Boo Hoo: A Dot-com Story* and are planning to produce a film starring Richard E Grant and Famke Jansen, depicting the story of Boo.com in autumn 2002.

CASE QUESTIONS

1 What are the lessons that can be learnt from the experiences of Boo.com?
2 If you had been CEO of Boo.com how would you have done things differently?
3 Design a strategy for Boo.com to succeed today.

THE DOT COM SHAKEOUT

Webmergers.com is one of the leading providers of research and services for buyers and sellers of Web and technology properties, producing regular reports on the state of mergers, acquisitions and bankruptcies of Web-based companies. In a report by Webmergers in 2002, they estimated that in the period 2000–2001, there were around 762 closures – 233 in 2000 and 537 in 2001.[40] The chart in Figure 6.2 plots the monthly shutdown or declared bankruptcies of Web-based companies. The research is based on surveying published and personal sources, tracking shutdowns and bankruptcies of 'substantial' Web-based companies around the world. Substantial is defined as those that have received significant funding from venture capitalists, business angel investors or other formal investors.

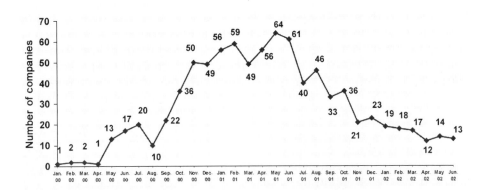

Figure 6.2 The number of Web-based company shutdowns (2000–2001)

Source: www.webmergers.com

The height of dot com closures peaked between November 2000 and August 2001 and seems to be slowing despite the economic slowdown in the USA and some European countries in late 2001. It is broadly estimated that nearly two-thirds of the closures are US-based companies, around 10 per cent are Western European, around 2 per cent are from the Asian-Pacific region and one-quarter come from the rest of the world. The kinds of companies that were largely affected were those with a higher cash burn rate, mainly in the business-to-consumer sector, and nearly half were e-commerce based businesses (i.e. conducting transactions such as e-market-places and e-tailers), followed by a quarter that were content providers such as news and entertainment websites. Some argue that the closure and bankruptcy rate of dot coms is slowing because there are no dot coms left. Webmergers believe this is like saying 'a decline in rabies rates is due to the fact that all dogs are dead'.

If these figures are put into perspective a different picture emerges. Webmergers conservatively estimate that there is a total of between 7,000–10,000 funded Web-based companies. This makes their failure rate around 8 per cent within the first 2–3 years of start-up. If this figure is compared to the average failure rate of 'bricks and mortar' start-up companies, most studies show that over 90 per cent fail within the first three years. The primary reason for such a high failure rate is that owners have to go through the learning curve of operating a specific type of business.[41] These figures suggest that there is more hype than substance in the reported failure of Web-based businesses. Far from being a failure, Web-based business on the whole has been a success (to date), with the stock market crash and the reporting of the high-profile failures (such as Boo.com) overshadowing the reality of the situation.

As well as the much reported closures of the dot coms, there has been even more activity in their mergers and acquisitions (M&A). For every closure in 2000 Webmergers found that there were almost four times as many Web-based companies being merged or acquired. This slowed in 2001, where for every closure there were nearly two Web-based companies that were merged or acquired. Figure 6.3 charts the volume and value of mergers and acquisitions over four years since 1998.

At the peak of the dot com frenzy, as cash burn rates reached unsustainable proportions, investors were reluctant and unwilling to invest any more funds in these companies. Web-based companies saw mergers as an alternative way of obtaining funding. In 2000, the time frame to get the deals done quickly for fear of being outbid was weeks, and often the merging and acquiring companies were not fully aware of what they were buying and how they were buying it. At the height of the frenzy, AOL (the Internet service provider) and Time Warner (the multimedia empire) merged in one of the biggest deals of the period valued at around US$157 billion in early 2000. It has since had to make a one-off write-down of between US$40bn and US$60bn of goodwill in its accounts for the three months to March 2002 to reflect 'overall market declines'.[42]

As time went on, the dot coms consolidated their finances in the face of more realistic and reluctant investment making the companies

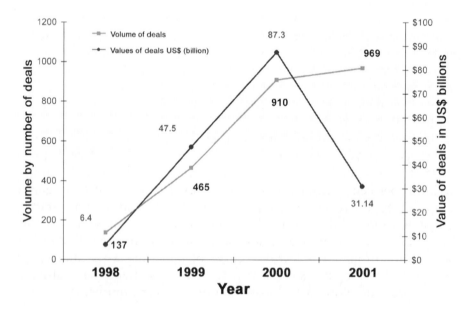

Figure 6.3 Mergers and acquisition activity of Web-based companies (1998–2001)

Source: www.webmergers.com

'cheaper'. The average deal fell from US$10.2 million in 1999 and US$9.5 million in 2000 to US$3.2 million in 2001, its lowest level over the four years and the timeframe for closing the deal became longer. The stock-market crash further eroded the valuation of the Web-based companies, making them cheaper still. The majority of mergers and acquisitions activity (over 90 per cent) originated from US companies in 1998–9, underlining the US advancement in e-commerce the lifecycle. By 2000, the rest of the world was catching up and was responsible for nearly 75 per cent of Web-based company M&A spending.

The pattern in the types of companies merging and being acquired followed that of the closures. Initially the major interest was in the business-to-consumer content provider websites, slowly changing more to the transaction and e-commerce websites and more recently concentrating on business-to-business related websites such as e-marketplaces. In 2001, there was a further shift towards acquiring Internet infrastructure companies that provide such infrastructure as e-business software, network tools and other 'e-business enabling' technology, which facilitates core Internet applications such as customer relationship management (CRM), e-procurement, on-line payments, supply chain management, collaboration and enterprise resource planning (ERP). Technology companies like IBM, PeopleSoft, Siebel Systems, Microsoft and SAP began taking advantage of the low valuations to fill gaps in their product lines cost effectively. The acquisition of content and e-commerce sites was extremely small by the end of 2001, reflecting the rock-bottom valuations. However, these kinds of deals were not entirely dead, as in the case of the record-setting deals of Cendant's (a travel/finance/re-location/real estate services conglomerate) US$2.9 billion acquisition of travel services provider Galileo International and Vivendi Universal's (the global media and communications corporation) US$373 million bid for on-line music property MP3.com.[43]

As more Internet companies got into difficulties, the bricks and mortar retailers acquired complete fully functional websites at a fraction of the set-up costs – they cashed in on the brand, the technology and the existing customer databases without the risk of the dot com start-up. For example, Great Universal Stores, the UK's largest home-shopping group (who own Argos and Burberry amongst others), bought jungle.com[44] in September 2000 for £37 million, which was thought to be well below the suggested stock exchange floatation valuation of £750 million. Jungle, one of the most recognised on-line-brands in the UK, had already spent £2 million on developing the website and £5 million on a high-profile marketing campaign, and had 370,000 registered customers and recorded sales of just over £75 million, but still made losses before tax of £11.4 million.

In March 2000, Kingfisher (owners of high-street retailers Comet, B&Q, Superdrug and Woolworths) bought a minority stake in the thinknatural.com website (Europe's leading on-line retailer of natural health products) for £3 million. As part of the deal, ThinkNatural would gain high-street promotion through Superdrug's 704 UK stores, and access to the supply chain and buying power of the health and beauty giant.[45]

WHAT ARE THE LESSONS LEARNT FROM DOT COM SHAKEOUT?

We have discussed the dot com phenomenon – its rise and fall. The reasons why the dot com phenomenon began and ended can be divided into three core factors – the macro-environment, the impact of the technology and the micro-environment at the level of the firm.

The macro-environment

Initially the technology and capabilities of the Internet were understood by very few. In this climate, demonstrations of Web pages and their ability to capture, manipulate and present information was very attractive. Hit counters would show the number of visitors reaching millions in a month and so financial projections were based on these volumes of visitors being translated into potential sales.

Venture capitalists were swayed by the projections, and the real world business sense of many hardened analysts was obscured by the new technology. Similarly with stock market and equity analysts. They were influenced by the amounts of capital investment the business plans could attract and the keen interest from potential investors.

Not only this, but the *sports-style coverage of the equity markets* created a hype machine fuelled by 'star' research analysts like Henry Blodget of Merrill Lynch & Co.[46] There were also suggestions and accusations of a clash of interests, where the large investment banks giving advice on the performance of stocks and equities were the same banks that were handling the flotation of the dot coms on the stock exchange and so were far from impartial advisors – but either way they were benefiting.

Another macro-environmental factor was the introduction of *Web-based stockbrokers* that enabled *individual non-professional traders* to buy and sell shares instantaneously and as many times a day as they required for a minimal commission fee (around £10). This, along with the *widely available company, market* and *economic information* on the Web and through other media, fuelled the *short termism*, which drove demand for dot com shares.

The growth of *the world economy* meant that vast quantities of funding were available from both institutions and individuals to invest in the new technology ventures or dot coms.

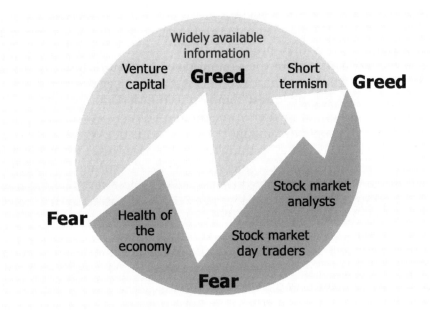

Figure 6.4 The dot com greed/fear spiral

All these events conspired to create *a greed spiral* upwards (see Figure 6.4), drawing in more investors and creating more of a demand for shares that were increasing in value by multiples of ten within days of issue. However, the failure to realise the projected levels of sales and profits and the inordinate rate of cash burn, coupled with the downturn in the economy, meant that further funding for investment was not forthcoming. Thus without further cash injections and with the heavy losses being experienced, the high-profile new start-ups were unable to continue and were either acquired or ceased to trade. The same factors that drove the greed spiral upwards now initiated the fear spiral downwards. The fear of losing further capital and any potential returns on investment exceeded the greed, which resulted in the different macro-environment factors impacting on each other compounding the slowdown further.

Impact of the technology

This relates directly to a number of issues relating to the use and access to the technology. For example, the *Internet penetration rates* during the period were still relatively patchy, and so a large number of potential users could not yet access the Internet and the boast of global reach was limited to certain regions and countries. Not only this, but the cost of connecting to the Internet was still relatively high and dependent on a 'pay as you go' basis rather than a flat rate. Penetration rates of *Internet-compatible comput-ing equipment* were also overestimated and so again the number of potential users was much lower than projected. In the case of Boo.com the website was far too sophisticated for the computing equipment of the majority of its users and so it became inaccessible. Boo.com were adamant they were not going to cater for the lowest common technical denominator.

As time went on, more users came on-line, so there was an increase in *user 'Web savvy'*; people became more familiar with the World Wide Web, and no longer clicked on everything on a Web page to see what it would do. This in turn reduced the impact of Web advertising and so *Web advertising revenues* almost halved in early 2001. These revenues fell even further later on in the year, causing many dot com businesses that relied on advertising as an integral part of their revenue stream to collapse.

The dynamics of the Internet and World Wide Web mean that there is almost *infinite space on the Web*. With the increasing number of start-ups that transferred an existing business model onto the Web or, even worse, copied other companies (largely because funding was available), the advan-tages of the power of the Internet were not harnessed by many and so *too many sellers were seeking too few buyers*. Many of the business models required both a critical mass of buyers and a critical mass of sellers at the same time. Many of the e-marketplaces fell into this category and many failed because it was impossible to create the same level of critical mass at the same time.[47] The more creative start-ups leveraged Internet tools to produce such innovations as collaborative buying, price comparison facil-ities, e-procurement and bidding systems for a number of different prod-ucts or services rather than just duplicate a mail-catalogue on the Web.

Because of the early stage of adoption of the Internet there was no empirical evidence or precedence of how to measure or interpret the success of websites. Different metrics, such as visitors to the site and number of page downloads, were used but there was a question mark over how effective they were in representing success. So as the general economic slowdown continued, advertisers and Internet sponsors were increasingly unsure of the wisdom of investing large amounts in websites.

Micro-environment – the business

As with any business since the beginning of the history of commerce, a well thought-out and realistic business plan is crucial to its success. In the case of the failed dot coms, the *business plans and the business models were not thought through properly*. They were put together on the back of the dot com hype and were largely implemented by *inexperienced managers* and executives who were young, IT literate and understood the technology, but who were unable to manage the large sums of venture capital. This led to a large amount being spent on technology which was largely put before the business, the revenue streams were overestimated, the salaries were over inflated, the borrowing was far too high and the cash burn rates were obscenely high (relative to other businesses). There was also a problem with the technology because, as one commentator said, 'we would get the orders for the website first and then figure out how to deliver it'. The bad planning not only extended to the revenue streams but also the logistics streams. In the case of etoys.com, they were too successful and could not cope with the logistics of delivery – which involved more frequent, geographically disparate deliveries of small packages to customers.

WHAT ABOUT THE SUCCESS STORIES?

The story of successful Internet start-ups is largely as a result of doing the opposite of the failed dot coms. These Internet start-ups concentrate on a specialist or niche area of a product or service. Some initially involve home working to minimise costs. This is a crucial part of competent financial management needed to drive a successful business start-up which means reduced *not* inflated salaries and very little or no debts or borrowing.

With the lack of loans and borrowing, there will also be limited outside involvement, which for the entrepreneurial and competent management team would be more of a hindrance than a benefit. Advertising and promotions budgets are also minimised. It was estimated that the average dot com spent some £3–5 million on promotions and advertising. In the case of the successful start-up, advertising is initially mainly through word-of-mouth (or viral marketing) and electronic means (such as newsgroups), which has been found to be the most effective means of promotion over the Web.

Another factor is in-house technology or website-development skills. The profile of the management team should, if it is an Internet or Web-based business, consist of at least one member of the team with the necessary IT skills, otherwise there will be problems attracting and maintaining loyal IT staff critical to operations.

Finally, those Internet companies who have succeeded have projected and realised modest profits which grow at a steady rate year on year. There should also be no immediate plans for flotation on the stock exchange in order to make a 'quick buck', cash in the shares and retire on the proceeds, as was the intention of large number of people involved in the initial wave of dot com start-ups. Some examples of successful Internet start-ups that are still in existence in 2002 and have been so for over two years include:

- *Tesco.com* (www.tesco.com) – the retail supermarket giant's on-line shopping service is one of the most successful in the food retailing sector.
- *Hard to find records* (www.htfr.com) – a specialist site that locates vinyl records and sells equipment for DJs.
- *The Alternative Gift Company* (www.alt-gifts.com) – a specialist site that provides a service to locate gifts for specific occasions and people and also supplies and ships those gifts.
- *Jobserve Recruitment* (www.jobserve.com) – the on-line recruitment agency is still privately owned and has won numerous accolades and awards as one of the most successful and fastest growing Internet start-ups since its inception and is only recently moving into multi-million pound premises to accommodate the growth in the company.
- *Online medical consulting service* (www.med4u.co.uk) – the on-line medical consulting service run by a couple of qualified medical experts and practitioners who offer a fee-paying consultancy on-line, giving patients piece of mind and advice on their conditions and medication.
- *Internet estate agent* (www.findaproperty.com) – has also grown from strength to strength and is a website where agents can post the properties for sale or let and potential buyers can then contact the agent themselves around the world.

All of these sites not only offer the basic goods or services but also include information relevant to the visitor and the industry sector in which they are operating.

SUMMARY

The dot com boom was fuelled by the introduction of new Web and Internet technology into the world of business. The Internet's ability to reach a global audience, and so access global markets across time and geographical barriers cheaply and effortlessly, was the basis of many business plans that attracted hundreds of millions of pounds of investment and funding. Conventional wisdom was that the first to grab a substantial market share would win and retain their position as market leaders. The unrealistic projections of the business plans fuelled a frenzy amongst investors, stock markets, the media and the business community to get in on the act and benefit from the bonanza. The demand for shares in Internet and Web-based companies far exceeded supply and companies that were only weeks old, with little or no information on their actual financial performance, were valued at hundreds of millions of pounds. This made them bigger than the 'traditional' multinational corporations and institutions that had been in existence for decades with a successful financial history. The spending on marketing and technology (seen as core to the strategy for capturing market share) spiralled out of control with some companies paying 400 per cent of their revenues on advertising. The dot com entrepreneurs were chasing growth at all costs – 'It's too soon for profits – they're just not important,' Forrester reported one dot com executive as saying.

The 'burn rate', the term analysts gave to the frenetic rate that firms spent money, was unsustainable and venture capitalists were unwilling and unable to pump more funds into ventures that were showing no financial returns. As more and more websites were launched, the market became overcrowded and it became difficult for consumers to differentiate between different sites. Companies like Boo were unable to build up numbers of buying customers fast enough to generate revenues to offset the high set-up costs and exceedingly high cash-burn rates. Since the high stock prices were based on unrealistic estimates of how fast profits and sales could rise, when losses began to mount, share prices plunged, which in turn hit confidence in the corporate sector. And so there was a return to rationality, which led to the demise or acquisition of many unsustainable dot coms.

With the consolidation of the dot com sector, so the economy returned to a semblance of stability with wages becoming more realistic, alleviating fears of potential inflationary effects and subduing the greed spiral. But just like the exaggerated and over-hyped report of the dot com bonanza, its demise has similarly been over-hyped and exaggerated.

Boo, and companies like it, taught many people some very hard lessons about remembering that a business plan is based on achievable and sustainable financial objectives.

DISCUSSION QUESTIONS

1 What were the major catalysts for the rise of the dot coms?
2 What were the major catalysts for the fall of the dot coms?
3 Explain how the same factors worked together to first create the rise in the dot coms and then lead to their downfall.
4 Where do you think the dot coms of today will be in 2 years time and where will they be in 5 years time?

REFERENCES

1 I. Rodger, 'E-business: opportunity or peril?' BBC News Online, 4/2/2000: http://news.bbc.co.uk/low/english/business/newsid_535000/535247.stm

2 I. Rodger, 'E-business: opportunity or peril?' BBC News Online, 4/2/2000: http://news.bbc.co.uk/low/english/business/newsid_535000/535247.stm

3 J. Arlidge, '"Dot com" millionaires log on as Britain's new elite', Guardian On-line, 19/9/1999: http://www.guardian.co.uk/Archive/Article/0,4273,3903512,00.html

4 'UK internet shopping set to boom', BBC Online, 7/12/1999: http://news.bbc.co.uk/low/english/business/newsid_535000/535247.stm

5 I. Rodger, 'E-business: opportunity or peril?' BBC News Online, 4/2/2000: http://news.bbc.co.uk/low/english/business/newsid_535000/535247.stm

6 'UK the place "for e-commerce explosion"', BBC News Online, 22/06/1999: http://news.bbc.co.uk/low/english/business/the_company_file/newsid_375000/375326.stm

7 I. Rodger, 'E-business: opportunity or peril?' BBC News Online, 4/2/2000: http://news.bbc.co.uk/low/english/business/newsid_535000/535247.stm

8 'UK Logs on to E-commerce', BBC On-line, 24/8/1999: http://news.bbc.co.uk/low/english/business/the_economy/newsid_429000/429406.stm

9 I. Rodger, '1999: The year of the Net', BBC On-line, 30/12/1999: http://news.bbc.co.uk/low/english/business/newsid_574000/574132.stm

10 'UK the place "for e-commerce explosion"', BBC News Online, 22/06/1999: http://news.bbc.co.uk/low/english/business/the_company_file/newsid_375000/375326.stm

11 'Sun Microsystems' Louise Proddow – It's dot com or die in the digital world', Guardian On-Line, 11/12/1999: http://www.guardian.co.uk/Archive/Article/0,4273,3940621,00.html

12 'E-bookers shares soar on debut', BBC On-line, 15/11/1999: http://news.bbc.co.uk/low/english/business/the_company_file/newsid_517000/517180.stm

13 'Internet stock frenzy', BBC On-line, 8/1/1999: http://news.bbc.co.uk/low/english/business/the_company_file/newsid_251000/251282.stm

14 M. Horsman, 'Net profit can also be gross', Guardian On-line, 6/12/1999: http://www.guardian.co.uk/Archive/Article/0,4273,3938435,00.html

15 J. Martinson, 'Analyst offered $7.5m lure', Guardian On-line, 16/12/1999: http://www.guardian.co.uk/Archive/Article/0,4273,3942150,00.html

16 J. Arlidge, '"Dot com" millionaires log on as Britain's new elite', Guardian On-line, 19/9/1999: http://www.guardian.co.uk/Archive/Article/0,4273,3903512,00.html

17 J. Arlidge, '"Dot com" millionaires log on as Britain's new elite', Guardian On-line, 19/9/1999: http://www.guardian.co.uk/Archive/Article/0,4273,3903512,00.html

18 The First Tuesday network includes 100 cities in more than 40 countries around the world and brings together the leading players in the technology sector: entrepreneurs and managers of new ventures; venture capitalists and investors; service providers; and 'intrapreneurs' and technology managers in corporate entities. The First Tuesday network includes over 100,000 members worldwide. www.firsttuesday.com

19 'Internet stock frenzy', BBC On-line, 8/1/1999: http://news.bbc.co.uk/low/english/business/the_company_file/newsid_251000/251282.stm

20 'Business: Your money all in a day's work', BBC On-line, 9/2/1999: http://news.bbc.co.uk/hi/english/business/your_money/newsid_275000/275572.stm

21 J. Cassy, 'Suddenly investors are going dotty', Guardian On-line, 18/11/1999: http://www.guardian.co.uk/Archive/Article/0,4273,3931690,00.html

22 J. Cassy, 'Suddenly investors are going dotty', Guardian On-line, 18/11/1999: http://www.guardian.co.uk/Archive/Article/0,4273,3931690,00.html

23 I. Rodger, '1999: the year of the net', BBC News Online, 30/12/1999: http://news.bbc.co.uk/low/english/business/newsid_574000/574132.stm

24 'Business: Your money all in a day's work', BBC On-line, 9/2/1999: http://news.bbc.co.uk/hi/english/business/your_money/newsid_275000/275572.stm

25 K. Anderson, 'Dot.com gold rush ends', BBC On-line, 30/5/2000: http://news.bbc.co.uk/low/english/business/newsid_766000/766098.stm

26 'Short burn rates leave dot.coms exposed to increasingly selective equity markets', PriceWaterhouseCoopers, 17/5/2000: http://www.pwcglobal.com/extweb/ncpressrelease.nsf/DocID/7ACD939A10B1C06E852568E4004D42C4

27 The research used the most recent financial statements and calculated the burn rate by dividing cash on balance sheet by cash operating expenses minus gross profit, and assumed that cash operating expenses and gross profit grow at the same rate as internet commerce (130 per cent per annum).

28 Launched in 1999, techMARK is an international market for shares in innovative technology companies. www.londonstockexchange.com

29 AIM is a global market for a wide range of small, young and growing companies either by direct investment in AIM stocks or through funds specialising in AIM. Investors should take into account that whilst potential returns may be high, AIM companies may be a higher risk. AIM companies are unquoted for tax purposes and there are certain tax advantages available to investors in qualifying quoted companies. www.londonstockexchange.com

30 S. Jordon and T. O'Sullivan, 'Sweden – The most wired country in the world', Guardian Unlimited, 12/3/2000: http://www.guardian.co.uk/Archive/Article/0,4273,3973149,00.html

31 J. Cassy, 'Boo opens online', Guardian On-line, 4/11/1999: http://www.guardian.co.uk/Archive/Article/0,4273,3925500,00.html

32 A. Hyland and J. Martison, 'High-profile internet companies cut jobs', Guardian On-line, 29/1/2000: http://www.guardian.co.uk/Archive/Article/0,4273,3956477,00.html

33 J. Cassy, 'Boo.com investors press for sale: E-finance special report', Guardian On-line, 4/5/2000: http://www.guardian.co.uk/Archive/Article/0,4273,4014469,00.html

34 N. McIntosh, 'Bye, bye Boo', Guardian Unlimited, 18/5/2000: http://www.guardian.co.uk/Archive/Article/0,4273,4019532,00.html

35 J. Cassy J, 'Boo's Swedish founder to spend more time with his family: E-finance special report', Guardian On-line, 10/2/2000: http://www.guardian.co.uk/Archive/Article/0,4273,3961723,00.html

36 N. McIntosh, 'Bye, bye Boo', Guardian Unlimited, 18/5/2000: http://www.guardian.co.uk/Archive/Article/0,4273,4019532,00.html

37 J. Snoddy, 'Boo is reborn in confident fashion', Guardian On-line, 27/10/2000: http://www.guardian.co.uk/Archive/Article/0,4273,4082284,00.html

38 J. Snoddy, 'Boo is reborn in confident fashion', Guardian On-line, 27/10/2000: http://www.guardian.co.uk/Archive/Article/0,4273,4082284,00.html

39 J. Cassy, 'From boo to bust – and back', Guardian On-line, 31/10/2001: http://www.guardian.co.uk/Archive/Article/0,4273,4288452,00.html

40 'February 2002. Year end shutdowns report: shutdowns more than doubled in 2001', WebMergers report: http://www.webmergers.com/editorial/article.php?id=49

41 http://www.ounceofprevention.ca/busopp.htm

42 'AOL Time Warner shaves forecasts', BBC News Online, 8/1/2002: http://news.bbc.co.uk/hi/english/business/newsid_1748000/1748159.stm

43 'February 2002. 2001 year-end Internet M&A report', Webmergers: http://www.webmergers.com/editorial/article.php?id = 50

44 'Jungle.com goes cheap', BBC On-line, 1/9/2000: http://news.bbc.co.uk/hi/english/business/newsid_905000/905796.stm

45 Think Natural press release, 22/3/2000: http://www.thinknatural.com/ThinkNatural/PressReleases/220300.jhtml;$sessionid$UFEMUTQAABWSRLA4AIKSFEQ?affiliate = ThinkNatural&req = 9593

46 R. Buckman, 'Who Caused the Dot-Com Crash?' *Wall Street Journal*, 5/3/2000: http://www.infopoint.com/articles/dotcomcrash.html

47 T. Miller, 'February 2002. Top ten lessons from the Internet shakeout', Webmergers: http://www.webmergers.com/editorial/article.php?id = 48

Public policies and legal issues

LEARNING OBJECTIVES

- To identify the main political and legal issues relating to electronic commerce and business.
- To understand the different measures that have been introduced to manage e-commerce in a commercial framework.
- To be able to identify issues of corporate policy and ethics relevant to organisations.

INTRODUCTION

In the first chapter, political factors were identified as key drivers of e-commerce and a major part of its infrastructure. A lack of infrastructure was identified as a barrier to e-commerce. This area is crucial to the development and advancement of e-business and e-commerce. This chapter will look specifically at three main areas:

(a) *Political* – the role of national governments and international organisations to foster and support e-commerce growth.
(b) *Legal* – laws, rules and regulations that control behaviour in the 'cyberworld'.
(c) *Ethical* – the role of organisations in implementing policies and procedures to safeguard stakeholders.

Each country has different legal and political frameworks and it would be impossible to cover all of them in this book. This chapter highlights the frameworks that are particularly relevant to e-commerce and business, being developed by international bodies such as the United Nations (UN), the Organisation for Economic Cooperation and Development (OECD) and the European Union (EU). These have a wide international significance because they are often the foundations on which international laws and policies are built. The UK will be used in instances where specific examples are required. Non-UK readers should use these examples to compare laws and regulation in their own country.

Because of the rapidly changing nature of the environment, the content in this chapter describes the situation as it stood at the beginning of 2002 and is very much subject to change. The aims of this chapter are to highlight the legal, political and ethical issues that current and future managers must be aware of and conversant with when implementing and conducting e-commerce. This chapter is intended to put the laws and regulation in context, and ensure that managers address the issues necessary to protect their employees, their organisations and other stakeholders, rather than being a module in Internet law. Due to our increasingly litigious climate, I am left with the inevitable necessity to request that all readers consult legal and other advisers before acting on any information contained in this book and to read the legal disclaimer in the preface of this book before continuing.

POLITICAL ISSUES – AN OVERVIEW

No one body controls or owns the World Wide Web and, given the global infrastructure, it is nigh impossible to police the content. One of the ways of controlling the Web is through technical protocols that govern how data is transmitted, stored and displayed over network infrastructures (see Chapter 2). However, in order for the Internet and the Web to be a serious business tool there must at least be some modicum of order and regulatory control, and thus the need for government intervention to support commercial transactions; prevent, police and punish fraud and 'cyber' crime; protect intellectual property and user privacy; and facilitate dispute resolution.

These issues will be dealt with in more detail in the remainder of this chapter.

SUPPORTING COMMERCIAL TRANSACTIONS

Government bodies and international organisations are striving to develop an infrastructure to bring the Internet under the jurisdiction of international and national trade law and practice. The United Nations Commissions on International Trade Regulations and Law (UNCITRAL) produced a Model Law on Electronic Commerce[1] in 1996, which was modified in 1998, based on the realisation that there was a need to recognise, in law, computer records, electronic data transactions, electronic data interchange

(EDI) which involves the use of alternatives to paper-based methods of communication and storage of information and incorporating concepts such as 'writing', 'signature' and 'original'. This Model Law is seen as a blueprint for governments to facilitate and unify the use of electronic communication and commerce between nations with different legal, social and economic systems. UNCITRAL suggested that this law needed to be implemented by governments in order to:

- Have tangible evidence of the parties' intent to enter a binding contract and be aware of the consequences of it.
- Ensure that the document would be legible to all and would remain unaltered over time, providing a permanent record of the intent of the author to 'write'.
- Provide reproduction of the document so that each party would hold identical copies of the same data.
- Authenticate data via a digital 'signature'.
- Be acceptable and recognised in a court of law, for taxation or other authorities.
- Allow for the easy storage of data in a tangible form.

E-COMMERCE LEGISLATION IN EUROPE[2]

The EU takes the similar view that the take-up of e-commerce by consumers and business depends upon the creation of an EU-wide framework that provides substantial legal guarantees for electronic commercial transactions and allows for the free movements of electronic services. EU legislation incorporates the main point outlined in the UNCITRAL Model Law in its directives on e-commerce, but also includes issues such as the protection of copyright in the information society and distance marketing of financial services.

LEGISLATION IN THE UK

UK legislation is based on EU directives. Several laws relating specifically to e-commerce and the use of the Internet and other electronic transactions have been passed in the past few years (2000–1) and there is still more to come (2002).

The Electronic Communications Bill 2000

Enacted in May 2000, the aim of the bill was 'to make provision to facilitate the use of electronic communications and electronic data storage;

to make provision about the modification of licences [for cryptography support service providers]'.[3] Under this Act, there is legal recognition of electronic data and documents and legal recognition of digital signatures. Furthermore, there is also to be a registration process under this Act to register and grant official approval of cryptography service providers. This register will be published in the public domain and will be updated to reflect the removal or addition of approved organisations onto the list. However under this law, key escrow[4] or recovery will not be imposed.

The UK Regulation of Investigatory Powers (RIP) Act 2000[5]

Enacted in July 2000, this clarifies the law as it relates to interception of communications over the Internet, surveillance and access to encrypted data. There is much controversy over this Act in the UK, with critics arguing that it is a gross invasion of privacy and is contrary to the European Convention of Human Rights defending employee and individual rights to privacy. The Act will enable employers to intercept e-mails and Internet use by their staff on the grounds of protecting the organisation from harm, for example preventing computer viruses.

The main areas of controversy are the 'black boxes' – devices that will enable security services to monitor users' activities over the Internet, namely the websites and chat rooms they visit and addresses of emails received or sent. Some Internet Service Providers (ISPs) will also be asked to 'maintain a reasonable intercept capability' to monitor the flow of data (a highly expensive and almost unmanageable task considering the fast-changing nature of the technology and ever increasing volume of Internet traffic). Warrants will be needed for interception, and these will be awarded by the Home Secretary upon fulfilling stringent criteria laid down in the Act.

The Act also requires a reverse burden of proof for surrendering private (decryption) keys. If intercepted communications are encrypted the Act will force the individual to surrender their private keys. The key holder must show they are doing everything they can to provide the keys but, if they are unable to present them, they may incur a jail sentences of up to two years and/or a fine. Russia, Malaysia and Singapore have passed similar laws.[6]

New E-Commerce Legislation by 2002

In accordance with EU directives, new legislation to cover e-commerce is due to be passed in the UK in 2002. This law will govern:

- The fixed establishment concept – defining where operators are established and pursue an economic activity whether trading over the Internet totally or partially.
- Transparency requirements for commercial communications to ensure fair trade and consumer confidence.
- Requirements relating to electronic contracts.
- Limitations to the liability of Internet intermediaries – removing liability for content when acting as a conduit, for example an ISP or Web host.
- Requirements regarding on-line dispute settlement to provide for fast efficient legal redress and ensure sanctions for violations.
- Requirements regarding the role of national authorities if it impacts on the protection of public interest.

This is a snapshot of the kind of legislation passed in the UK to support the commercial rise of e-commerce.

WHAT ARE 'BIT TAXES'?

Taxation of electronic commerce is a complex issue, especially in consumer-to-business relations. Business-to-business commerce is more used to dealing with international taxation rules and procedures and so is less problematic. With the development of e-commerce and in particular the use and access of the Internet, a number of proposals have been put forward about taxing Internet use and access – so called 'bit taxes'. For example: addressing social and international inequalities in access to the World Wide Web, where it is suggested that industrialised nations tax their citizens' access to the net to finance underdeveloped countries infrastructure; charging users a small fee for sending a certain number of e-mails over the net.[7]

The OECD agreed a draft policy[8] on the taxation of electronic commerce in 1998. They ruled out a flat-rate 'bit-tax' on all Internet deals, supporting the continuation of traditional tax principles of indirect taxes being levied on the basis of where the goods or services are consumed, not where they are produced. Taxation should seek to be neutral and equitable between electronic and conventional forms of commerce.

Direct taxation embraces the concept of 'permanent establishment', where a company is liable to the taxation regulations and laws in the country where it is deemed to have permanent establishment. The OECD expects that international taxation treaties and jurisdictions will still apply in the case of organisations conducting electronic commerce.

The EU[9] is following the policy on taxation suggested by the OECD and currently has no intention of taxing e-commerce. With regards to indirect taxation, the Commission believes that the EU value-added-tax (VAT) system can continue to serve as a model for the taxation of global electronic commerce. Since the EU publishes directives for its Member States to incorporate into national law, EU members will have similar policies. In the UK, according to the Inland Revenue,[10] the following do not constitute permanent establishment:

- Websites.
- Web host – whether the server on which data is stored is co-located or hosted by a third party.
- ISP is not considered a dependent agent of another enterprise and so has no part in determining permanent establishment.
- While a place where computer equipment such as a server is located may in certain circumstances constitute a permanent establishment, this requires that functions performed at that place be significant and an essential or core part of the business activity of the enterprise.

Permanent establishment by an e-business is where the company is registered and is the location where the essential part of the business activity is performed.

In the USA, however, Congress adopted the Internet Tax Freedom Act (ITFA), providing for a limited and temporary exemption from new state and local taxes on Internet access in October 1998. This Internet Tax Moratorium (HR1552) preventing Internet access taxes and multiple and discriminatory taxes on the Internet[11] was extended to 1 November 2003.

In order for the continued growth of international e-commerce, an international consensus on consumption taxation is critical. Uncoordinated action will be harmful to the development of electronic commerce and undermine compliance efforts.

WHAT ABOUT CLASSIFICATION OF DIGITISED PRODUCTS?

There is a view that the on-line supply of digitised products should not be treated as a supply of goods, but as a supply of services. It is inconsistent to treat a digitised product differently from its conventional counterpart (e.g. products such as books, software, images, music or information) and each should have the same rate of taxation regardless of the method of delivery to ensure neutrality. If digitised products are treated as services, then further guidance is needed to specify which of the many different sources of supply rules for services will apply. This has yet to be clarified.

LEGAL PREVENTION OF 'CYBER' CRIME AND FRAUD

Data espionage and data theft, credit card fraud, child pornography, far-right extremism and terrorists are ever more common on the Internet. (Joschka Fischer, German foreign minister)[12]

Cybercrime is defined by British police as the use of any computer network for crime. It is inevitable that with the growth of e-commerce, business transactions on-line, the increased use of networks and computers, so there will be a synonymous growth of crime facilitated by networks and computers. According to the Computer Emergency Response Team Coordination Center (CERT/CC) in the USA, the number of reported incidences of security breaches in the first three quarters of 2000 rose by 54 per cent over the total number of reported incidences in 1999.[13] The kinds of crimes that can occur were outlined in Chapter 4.

In the majority of countries around the world, existing regulations and laws are being used to tackle cybercrime. There have been a number of prosecutions and case law is being built up. However, some argue that law enforcement agencies are unable to fight twenty-first-century cybercrime with twentieth-century tools and legal authority, and that existing laws are likely to be unenforceable against such 'new' crimes. A report by the technology policy consultancy McConnell International,[14] analysing the state of legislation in 52 countries, identified four major areas (summarised in Table 7.1) that must be addressed by new or modified legislation in order for any country to be able to compete effectively in the new economy. The report found that there was no consistency or coordination amongst different countries either in the legislation for crimes or the kind of punishment. It confirmed the need for a cybercrime model law to be introduced to act as a blueprint for national governments around the world.

'CYBER-LIABILITIES' – HUMAN RESOURCE AND EMPLOYMENT ISSUES

In an increasingly litigious commercial and social environment, the facilitation of electronic communication has introduced another potential source of litigation and liability to organisations and individuals. The main ones are defamatory/harassing e-mails, the downloading of illegal and indecent material, and negligent virus transmission.

E-mail is informal and often less care is taken than when writing a conventional letter or memo. It is often used in a way similar to conversations, where loose emotive language can be used leading to misunderstandings and disputes in a permanent record. Suggestive e-mails to

TABLE 7.1 Areas of cybercrime

Area to be covered by legislation	Type of crime committed
Data crimes	Data interception: interception of data in transmission Data modification: alteration, destruction or erasing of data Data theft: taking or copying data, regardless of whether it is protected by other laws, e.g. copyright, privacy
Network crimes	Network interference: impeding or preventing access for others, e.g. a distributed denial of service (DDOS) attack Network sabotage: modification or destruction of a network or system
Access crimes	Unauthorised access: hacking or cracking to gain access to a system or data Aiding and abetting: enabling the commission of a cyber crime
Related crimes	Computer-related forgery: alteration of data with intent to represent as authentic Computer-related fraud: alteration of data with intent to derive economic benefit from its misrepresentation Virus dissemination: introduction of software damaging to systems or data

employees may be interpreted as sexual harassment. An employee may send defamatory remarks by e-mail about another person. The existence and availability of such e-mails could damage a company's defence in litigation. Proceedings can be brought against the author of the e-mail, the employer of the author or both.

CASE
STUDY

In 1997, Western Provident Association Limited (a private medical insurance company) were the subject of an internal e-mail memo by staff at Norwich Union falsely suggesting that it was in severe financial difficulties and was being investigated by the UK Department of Trade and Industry. Libel proceedings were instituted by Western Provident against Norwich Union holding it responsible for the action of its employees in sending defamatory messages through their e-mail system. Norwich Union settled the case, apologised, and paid £450,000 in damages.[15]

In 1997 three major US corporations were sued by black employees claiming discrimination over what appeared on their computer screens. They were offended by an e-mailed parody of African-American speech patterns.

Oil giant Chevron had to pay out US $2.2m after a female employee complained of sexual harassment when she found sexist jokes under the heading 'why beer is better than women'.[16]

A similar case in the UK recently resulted in the dismissal of two employees at an engineering company in Huddersfield. The two employees forwarded e-mails ranging from a cartoon frog in a blender to smutty drawings and jokes among a group of 40 willing employees. However, one e-mail ended up being sent to a colleague who did not share their sense of humour. He complained and an investigation and surveillance operation was launched, resulting in the sacking of the two employees for forwarding more e-mails than anybody else. An industrial tribunal found the company within its rights to sack the employees not only for sending the e-mails but also for the amount of time wasted in the process. In this case, the company had a clear policy stating precisely what was acceptable material for inclusion in e-mails.[17]

The basis for the proceedings against Norwich Union and the other corporations was that the company was vicariously liable for the acts of its employees. However, it might be possible to bring proceedings against an employer on a separate basis, namely that it is the publisher of the allegedly defamatory material because it supplied the equipment through which the message is transmitted and on which it appeared. European courts are increasingly assigning liability for on-line content to the publisher – in this case the employer – rather than the author. For example, in the case of British Gas: 'In June 1999, British Gas paid compensation for a libellous e-mail. The High Court ruled that an e-mail sent out in 1997 libelled a rival gas connection firm. British Gas paid over $100,000 in damages.'[18]

It is necessary and legitimate therefore for businesses to protect themselves to stop viruses or block obscene or libellous material. The RIP Act in the UK states clearly that only 'communications relevant to the system controller's business' can be monitored and recorded. There is a growing industry in software designed to monitor e-mails sent from company servers by using a keyword search to filter and monitor material being sent or received. According to a survey by software distributor Peapod,[19] 38 per cent of British companies can already monitor the content of e-mails and 18 per cent are able to track their destinations.

Companies must develop and disseminate clear guidelines, policies and even additional clauses in employee contracts to make sure employees understand they are being monitored and that their e-mails are not private and explain the reasons for this; for example, excess non-company traffic clogs up networks, increasing the potential for spread of viruses and potentially obscene, offensive or libellous material. In the USA, federal government employees are warned each time they log on to their PCs that they are being monitored.

A survey published by Dotadult.co.uk (a search engine for sex-related sites) in 2000[20] found that 40 per cent of all searches using the engine were conducted from the office, with peak times being the lunch hour and the early evening. It has been estimated that

CASE STUDY

staff surfing the Web for non-work purposes could be costing major companies as much as £2.5m a year.

In the first case of its kind in the UK, a 29-year-old office manager from Winsford in Cheshire was dismissed after her boss discovered she had been arranging her holiday during work hours. The employee protested that the amount of work time had been minimal because she had mainly used her lunch breaks. And that in total she had spent less than two hours over four days searching for a holiday. The tribunal said her personal use of the computer had made her guilty of misconduct.[21]

Not only this, but the survey also found that office workers are frequently using the Internet to search for what many employers would regard as inappropriate material, with city firms, telecommunication and IT companies amongst the heaviest users.

Companies can find themselves open to legal, business and ethical consequences as a result of their employees inappropriate use of the Internet – including damaged reputation with clients, lawsuits for sexual harassment or discrimination. For example:

Ford suspended three workers at its Dagenham plant in Essex on suspicion of accessing pornographic material on the internet while at work. One of the suspended workers spent up to four hours a shift accessing the material.[22]

Orange sacked up to 40 workers after an internal investigation revealed they were downloading pornography from the Internet.[23]

The White House, Dow Chemicals and the Houses of Parliament have also had to discipline or dismiss members of staff caught downloading pornography from the Web. Existing general laws in the UK governing obscene material and publishing of material that might be considered obscene apply in the e-commerce world. Furthermore, under the Telecommunications Act of 1984 in the UK, it is an offence to send 'by means of public telecommunication systems a message or other matter that is grossly offensive or of an indecent obscene or menacing character'.[24] It is also an offence for any person to have in his possession any indecent photograph or pseudo-photograph of a child under section 160 of the Criminal Justice Act 1988.

Firms have introduced a range of specialist software to try to stop employees misusing work equipment – such as software that detects words in e-mails or messages that could potentially be actionable (sexist, racist, obscene, names of competitors, derogatory words); software that detects employees surfing patterns, sites accessed and downloads. However, this is only one tool in the company's arsenal to protect itself; company policy

and employee contracts must also be clarified and disseminated by organisations to their workforce.

PROTECTING INTELLECTUAL PROPERTY

Issues of intellectual property have been given particular prominence in
the information age where ways of doing business and electronic data
(such as sound, text, video or graphics) can be displayed, copied, collected,
exchanged and shared easily and quickly over an open global network.

The UN set up the World Intellectual Property Organisation (WIPO)[25]
in Geneva, Switzerland, to administer international treaties dealing with
different aspects of intellectual property. However, each country has a
national infrastructure for protecting intellectual property. Some of the
'traditional' forms of protection can still be applied and include:

- *Copyright* © – a statutory grant that provides the creators of intellectual
  property with ownership. There is no official register for copyright. It is
  an *unregistered right* (unlike patents, registered designs or trademarks).
  So, *there is no official action to take* (no application to make, forms to fill
  in or fees to pay). Copyright comes into effect immediately, as soon as
  something that can be protected is created and 'fixed' in some way, for
  example on paper, on film, via sound recording or as an electronic
  record on the Internet. Normal practice is to copyright work with the
  copyright symbol ©, followed by name and date, to warn others against
  copying it, but it is not legally necessary in the UK. Works are protected
  by copyright, regardless of the medium in which they exist and this
  includes the Internet. Copyright does not protect ideas but protects the
  way the idea is expressed in a piece of work. Copyright in a literary,
  dramatic, musical or artistic work (including a photograph) lasts until
  70 years after the death of the author. Sound recordings, broadcasts and
  cable programmes are protected for 50 years, and published editions are
  protected for 25 years.[26]

  In the UK the government patent office feels that 'current UK law
  generally provides a sound basis to meet the challenges of new technology',[27] but some adjustments have been made to the law to incorporate
  changes suggested by the EU directive.[28] The main adjustments include
  performers' exclusive rights to control 'on demand' transmissions of
  recordings of their performances; amendments to comply with the
  more comprehensive and legal protection for technological systems
  and the introduction of provisions for the protection of electronic
  rights management.
- *Patents* – a patent for an invention is granted by government to the
  inventor, giving the inventor the right for a limited period to stop

others from making, using or selling the invention without the permission of the inventor. When a patent is granted, the invention becomes the property of the inventor, which – like any other form of property or business asset – can be bought, sold, rented or hired. Patents are territorial rights; UK Patent will only give the holder rights within the UK and rights to stop others from importing the patented products into the UK.[29] In the UK, once a trademark is registered, renewal fees are payable to the Registry every 10 years, to keep the registration in force. A registration may be renewed indefinitely. However, particularly relevant to e-commerce is the fact that in the UK an invention is not patentable if it is 'a scheme or method for performing a mental act, playing a game or doing business; the presentation of information, or a computer program'.[30]

The patent and trademark laws differ in the USA, where Priceline .com have a trademark on their service and Amazon.com have patented their 1–Click ordering system.

CASE STUDY

There is an ongoing debate about the negative impact of patenting such business ideas. Tim O'Reilly, a publisher of computing books,[31] maintains that the Amazon '1–Click' patent should never have been allowed since this is not an invention but a trivial application of cookies – an unpatented technology introduced several years before Amazon. He argues that to patent obvious ideas that are already in wide use is an abuse of the system:

> to . . . patent something like '1–Click ordering' is a slap in the face of Tim Berners-Lee and all of the other pioneers who created the opportunity that Amazon has done such a good job of exploiting. Amazon wouldn't have existed without the generosity of people like Tim, who made legitimate, far-reaching inventions, and put them out into the public domain for all to build upon. Anyone who puts a small gloss on this fundamental technology, calls it proprietary, and then tries to keep others from building further on it, is a thief. The gift was given to all of us, and anyone who tries to make it their own is stealing our patrimony.[32]

Jeff Bezos of Amazon responds by arguing that giving up the patents will not benefit anybody, but rather patent laws governing business method and software should be changed and that he is working to attempt to instigate the changes. He wants 'fewer patents, of higher average quality, with shorter lifetimes [3–5 years instead of 17 years]. Fewer, better, shorter. A short name might be "fast patents".'[33] Doubtless, the debate will rage on. In the UK, however, neither patent would be accepted.

- *Trademarks* – a trademark is any sign which can distinguish the goods and services of one trader from those of another. A sign includes, for example, words, logos, pictures, or a combination of these. In the case of the Web, trademarks are equally applicable and recognised.
- *Digital watermarks* – this new technology, sometimes called 'fingerprinting', is similar to traditional watermarks used in print media (such as

paper currency) to establish proof of authenticity. Digital watermarks produce unique encoded messages that are indelible and invisible to the naked eye, embedded in the digital file so that they are hidden in the source code. Special viewing software can be used to reveal the item's authenticity, including the creator's unique code, name contact details, distribution details and the like. This technology is another tool that can be used to protect digital intellectual property and enforce the law in the e-commerce world.

WHAT ABOUT CYBERSQUATTING?

Since the beginning of domain name registrations, a number of individuals and companies have applied for and reserved domain names that they think someone else will want, either now or in the future, and over which they have no legitimate claim. Their sole purpose is to sell them on (at a profit) to those who would want the domain names. This practice is known as 'Cybersquatting', which is fuelled by cheap annual registration fees for domain names (between £6–£60 from any authorised ICANN registrar) and no screening process of domain name applications. Some cybersquatters have reserved a long list of names, including common English words, well-known companies or their products, sports figures, celebrities and political candidates.

In October 1999, the US Senate passed a bill to outlaw cybersquatting, with a US $100,000 fine for registering an internet name in 'bad faith'.[34] Although trademark laws may offer some protection, the World Intellectual Property Organisation (WIPO) has established a uniform dispute resolution procedure to deal with disputes concerning bad faith registration and use of trademarks as domain names. The WIPO Arbitration and Mediation Centre[35] is the leading service provider of the procedure known as the Uniform Domain Name Dispute Resolution Policy (UDRP). The process has proven to be an efficient and cost-effective international mechanism, with over 90 per cent of the 3,262 complaints received by the end of November 2001 having been resolved for a fee starting from US $1,000. Around 80 per cent of the cybersquatting cases filed with WIPO since December 1999 have resulted in an order to transfer the domain name. Some of the winners and losers are outlined in Table 7.2.

The Second WIPO Process[36] is in the stage of broadening the framework to include identifiers other than trademarks as domain names and is directed at examining the bad faith and misleading registration and use of these. These other identifiers, which form the basis of naming systems used in the real or physical world, are:

- International Non-proprietary Names (INNs) for pharmaceutical sub-stances, a consensus-based naming system used in the health sector to establish generic names for pharmaceutical substances that are free from private rights of property or control.
- The names and acronyms of international intergovernmental organisa-tions (IGOs).
- Personal names.
- Geographical identifiers, such as indications of geographical source used on goods, geographical indications and other geographical terms.
- Trade names, which are the names used by enterprises to identify themselves.

There is a debate over whether registering common or highly generic words is in fact cybersquatting since they reflect an industry or are generally descriptive and so there is no real trademark at issue. A whole industry has emerged around this and one of the companies that provides a forum for the buying and selling of such domain names is the US company Greatdomains.com.[37] The following is a selection of the types of bids listed on the site:

- America.com at $15 million.
- media.com at $975,000.
- nicotine.com at $100,000.
- findbinladen.com $20,000.
- selectaschool.com $3,000.

In 1997 a Texas-based company paid US $150,000 for the generic URL business.com and later sold it for a reported US $7.5 million. The same company that had registered eflowers.com later sold it to the company Flowers Direct for over US $38,000 plus a 50 per cent cut of all future transaction fees and a complementary bunch of flowers sent to the CEO's wife each month.[38] The BBC also spent a considerable sum on buying the address bbc.com from Boston Business Computing who had registered it legitimately.

WHAT ABOUT PRIVACY?

In the information economy, one of the most abundant commodities is information. We are all data subject and all types of organisations hold information about us. The advent of the Internet and the World Wide Web means that there is a further channel for collecting and using information. However, this new medium is largely 'invisible', where the processes of

TABLE 7.2 Winners and losers of cybersquatting cases

Winners	Losers
Harrods,[1] the London department store, evicted a cybersquatter through the courts to claim ownership of the domain name harrods.com	Armani.[10] Anand Mani, a graphic designer based in Vancouver had a business that had operated under the name A. R. Mani since 1981 and had registered the domain name www.armani.com for his business. The fashion house, which included Armani, the Italian designer, argued that Mr Mani had taken the name with intent to confuse users. The WIPO dismissed Armani's complaint and ruled in favour of Mr A. R. Mani.
The same result was seen with Scottish Widows, Marks and Spencer and Dixons,[2] where the courts found that those who registered the domain names did not have a legitimate excuse for using the name and had to transfer it to the appropriate party.	
One in a Million Group[3] registered a number of well-known names including ladbrokes.com, burger-king.com, buckinghampalace.org and cellnet.net but it was ordered in court to return them to the corporate owners of the business name.	Sting.[11] Pop musician Sting, failed to evict an alleged cybersquatter who owns the website address www.sting.com. Sting claimed the American holder of the site, Michael Urvan, had offered to sell it for US$25,000 (£16,500) but could offer no proof to support it. Mr Urvan had demonstrated he had used the word 'sting' to identify himself in e-mail and Internet addresses for some time. He also showed printouts of the on-line game Quake, evidencing the use of the word 'sting' by many of the game players. The WIPO panel acknowledged that Sting is a 'world famous entertainer' known by that name but also ruled it was also a common English word, listing its multiple meanings in a dictionary. The WIPO ruled that the word is undistinctive and most likely is used by numerous people in cyberspace.
The Post Office.[4] Mr. Nelson, who registered a number of well-known domain names including www.royal-mail.co.uk. He told the Post Office that it could only have it if they put a golden post box outside his station, and let children post letters to anywhere in the world for free for a year from it. The Post Office refused and began legal proceedings. Mr. Nelson returned the domain name to its rightful owners.	
The BBC[5] won a battle against a US-based Corporation (Data Art) who registered bbc.news.com. The WIPO found that the company had no rights to the tradename and that it had been registered in bad faith. It was ordered to transfer it to the BBC.	Bruce Springsteen[12] lost his attempt to evict a fan club from an Internet website which bears his name. The WIPO ruled that Canadian Jeff Burgar, who registered the Springsteen site on behalf of the Bruce Springsteen Club, had not violated the rock singer's rights by registering the website brucespringsteen.com. The WIPO panel said that Burgar had 'demonstrated that he has some rights or legitimate interests in respect of the domain name and [Springsteen] has failed to demonstrate that the domain name was registered and has been used in bad faith'. Springsteen had put forward no evidence that Burgar had ever tried to sell the domain name.
Julia Roberts,[6] the American actress, won a legal battle to prevent anyone using her name as an Internet domain name. The WIPO granted Roberts exclusive rights to her name and ordered US cybersquatter Russell Boyd to transfer the domain name juliaroberts.com back to the actress.	
Jeanette Winterson,[7] the British author, won the rights to her name from a Research Fellow in the Department of History and Philosophy of	

TABLE 7.2 Continued

Winners	Losers
Science at Cambridge University who had registered 132 of 'the world's favourite writers', including Winterson. The WIPO found that the domain names had been registered and used in bad faith and ordered Mark Hogarth to transfer the domain name to Winterson.	
Oxford University.[8] An Australian cybersquatter changed his name from Doc Seagle to Oxford University and claimed he was now called Oxford by his friends and family. He registered the domain name oxford-university.com, claiming he had legitimate rights to it because of his name. He was ordered to transfer the domain name back to Oxford University after it was found that he had registered the domain name to be used in bad faith.	
Madonna.[9] US pop singer. Dan Parisi, an American, bought the domain name madonna.com in 1998 for $20,000 and used the site to feature sexually explicit photographs and text. He claimed that Madonna had no greater right to the website than any other individual or organisation with the Madonna name since Madonna was named after the Virgin Mary, as was her mother and hundreds of thousands of other people throughout the world. However, the WIPO found that Parisi had not registered the name in good faith and that he 'lacks the rights and legitimate interest in the domain name' and ordered that he transfer it to Madonna.	
Actress Nicole Kidman, tennis players Venus and Serena Williams, Christian Dior and Nike have also successfully won back their names.	

Notes:

[1] 'Cybersquatting: Get off my URL' 15 November 1999: http://news.bbc.co.uk/hi/english/special_report/1999/02/99/e-cyclopedia/newsid_440000/440914.stm (accessed December 2001).

TABLE 7.2 Continued

2 'Firm accused of net name piracy', 26 January 2000: http://news.bbc.co.uk/hi/english/uk/scotland/newsid_619000/619312.stm

3 'Cybersquatting: Get off my URL' 15 November 1999: http://news.bbc.co.uk/hi/english/special_report/1999/02/99/e-cyclopedia/newsid_440000/440914.stm (accessed December 2001).

4 'Cybersquatting part 2: Giving it a good name', 16 November 1999: http://news.bbc.co.uk/hi/english/special_report/1999/02/99/e-cyclopedia/newsid_516000/516426.stm

5 'BBC's cyber victory', 6 October 2000: http://news.bbc.co.uk/hi/english/uk/newsid_957000/957866.stm (accessed December 2001).

6 'Roberts wins cybersquatter battle', 2 June 2000: http://news.bbc.co.uk/hi/english/entertainment/newsid_774000/774850.stm (accessed December 2001).

7 **WIPO Arbitration and Mediation Center** Administrative Panel Decision: Jeanette Winterson v. Mark Hogarth, Case No. D2000-0235: http://arbiter.wipo.int/domains/decisions/word/2000/d2000-0235.doc (accessed December 2001).

8 'Oxford University in cybersquatter row', 29 March 2000: http://news.bbc.co.uk/hi/english/education/newsid_694000/694871.stm; WIPO Arbitration and Mediation Centre Administrative Panel Decision: **The Chancellor, Masters and Scholars of the University of Oxford v. DR Seagle Case No. D2000-0308:** http://arbiter.wipo.int/domains/decisions/word/2000/d2000-0308.doc (accessed December 2001).

9 WIPO Arbitration and Mediation Centre Administrative Panel Decision: **Madonna Ciccone, p/k/a Madonna v. Dan Parisi and 'Madonna.com' Case No. D2000-0847:** http://arbiter.wipo.int/domains/decisions/word/2000/d2000-0847.doc (accessed December 2001).

10 'Armani loses website fight', 2 August 2001: http://news.bbc.co.uk/hi/english/business/newsid_1470000/1470671.stm (accessed December 2001).

11 'Sting stung online', 28 July 2000: http://news.bbc.co.uk/hi/english/entertainment/newsid_855000/855523.stm (accessed December 2001).

12 'Springsteen loses website fight', 7 February 2001: http://news.bbc.co.uk/hi/english/entertainment/newsid_1158000/1158977.stm (accessed December 2000).

data capture, transmission and storage is not obvious to the user. A visit to a single website can result in global collection and transmissions of personal data, for example via search engines, 'cookies', on-line shopping, payments, Web-casting, log analysis and games, to identify just a few of the activities. So there is an additional element of concern about privacy and protection of Internet and Web users. Data protection is a necessity if trust and confidence is to be engendered in the Internet and Web.

A survey by the Graphic, Visualization, & Usability Center's (GVU) 10th WWW User Survey[39] found that over 70 per cent of respondents felt that privacy laws were needed and over 85 per cent disagreed with reselling information by organisations. When questioned about the most important issue facing the Internet,[40] 19 per cent cited privacy which was the highest response rate of all the other criteria.

Directives covering Data Protection in Europe[41] have been developed and are incorporated in the UK Data Protection Act 1998[42] which was fully in force in 1999. It pertains to personal data, that is information, facts or opinions about living identifiable individuals or 'data subjects'. The new Act has some changes in it, which are significant for the security of that information and states, amongst others, that data:

- Can only be collected and processed, e.g. 'obtaining', 'holding' and 'disclosing', with explicit permission.
- Cannot be transferred to any third party without agreement from the data subject.
- Must be accurate, complete and kept up to date.
- Must be protected and security measures must be taken to protect the personal data against any accidental or unlawful destruction or accidental loss.
- Subject must have the option to opt out, correct or delete information.
- Cannot be transferred to countries without 'adequate' data protection laws, for example the USA or Switzerland that do not have similar data protection laws. However, there is a Safe Harbour[43] clause which has been approved by the European Commission which enables organisations to commit themselves to complying with a set of data protection principles approved by and consistent with those in the EU.
- Can be processed for limited purposes but must not be kept longer than necessary.
- Subjects must have recourse for complaint if they are unsatisfied with the organisation's practices and there must always exist a method of enforcement and remedy.

Appendix 6 (www.tassabehji.co.uk) gives further information from the Data Protection Office for data controllers using the Internet.

A warning to organisations that use data collected over the Internet: in the GVU survey mentioned, only 1 per cent always register on websites (twice as many in the USA than in Europe) and of those that do register, nearly half falsified information[44] some or all of the time but the other half never falsified information. US respondents were less likely ever to falsify information (51 per cent) than European respondents (35 per cent). The Internet facilitates anonymity and enables users to adopt different roles, and the survey's findings suggest that this is a particularly attractive feature with 87 per cent of respondents liking the anonymous nature of the Web and more than 60 per cent of respondents wanting to assume different roles. So organisations must question the veracity of the data they collect and assess how to use it most effectively.

WHAT ABOUT ON-LINE CONSUMERS?

Each country has a different set of rules and regulations that govern consumer protection both when buying by mail, telephone, Internet, digital TV, or physically in a shop. The fact that the Internet connects the world and enables purchasing from any country opens up a minefield of potential problems for the consumer and the respective rights they have when buying goods or services. Until there is a uniformity of these consumer protection laws and regulations, consumers must make sure they are confident of the company from which they are buying the goods or services if they are not in their respective country of establishment.

Work is afoot to develop and implement international codes of practice to help to protect consumers' rights and offer a higher level of consumer protection and service than the basics set down in law. This will improve consumer confidence but must be flexible and keep pace with rapid market developments. The UK is one of the leading players in this area, and recent private sector and government initiatives include:[45]

- *Internationally*: the UK plays a leading role, as a Vice Chair of the OECD Consumer Policy Committee, which publishes the *OECD Guidelines for Consumer Protection in the Context of Electronic Commerce*.[46] These guidelines advise governments, businesses, consumers and their representatives on the core characteristics of effective consumer protection for e-commerce. They cover information provision, advertising and marketing, transaction procedures, payment security, data privacy, dispute resolution and redress.
- *In Europe*:[47] as part of its e-confidence initiative the European Commission is working with business and consumer partners to develop an EU scheme for e-commerce codes based on the TrustUK approach. The purpose of this is to increase consumer confidence and strengthen the single European market by providing an agreed minimum level of

consumer protection throughout the EU. The directive does not apply to business-to-business transactions.

- *TrustUK*:[48] a UK private-sector-led scheme launched in July 2000 to approve codes of practice for retail e-commerce. On-line businesses that meet the TrustUK criteria display an 'e-hallmark' on their websites, indicating that consumers can shop with confidence.

Co-regulation is also high on the agenda in bi-lateral talks with countries such as Japan, Hong Kong and Singapore. One of the challenges is to develop links between national codes so that consumers can have more confidence in shopping further afield. In the UK, consumers largely get the same degree of protection from the law as they would if they were buying goods or services from a bricks and mortar store. Consumer Protection (Distance Selling) Regulations 2000[49] apply to businesses selling goods or services to consumers on the Internet or digital television; by mail order, including catalogue shopping; and by phone and by fax. The scope of the Regulations is very broad. They cover both goods and services, where the contract is made without any face-to-face contact between supplier and consumer.

Many businesses already use terms and conditions that meet these regulations, but all need to check that they do comply. Key features of the Regulations[50] state that:

- The consumer must be given clear information about the goods or services offered. The seller must provide clear and comprehensible information to enable the consumer to decide whether to buy. This must include the seller's contact details; a description of the goods or services; the price including all taxes and delivery costs where they apply; arrangements for payment; arrangements and date for delivery (where no delivery date has been agreed then delivery must be within 30 days); the right to cancel the order; and how long the offer or the price remains valid.
- After making a purchase the consumer must be sent confirmation of the order in writing (including e-mail).
- The consumer has a cooling-off period of seven working days in which they can withdraw from the contract. The aim of the cooling-off period is to give consumers an opportunity to examine the goods or services being offered, as they would have when buying in a shop. The right to cancel is fundamental; however, this is balanced in the Regulations by the consumer's responsibility to take care of the goods before returning them within 30 days. Cancellation can be sent by e-mail.
- Protection from credit-card fraud if payment is made with a credit card, then claims for non-delivery from the credit-card company or fraudulent use of it can be made.

Because of the ease of changing and updating information on the Web, terms and conditions can also be changed. In order to ensure both consumer and trader are protected, a copy of any terms and conditions that appear on the website should be kept with the order, in case of any disputes or problems.

DISPUTE RESOLUTION AND REDRESS

The OECD and the EU are working with member nations to develop schemes for e-commerce and other commercial dispute resolution and redress. Consumers need to know that if something goes wrong with a transaction, there are effective ways of handling complaints and getting redress that is not as costly or time consuming as going to court – especially if the trader is in another country.[51] A number of Alternative Dispute Resolution (ADR) schemes (such as ombudsmen and arbitration) are being developed to offer low-cost, user-friendly alternatives to going to court.

The UK Government believes[52] that such schemes, including on-line ones, can make a valuable contribution to consumer confidence in the single market and in electronic commerce. The DTI is developing the European Extra-Judicial Network (EEJ-Net) working through the OECD to promote cross-border ADR internationally. EEJ-Net will give consumers access to schemes in other EU Member States which will help settle consumer disputes out of court – such as ombudsmen and arbitration schemes. EEJ-Net started its pilot phase in October 2001. Each Member State has agreed to set up a national 'clearing house' to provide the necessary links. The National Association of Citizens Advice Bureaux (NACAB) will undertake this function for the UK and it has set up a temporary UK clearing-house website,[53] which provides guidance on how to resolve complaints and accessing the network. The detailed functions of clearing houses, ADR schemes and EEJ-Net procedures are still in the process of being developed through discussions between the Commission,[54] Member States and clearing-house representatives.

WHERE DOES SPAM FIT IN

One of the issues currently not covered by law is spam:[55] 'The practice of indiscriminate distribution of messages (for example junk mail) without permission of the receiver and without consideration for the messages' appropriateness.'[56] Although not strictly illegal, spam is deemed to be unethical. The sending of high volumes of unwanted commercial solicitations via e-mail and other electronic means has a number of negative effects. Apart from being an annoyance to the majority of users receiving large numbers of 'junk mail',

- It is potentially a source of widening the spread of viruses.
- The volume of spam traffic slows down the Internet in general.
- Spam could potentially shut down Internet Service Provider mail servers because of the sheer volume of traffic at one time. In fact Internet Service Providers take a very harsh view of spam and tend to close down the sources of spam without any prior warning.
- Spam also has a limited impact on the objectives of the spamming organisation – if a spammer sent out 100,000 e-mails and got a 1 per cent response rate, ostensibly that would mean 1,000 potential 'customers'. However, if 5 per cent of people who received the spam complained, that would mean potentially 5,000 e-mails back to the spamming organisation, which means overloaded networks and mail servers for the organisation itself, as well as bad publicity from 5,000 people who would never become customers.

There are a number of practical measures for cutting spam, such as the installation of software packages such as spamweasel[57] and mailtalkx;[58] deleting spam immediately and not responding in any way which could validate an e-mail address. But it is the user who must be proactive in initiating these measures.

WHAT ABOUT ETHICS IN E-COMMERCE?

There is often confusion between legal and ethical issues, and although they are very much related, as we will see, they are not the same. Laws are enacted by government and built up through case precedents to form common law. Ethics on the other hand deals with the philosophical consideration of what is right and wrong. This is largely a subjective area because the definitions of right and wrong are not always clear. What is unethical is not necessarily illegal and what is ethical is not necessarily legal. It is a complex area where one group could refute the ethics of another group as unethical – this is particularly obvious across different cultures and countries. However, with the advent of the Internet, globalisation and a new way of conducting business, there is a need for guidelines to cover the unregulated activities of this new digital environment.

Many companies and professional organisations develop their own codes of ethics and put together a collection of principles intended as a guide for both its internal (e.g. employees) and external (e.g. customers) stakeholders. For example the Co-operative Bank (www.co-operativebank.co.uk) in the UK publish an ethical policy which restricts its business dealings with any organisation contravening human rights, animal and ecological welfare, and a range of other social and ethical issues.

Organisations can register with trusted trade associations and obtain hallmarks by abiding with an ethical and trustworthy code of practice that promotes policies of disclosure, honesty, trustworthiness and informed consent (such as the Which? consumer association).

Organisations can also clearly post their privacy policy that outlines their organisation's practices regarding user privacy and data. However, a report by Harris Interactive[59] in December 2001 found that only 3 per cent of consumers bother to read on-line privacy policies when they visit new websites, largely because they are too long and wrapped in hard-to-understand legal language. Organisations can overcome this problem by simplifying their privacy statements, clearly outlining exactly what data is collected about users, exactly how it will be used and whether it will be shared with a third party – rather than have a longwinded legal document that is too time consuming and difficult to decipher by most users.

From the internal stakeholders' point of view, there is the issue of censoring, monitoring and controlling employees' use of the World Wide Web and electronic messages. Organisations must protect themselves from legal action in an increasingly litigious society. From the examples we have seen earlier in this chapter, organisations have been deemed to be liable for the messages sent by their employees. As with external stakeholders, organisations must raise the awareness of employees and must ensure openness and clarity about what actions they are taking. This can be done by:

- Introducing policies at work – including e-mail and Internet usage policies with clear guidelines for employees about using the Internet (whether they can use it for personal use, when and for how long, forbidden sites, not downloading material) and protocols for sending electronic messages from work.
- Revising contracts to incorporate personal employee liability if they do not abide by the organisation's policies.
- Raising awareness of the dangers amongst employees by providing training sessions and on-line reminders.
- Keeping employees aware of all the measures being taken by the organisation and making sure there is a forum for participation and discussion.

These are a few measures that organisations must take to support and uphold the legal and regulatory requirements, to protect users, employees and organisations from the potential dangers and liabilities of using the Internet.

SUMMARY

Discussions about the Internet often focus on its enormous commercial potential and the benefits to consumers and businesses alike. In this chapter we have identified how the power of the Internet can be abused and some of the political, legal and regulatory measures that are being introduced to minimise this abuse.

The legal infrastructure governing e-commerce is still in its infancy. However, national and international governments are very much aware of the need to introduce new laws, change and modify old laws in order to keep up with the growth in development and use of the Internet and World Wide Web by all sectors of the community.

International organisations have been proactive in developing directives to member states to ensure that their citizens are protected by the law. But there is still much to be done to ensure there is a consistent and coordinated infrastructure to govern international transactions over the Internet which cover:

- The legal recognition of electronic documentation, contracts and signatures.
- Governance of direct and indirect taxation of e-commerce and digitised products.
- Legal detection, prevention, protection and punishment of 'cybercrime'.
- Liabilities for organisations, employees and individuals using the Web and e-commerce.
- Protection of the rights and privacy of individuals and consumers over the Internet.

Until this infrastructure is developed fully, organisations and individuals must take technical and other measures to protect themselves from the potential pitfalls of taking part in e-commerce.

DISCUSSION QUESTIONS

1 How effective do you think the current laws are in stopping 'cybercrime'?
2 What recommendations would you make to improve these laws?
3 Taking one other country, identify the laws that govern e-commerce in that country. How do they compare to the international frameworks introduced by the OECD and UN?
4 What measures has your organisation taken to protect itself from cyber liabilities such as libel, indecent material and harassment?

REFERENCES

1 UNCITRAL Model Law on Electronic Commerce with Guide to Enactment (1996), with additional article 5 *bis* as adopted in 1998: http://www.uncitral.org/english/texts/electcom/ml-ecomm.htm (accessed November 2001).

2 Amended proposal for a European Parliament and Council Directive on certain legal aspects of electronic commerce in the Internal Market, document delivered on 19/02/2001: http://europa.eu.int/eur-lex/en/com/dat/1999/en_599PC0427.html (accessed December 2001).

3 *Electronic Communications Act 2000*, Chapter c.7, The Stationery Office Limited © Crown Limited: http://www.hmso.gov.uk/acts/acts2000/20000007.htm#7 (accessed November 2001).

4 The United States and other national governments have sought to prevent widespread use of cryptography unless 'key recovery' mechanisms guaranteeing law enforcement access to plaintext are built into these systems. Key recovery also known as 'key escrow.' The term 'escrow' became popular in connection with the U.S. government's Clipper Chip initiative, in which a master key to each encryption device was held 'in escrow' for release to law enforcement. Today the term 'key recovery' is used as a generic term for these systems, encompassing the various 'key escrow,' 'trusted third-party,' 'exceptional access,' 'data recovery,' and 'key recovery' encryption systems introduced in recent years. ('The risks of key recovery, key escrow, trusted third party & encryption', a report by an ad hoc group of cryptographers and computer scientists: http://www.cdt.org/crypto/risks98/ [accessed December 2001]).

5 *Regulation of Investigatory Powers Act 2000*, ISBN 0 10 542300 9 © Crown Publications: http://www.legislation.hmso.gov.uk/acts/acts2000/20000023.htm (accessed December 2001).

6 J. Glover and P. Barkham, 'The RIP Act – special report: Privacy on the net, Guardian Online 24/10/2000: http://www.guardian.co.uk/Archive/Article/0,4273,4031280,00.html (accessed December 2001).

7 'Developing nations want better net access': http://news.bbc.co.uk/hi/english/sci/tech/newsid_543000/543668.stm (accessed November 2001).

8 Electronic Commerce: Taxation Framework Conditions, a Report by the Committee on Fiscal Affairs 8 October 1998: http://www.oecd.org/pdf/M000015000/M00015517.pdf (accessed November 2001).

9 For more information on tax and e-commerce, try these sites: Taxation and Customs Union Directorate General: http://europa.eu.int/comm/taxation_customs/index_en.htm; E-Revolution website's taxation legislation page at: http://www.ispo.cec.be/ecommerce/legal/taxation.html; Electronic Commerce Legal Issues Platform (click on documents button and download relevant documents): http://www.jura.uni-muenster.de/eclip/eclip_I.htm

10 'Permanent establishment': www.inlandrevenue.gov.uk /e-commerce/ecom15.htm (accessed March 2001).

11 'AeA commends Senate on Internet tax moratorium extension; Internet tax ban that expired Oct. 21 back On track with senate vote', Business Wire, 15 November 2001: http://globalarchive.ft.com/globalarchive/article.html?id=011115010033&query=%22Internet+tax%22

12 'Life of crime, Part 5', BBC On-line Series: http://news.bbc.co.uk/hi/english/static/in_depth/uk/2001/life_of_crime/cybercrime.stm (accessed November 2001).

13 See www.cert.org. Although the following organisations also track reported incidents, global statistics have yet to be compiled: the National Infrastructure Protection Center (NIPC) (www.nipc.gov), the Computer Security Institute (CSI) (www.gocsi.com) and the Internet Fraud Complaint Center (www.ifccfbi.gov).

14 'Cyber crime . . . and punishment? Archaic laws threaten global information', A report prepared by McConnell International with support from WITSA December 2000: http://www.mcconnellinternational.com/services/CyberCrime.pdf (accessed November 2001).

15 'Libel and internal e-mail systems: The impact of the Norwich Union case', August 1997: http://www.mccannfitzgerald.ie/legal_briefing/litigation_arbitration/email_libel.html (accessed December 2001).

16 'Sexual harassment – e-mail style', http://www.peapod.co.uk/index_fl.html (accessed December 2001).

17 P. Inman and J. Wilson, 'Why that joke email could get you the sack – your in-box is not as private as you thought', Net news, Guardian, 2 December 2000: http://www.guardian.co.uk/Archive/Article/0,4273,4099488,00.html (accessed December 2001).

18 'British Gas commits e-mail libel': http://www.peapod.co.uk/index_fl.html.

19 http://www.peapod.co.uk/index_fl.html

20 R. Cellan-Jones, 'Software targets porn sneaks', 20 September 2000: http://news.bbc.co.uk/hi/english/sci/tech/newsid_933000/933330.stm (accessed December 2001).

21 'Business: The company file sacked for surfing the Net', 16 June 1999: http://news.bbc.co.uk/hi/english/business/the_company_file/newsid_370000/370497.stm

22 'Ford workers "accessed porn"', 17 January 2001: http://news.bbc.co.uk/hi/english/uk/newsid_1121000/1121618.stm

23 'Sacked for downloading porn', 1 September 2000: http://news.bbc.co.uk/hi/english/uk/newsid_906000/906391.stm

24 'Webwise basics – law and copyright': www.bbc.co.uk/webwise/basics/userbeware01_print.shtml (accessed March 2001).

25 www.wipo.org (accessed December 2001).

26 Ownership and duration of copyright: http://www.patent.gov.uk/copy/indetail/ownership.htm

27 Implementation of the Copyright Directive in the UK: http://www.patent.gov.uk/copy/notices/implement.htm (accessed December 2001).

28 Published in the *Official Journal of the European Communities* (Directive 2001/29/EC – OJ Reference: L 167/10; 22.6.2001). The Directive has therefore entered into force, and as required by Article 13 it must now be transposed into the national laws of EU Member States before 22 December 2002: http://www.patent.gov.uk/copy/notices/implement.htm (accessed December 2001).

29 'What is a patent?': http://www.patent.gov.uk/patent/definition.htm (accessed December 2001).

30 'What is a patent?' http://www.patent.gov.uk/patent/definition.htm (accessed December 2001).

31 'Ask Tim Forum', February 2000: http://www.oreilly.com/ask_tim/amazon_patent.html (accessed December 2001).

32 'Ask Tim Forum', February 2000: http://www.oreilly.com/ask_tim/amazon_patent.html http://www.oreilly.com/ask_tim/bezos_0300.html (accessed December 2001).

33 'An open letter from Jeff Bezos on the subject of patents': http://www.amazon.com/exec/obidos/subst/misc/patents.html/002–1619671–0862405 (accessed December 2001).

34 http://news.bbc.co.uk/hi/english/world/americas/newsid_845000/845593.stm (accessed December 2001).

35 'WIPO Arbitration and Mediation Centre',: http://arbiter.wipo.int/center/index.html

36 The recognition of rights and the use of names in the Internet domain name system', Report of the Second WIPO Internet Domain Name Process: http://wipo2.wipo.int (3 September 2001); http://wipo2.wipo.int/process2/report/html/report.html (accessed December 2001).

37 'GreatDomains.com is the world's leading provider of secondary market services for the exchange of domain names. A subsidiary of VeriSign, GreatDomains.com offers its community of buyers and sellers a reliable and trustworthy marketplace in which they can conduct their transactions. GreatDomains has no knowledge of whether any Domain Names listed on this Web site violates any third party intellectual property rights. GreatDomains will promptly delist any Domain Name reasonably objected to by the Owner of a pre-existing trademark': www.greatdomains.com (accessed December 2001).

38 'The $7.5m net address', 2 December 1999: http://news.bbc.co.uk/hi/english/business/newsid_547000/547105.stm (accessed December 2001).

39 'GVU's 10th WWW User Survey: The 10th Survey was run from October 10, 1998 through December 15, 1998': http://www.gvu.gatech.edu/user_surveys/survey–1998–10/ (accessed December 2001).

40 Source: GVU's 10th WWW User Survey (conducted October 1998): http://www.gvu.gatech.edu/user_surveys/survey–1998–10/graphs/general/q66.htm (accessed December 2001).

41 'Third annual report on the situation regarding the protection of individuals with regard to the processing of personal data and privacy in the community and in third countries covering the year 1998': http://europa.eu.int/comm/internal_market/en/media/dataprot/wpdocs/wp35en.pdf (accessed December 2001).

42 The Data Protection Act 1998 © Crown Publications: http://www.hmso.gov.uk/acts/acts1998/19980029.htm (accessed December 2001).

43 'EU adopts decision on US Safe Harbour scheme', 27 July 2000: http://www.dataprotection.gov.uk/dpr/dpdoc1.nsf/24afa328dcbf83d8802568980043e730/4be369978f6832b28025692f003458cb?OpenDocument. For the EU decision (an Adobe PDF file [41 pages]): http://www.europa.eu.int/comm/internal_market/en/dataprot/adequacy/dec2000520ec.pdf. For the American Safe Harbour website (includes lists of companies who are Safe Harbour registered): http://www.export.gov/safeharbor/

44 http://www.gvu.gatech.edu/user_surveys/survey–1998–10/graphs/general/q65.htm

45 'Work Of consumer affairs directorate distance selling and e-Commerce': http://www.dti.gov.uk/CACP/ca/work9.htm#e_codes

46 http://www.oecd.org/oecd/pages/home/displaygeneral/0,3380,EN-document–0-nodirectorate-no–24–320–0,FF.html

47 http://econfidence.jrc.it/default/show.gx?Object.object_id = EC_
FORUM000000000000000D
48 http://www.trustuk.org.uk/
49 'Distance selling directive which was passed in October 2000 (SI 2000 No.
2334) implements directive 97/7/EC of 20 May 1997': http://www.dti.gov.uk/
CACP/ca/work9.htm (accessed December 2001).
50 'The consumer protection (distance selling) regulations 2000': http:/
/www.dti.gov.uk/CACP/ca/policy/distanceselling/newregs.htm; 'The Consumer
Protection (Distance Selling) Regulations 2000 Statutory Instrument 2000 No.
2334': http://www.hmso.gov.uk/si/si2000/20002334.htm © Crown
Publications (accessed December 2001).
51 'On-line shopping advice – Office of Fair Trading': http://www.oft.gov.uk/
html/shopping/noframes/border.html#goingjump
52 'Work Of consumer affairs directorate distance selling and e-commerce': http:/
/www.dti.gov.uk/CACP/ca/work9.htm
53 http://www.eej-net.org.uk/
54 The draft Commission memorandum of understanding on clearing house
functions and a full set of EEJ-Net documentation is available from the
European Commission website: http://europa.eu.int/comm/consumers/policy/
developments/acce_just/index_en.html
55 A first-hand report indicates that the term is derived from a famous Monty
Python sketch ('Well, we have spam, tomato and spam, egg and spam, egg,
bacon and spam . . .'): http://searchsystemsmanagement.techtarget.com/
sDefinition/0,,sid20_gci213031,00.html (accessed December 2001).
56 Spam: www.whatis.com (accessed March 2001).
57 Downloadable from www.mailgate.com
58 Downloadable from http://softbytelabs.com/
59 'Honesty about e-privacy, truly the best policy', by Keith Regan, E-Commerce
Times, 5 December 2001: http://www.ecommercetimes.com/perl/story/
15138.html#story-start (accessed December 2001).

Economics, management theory and e-commerce

The impact of 'e' on economic and management thinking

LEARNING OBJECTIVES

- To understand the importance of technology on the economy and business.
- To identify the impact of technology and the Internet on the economy.
- To explore the idea of webonomics and the network economy.
- To recognise the impact of the Internet on management theories and thinking.

INTRODUCTION

This chapter will explore the impact of technology and the Internet on a range of economic and management theories. It will first explain the importance of technology and innovation on the economy and business. It will then look at the concept of disruptive technologies and how to harness them, moving to an exposition of the network effects of the Internet and the impact of digitisation on economic laws of diminishing return. The influence of e-commerce on traditional frameworks such as Porter will be described and the concept of the 'killer application' as a new management strategy for the digital economy will be explored. The aims of this chapter are both to introduce the different strands of thinking on the effects of e-commerce and also to highlight a common premise that runs through them all, illustrating that each is not an independent view but that they are built upon and validate each other.

WHY IS TECHNOLOGY IMPORTANT TO ECONOMICS?

Business and the economy are inextricably linked with the development and implementation of new technology. Growth and development of any modern economy has been recognised by many economic theorists, such as Kondratieff, Schumpeter, Mensch and Porter, to be based on innovation and new technology. The old economic factors of production (capital, land, labour, enterprise) first identified by Adam Smith in his *Wealth of Nations*[1] are framed in physical terms of natural resources. This, it is argued, is no longer enough to determine the success of businesses in a 'modern' economy. The emphasis has shifted to other factors, such as innovation and the capacity of an industry or economic cluster to adapt new technology for business success, although these arguably could come under the factor of enterprise.

A BRIEF ECONOMIC THEORY

In the early twentieth century, the economist Kondratieff introduced his 'Long Wave Theory'[2] of economic growth based on a study of nineteenth-century price behaviour, which included wages, interest rates, raw material prices, foreign trade, bank deposits, and other data. From this, he suggested that a long-term order of economic behaviour existed and could be used for the purpose of anticipating future economic developments. He maintained that an economy goes through the phases of *prosperity, recession, depression,* and *recovery* (one wave) in cycles of around 50–60 years. He detailed the number of years that the economy expanded and contracted during each part of the half-century long cycle, which industries suffer the most during the 'downwave' and how technology plays a role in leading the way out of the contraction into the next 'upwave'.

Building on this theory, the economist Schumpeter[3] assigned techno-logical innovation an almost exclusive role, as the engine of economic development: 'the fundamental impulse that sets and keeps the capitalist engine in motion comes from the new consumers' goods, the new methods of production or transportation, the new markets, the new forces of industrial organisation that capitalist enterprise creates' (Schumpeter, 1943).[4] After each wave the new innovation builds on the framework that has been developed previously in an evolutionary way. Far from being mutually exclusive cycles, which occur independently, each new cycle is a product of the economic development and technical innovation that has gone before. Schumpeter insists that the opportunities for technical innovations are very unevenly spread across different sectors of the economy and are not continuous over time, but occur in explosive bursts as entrepreneurs realise the economic potential arising from new combinations of technical and organisational change.

Mensch[5] updates Schumpeter's theory, giving it an empirical base in history, where clusters of basic innovations take place and generate completely new sectors. He stresses that only innovation can overcome depression and that government must implement an aggressive innovation policy to stimulate the search for new and basic innovation. Technological innovations are also influenced by and a product of historical formation of social institutions and political environments, which give rise to innovative thinking and development, which in turn produce new technology and ways of implementing it.

These cycles of innovation and their impact on the factors of production can be illustrated by putting them in the context of major technical and historical occurrences over the past 200 years. Table 8.1 broadly summarises the periods of economic cycles, their socio-political milieux, the main influential technological innovation of the time and the impact on some of the economic factors of production. With each technological innovation, there is a shift in the relative importance of the four economic factors of production as the catalysts for economic growth. Porter[6] emphasises this fact, maintaining that the prosperity and competitive advantage of a nation is no longer as a result of a nation's natural resources and its labour force, but rather the ability of its industry to innovate and upgrade. This can be seen as disruptive technology on a macro-environmental level.

There is much debate within the economic community itself over the existence and veracity of economic/business cycle theory. Whether readers subscribe to this theory or not, the impact of new technology on the economy of a nation is indisputable.

WHAT ARE DISRUPTIVE TECHNOLOGIES AND HOW CAN THEY BE MASTERED?

Historically, innovation and new technology are nothing new in the world of business. The introduction of the Internet and the subsequent use of new technology to conduct business have raised awareness for the need to understand and manage technology at a micro level of the firm. Bower and Christensen,[7] Harvard Business School professors specialising in managing the commercialisation of advanced technology, conducted a study of leading companies in a variety of industries that have confronted technological change. They found that staying too close to customers' needs led to some companies being unable to adapt successfully to technological changes. One of the main problems they identified was that managers continue to do what has worked in the past and so continue to serve their

TABLE 8.1 Economic cycles in their historical context

Economic business cycles	Politico-economic influences	Technological innovation	Impact on factors of production
First cycle (1780s–1830s)	French Revolution	Industrial Revolution (I): iron industry/textile industry/steam technology	Land – iron and coal resources Capital – overseas trade, sophistication of trading and banking systems Labour – division of labour/factory workers/increased population Enterprise – investment by landowners in new industry
Second cycle (1830s–1880s)	Marx	Industrial Revolution (II): steel industry/railroads	Land – pig iron coal resources Capital – joint stock banks, issuing of notes alongside gold, stable banking system Labour – improved conditions and education for workers Enterprise – investment by the State and venture capitalists
Third cycle (1880s–1930s)	Capitalism	Electrical engineering/electricity/motor manufacturing	Land – coal, petroleum, other metals and semiconductor Capital – increased overseas trade, development of international financial markets Labour – more skilled labour, demise of child labour, improved education and conditions Enterprise – inter-war speculation
Fourth cycle (1930s–1990s)	Socialism Unionism Consumption	Nuclear technology/oil/electronics/micro-processing technology	Land – aluminium, silicone, petroleum Capital – increased international investment, sophisticated financial markets Labour – highly skilled labour, universal education and basic standards of living, integration of trade unions into common working practices Enterprise – international investment
Fifth cycle (1990s–	Globalisation International Integration	Information technology/telecommunications technology/bio-technology and genetic engineering	Land – recycled/ environmentally friendly materials Labour – workers skilled in knowledge-based products and services rather than in manufacturing Capital – money, like information, is now only data; single-market world Enterprise – Monopolistic media and IT, private institutional investment for the many (e.g. pension schemes)

current customers' needs, rather than focusing attention and resources into programmes developing technology for which current customers do not identify a need and where short term profit margins and cost structures seem unattractive. One of the main difficulties is being able to identify the innovative technology of the future and acting to maximise its benefits.

In order to recognise this technology, Bower and Christensen identified two categories of technological innovation (sustaining and disruptive) that had different *'performance trajectories'* – the rate at which the performance of a product has or is expected to improve over time. They cited the example of computer-storage capacity as a critical performance trajectory for computer hard drives and the amount of earth moved per minute as a critical performance trajectory for mechanical diggers. Figure 8.1 shows the difference between the effects of the two technologies. *Sustaining technologies* tend to maintain a rate of improvement in existing products, adding something more or improving on the product's performance attributes that are valued by existing customers. Thus companies tend to invest resources in building on existing investment and cost structures for sustaining technologies.

Disruptive technologies have a different set of performance attributes that are not currently valued by mainstream existing customers. The revenue from disruptive technologies is low to zero in the short term, because markets are being built up and projections are difficult. As a result, managers typically conclude that the technology cannot make a meaningful contribution to corporate growth and so investment in disruptive technologies is not worthwhile, and thus established companies may detrimentally lose out.

Figure 8.1 shows that technology/product lifecycles eventually come to a point where they descend into obsolescence. The idea of disruptive technology is that, well before reaching this stage of decline, organisations must recognise and support the development of new 'disruptive' technology as a way of continuing growth and improvement. Eventually, the performance attributes of the existing technology that is valued by existing customers will change rapidly once the new disruptive technology has been developed and marketed. The performance attributes of the established disruptive technology will become those required by mainstream customers. However, if the organisation has not recognised this, and concentrated on sustaining technologies at the expense of disruptive technologies, this can potentially be disastrous for the organisation.

One example is IBM in the 1970s, who had a core of large industry and government-based customers buying mainframe computers. IBM were working to improve this product for this select customer group, while largely ignoring the advent of mini and personal computers because they saw no immediate use for them. It was only once the personal computers

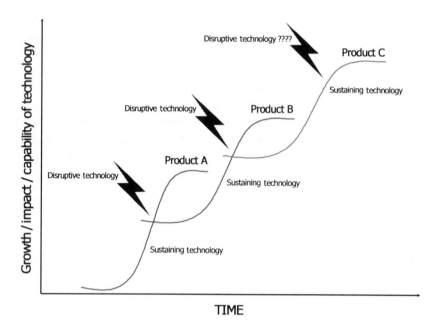

Figure 8.1 Disruptive and sustaining technologies

became established in the market that IBM customers' performance attributes changed and IBM had to compete with the pioneers who by then had dominated the market.

It should be noted that a disruptive technology does not necessarily surpass the capability of existing technology, and in some instances might be inferior, but it fulfils the needs of customers. For example, personal computers do not outperform mainframes, but personal computers with file servers meet the needs of organisations effectively even though the profit margins of IBM's mainframes are still higher than those of personal computers.

To be able to recognise and maximise the benefits of disruptive technology, Bower and Christensen recommend that managers:

- *Determine whether technology is disruptive or sustaining.* For example, by examining internal disagreements between technical and finance/marketing departments – this is usually a sign of disruptive technology that managers should explore.
- *Define the strategic significance of disruptive technologies* by asking the right questions of the right people about the strategic importance of the technology. Supplier companies usually ask mainstream and large customers to assess the value of innovative products. However, since

disruptive technology may not exceed the capability of existing technology, the feedback from this group will always be for sustaining
technology and against disruptive technology.

- *Locate the initial market for the disruptive technology* by creating information about these non-existent markets by experimenting repeatedly
with both the product and market to identify the customers, selling
factors of product performance and price. Market research in this
instance is unhelpful because it is often hard for respondents to
imagine the impact of the new disruptive technology because the
market does not exist. For example, in the case of the Polaroid camera,
very few respondents were able to imagine the uses of instant photo-
graphy and so the market research studies concluded that only 100,000
cameras would be sold over the product's lifecycle.

- *Place responsibility for disruptive technology business in an independent
organisation* that is small enough to be able to make changes necessary
in reaction to market conditions and where small successes seem
acceptably large in a new market start-up.

- *Keep the disruptive organisation independent.* Managers must not look to
re-integrate the spin-off company back into the larger corporation to
share fixed costs and economies of scale because of resource allocation
issues and decisions over whether or when to cannibalise established
products. Every organisation in the computer hard-drive manufacturing industry that has attempted to manage a disruptive business within
a single organisation has failed.

No matter what the industry, all products have a limited lifespan,
which will eventually come to an end. Companies which have recognised
the strategic importance of disruptive technology as a part of the product
lifecycle, and embraced the strategy for realising its full potential – even at
the expense of the mainstream business – will survive and grow. This
concept is also known as cannibalisation.

WHAT IS CANNIBALISATION?

Cannibalisation is not a new concept and companies have been struggling
with different strategies to maximise revenue from multi-products and
multi-channels that compete with each other. For example, General Elec-
tric (GE) produced CT scanners for hospitals – an expensive high-end
product. They learned that a Japanese company was entering the market
with a less expensive, smaller and more electronic model of the CT
scanner. GE had to make the decision whether to introduce a similar
machine into the market before the Japanese or whether to protect the
higher-profit margin on their large CT scanner. One manager settled the

argument by saying 'aren't we better off to cannibalise ourselves than to let the Japanese do it?'.[8]

The computer-processor manufacturing industry is one based on product cannibalisation, where they are constantly and regularly introducing new and improved processor speeds before critical mass for older processors has been achieved. This is the only way they can survive in a market that is driven by new and rapid introduction of products and components.

Moorthy and Png[9] have shown (mathematically) that where consumers agree on the quality ranking of available products but differ in their willingness to pay, a company offering two products should lower the quality (if possible) and price of the low-end product to make it less desirable to the high-end product buyers, while maintaining the price of the high-end product (or lowering it very slightly) to maximise profit and achieve the greatest reduction in cannibalisation. But this is only one strategy of many.

The advent of the Internet and World Wide Web has also introduced multi-channels. In the past, many companies sold to a single market through a single channel, but today whole numbers of channels are available including the Internet and mobile devices. With this comes conflict and control problems that are sometimes potentially disastrous to an organisation where different departments are competing for the same customer, and are unable to coordinate marketing and sales strategies, ending up with alienating or losing the customer. One of the important strategies for controlling channel conflict is to establish clear channel boundaries established on the basis of customer characteristics (for example, size or industry sector), geography or products. For example, in the business-to-business sector, an expensive face-to-face sales channel would be needed for large-account customers who need a specialist service, compared with the cheaper Internet channel, which can be used for a standard product or service for small-account customers.

A study by the American Banking Association[10] revealed that there were large cost differentials for different service delivery channels in the banking sector, with the Internet being the cheapest. These are summarised in Table 8.2. Each of these channels is suited to different kinds of

TABLE 8.2 Costs per transaction in the banking sector

Service Delivery Channel	Cost per transaction
Bank branch	US$1.07
Telephone banking	US$0.54
ATM/cash machine	US$0.27
Internet banking	US$0.01

customer needs at different times and for different products. Customers are encouraged to choose Internet banking with incentives of higher interest rate on-line savings accounts or lower interest rate on-line loans.

One of the more effective strategies to minimise the disruptive effects of cannibalisation is not to see the different channels as being in competition or conflict, but to see all the channels as contributing to the whole organisation, providing additional value to customers, leading to increased revenue generation. For example, moving employees around the different channels can enhance the feeling of complementarity, and enabling all customers to experience all the channels seamlessly would mean that employees and customers no longer feel they have a particular loyalty to any one channel at the expense of the other. This would ensure that each channel is perceived to be a part of the whole range of service offerings.

LAWS UNDERPINNING THE IMPACT OF 'E'

Much has been written about the impact of computing technology and the Internet on the economy and business. These observations have been encapsulated into laws that are meant to explain the phenomenon created by the Internet and technology. By understanding this phenomenon, businesses can enhance and develop their business plans accordingly. This section will describe these laws and their origins, and how they have been used to explain the rise of the 'new economy'.

Moore's Law

Dr Gordon Moore, a chemistry graduate from the University of California at Berkeley and a chemistry and physics postgraduate from the California Institute of Technology, Berkeley, went on to co-found Intel Corporation in 1968, serving initially as Executive Vice President. He became President and Chief Executive Officer in 1975 and held that post until elected Chairman and Chief Executive Officer in 1979. He remained CEO until 1987 and was named Chairman Emeritus in 1997. He is a director of Gilead Sciences Inc., a member of the National Academy of Engineering and a Fellow of the IEEE. He received the National Medal of Technology from President George Bush in 1990.

In his own words, Gordon Moore explains his law:

> I first observed the 'doubling of transistor density on a manufactured die every year' in 1965, just four years after the first planar integrated circuit was discovered. The press called this 'Moore's Law' and the name has stuck. To be honest, I did not expect this law to still be true some 30 years later, but I am

now confident that it will be true for another 20 years. By the year 2012, Intel should have the ability to integrate 1 billion transistors onto a production die that will be operating at 10GHz. This could result in a performance of 100,000 MIPS [millions of instructions per second], the same increase over the currently cutting edge Pentium® II processor as the Pentium II processor was to the 386! We see no fundamental barriers in our path to Micro 2012, and it's not until the year 2017 that we see the physical limitations of wafer fabrication technology being reached.[11]

So Moore predicted that the number of transistors the industry would be able to place on a computer chip (which provided more power to process instructions that drive electronic equipment) would double every year. While originally intended as a rule of thumb in 1965, it was modified to reflect changes every 18 months instead of one year, but this has proven to be accurate over the past three decades, as can be seen in the graph in Figure 8.2.

From this simple observation of a trend that was specific to the semiconductor industry, a number of consequences of this observation have been associated with it and extrapolated to create Moore's Law (also known as Moore's Law of the Microcosm). So, this Law maintains that 'every eighteen months, for the foreseeable future, chip density (and hence computing power) would double while cost remained constant, creating ever more powerful computing devices without raising their price'.

Moore's Law is increasingly being used as a metaphor for anticipated rates of rapid technological change accompanied by economic and social effects, with processing power, not circuit density, becoming the new basis of Moore's Law. But it is still validly applicable; for example, disk-drive

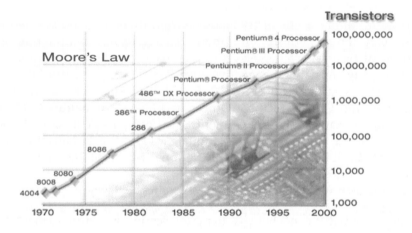

Figure 8.2 Moore's Law and Intel's processing capacity

Source: www.intel.com

magnetic-storage technology has followed a similar scaling path as semi-conductors. Standard computer hard drives have increased from capacities of megabytes (million bytes) to gigabyte (billion bytes) in about a decade. Analysts and experts in the fibre optic industry have also declared that Moore's Law applies to their industry, with the number of chips on an optical transceiver falling from 7 in 1999, 4 in 2002 and 2 in 2003, thus reducing costs, increasing efficiency and producing faster fibre optic networks.[12]

CASE STUDY

Bob Schaller[13] examined the wide range of uses, interpretations and applications of Moore's Law and the following are some of the interesting ones:

'Moore's Law' may one day be as important to marketing as the Four Ps: product, price, place, and promotion . . . If it is borne out in the future the way it has in the past, the powerful Pentium on your desktop will seem as archaic as a 286 PC in a few years (Koprowski, 1996)

We have become addicted to speed. Gordon Moore is our pusher. Moore's law, which states that processing power will double every year and a half, has thus far held true. CPU designers, always in search of a better fix, drain every possible ounce of fat from processor cores, squeeze clock cycles, and cram components into smaller and smaller dies. (Joch, 1996)

So holding 'Moore's Law' as the constant, the technology in place in classrooms today will not be anything like the classroom of five years from now! (Wimauna Elementary School, 1996)

The End of Moore's Law: Thank God! . . . The End of Moore's Law will mean the end to certain kinds of daydreaming about amazing possibilities for the Next Big Thing; but it will also be the end of a lot of stress, grief, and unwanted work. (CUUG, 1996)

Computer-related gifts must be the only Christmas presents that follow Moore's Law. (Sydney Morning Herald, 1995)

Moore's Law is why . . . smart people start saving for the next computer the day after they buy the one they have. . . Things are changing so fast that everyone's knowledge gets retreaded almost yearly. Thank you, Mr. Moore . . . [for] the internet, a creature of Moore's Law . . . (Hettinga, 1996)

However, there are limitations to the Law, as 'Gordon Moore himself jokingly cites that if similar progress were made in transportation technologies such as air travel, a modern day commercial aircraft would cost $500, circle the earth in 20 minutes, and only use five gallons of fuel. However, it may only be the size of a shoebox'.[14]

Metcalfe's Law

Dr Robert Metcalfe, a graduate of the Massachusetts Institute of Technology and postgraduate from Harvard University, went to the Xerox Palo

Alto Research Centre in 1972, where he invented Ethernet – the local-area networking technology that now connects over 20 million computers worldwide. In 1979, he founded 3COM Corporation, a computer networking company that over a period of 11 years grew to have US $400 million in sales. At 3COM he held various positions including chairman, chief executive officer, president, division general manager, and vice president of sales and marketing. In 1988, he was awarded IEEE's Alexander Graham Bell Medal for his work on the invention, standardisation and commercialisation of local area networks.

Metcalfe states: 'I made this law up. It is called Metcalfe's Law. I did not call it Metcalfe's Law, but I am delighted that other people are. And it says that the value of a network grows as the square of the number of users.'[15] This means that new technology is only valuable if many people use it and the more people use it the more valuable it becomes and that value grows exponentially. For example, one telephone or fax machine is of no value to anybody. Once two people have a fax machine or telephone, then they become more valuable to both parties. The more people with fax machines and telephones increases the usefulness and thus value of each individual machine or telephone. So every computer added to the network uses it as a resource, while adding resources in a spiral of increasing value and choice. This has been described mathematically as

$$\text{Network Value (V)} = \text{number of users squared (n)}^2$$

Figure 8.3 shows how each additional number of endpoints (users) to a network impacts on the total value of the network. The network that does

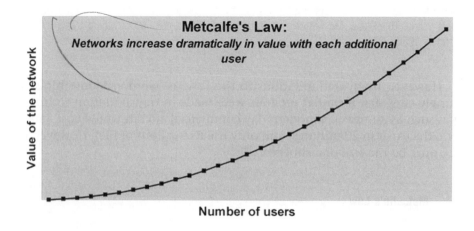

Figure 8.3 Metcalfe's Law illustrated

not reach everywhere is of little value. The power of the network increases exponentially by the number of computers connected to it. However, some argue that Metcalfe's law is only applicable in certain circumstances. For example, it can only apply to interconnected and networked machines and not to the value of human beings connected to the network because humans are only able to work sequentially. If they do work in parallel they can only do this for a short time and with a limited number of tasks.[16]

Another argument against Metcalfe's law is presented by Warren Packard, a venture capitalist, who maintained that it is just a 'temporal anomaly . . . Networks saturate for a variety of reasons. As the population of a network increases, the value of each additional member diminishes. How much value was gained when the 200 millionth individual jumped on the Internet? In addition, technologies mature and become obsolete causing once healthy networks to atrophy.'[17] Nobody who has used the Internet at 'peak times' and experienced slow or non-existent access can disagree with this view.

Metcalfe's Law assumes infinite capacity, but networks are reliant upon physical hardware (routers, cables, modems, servers, memory, and so on), all of which have finite capacity and physical limitations. Packard suggests that when looking at networks in isolation, Metcalfe's Law 'does not hold up'. However, from a macro perspective, 'Metcalfe is right on target' because he sees constant innovation as the key to fuelling the Internet economy. Consistent with the concept of disruptive technology is the idea that each new set of technological innovations will create another 'S' curve (representing the product's lifecycle) yielding exponential benefits. In aggregate the number of 'S' curves created will appear to be 'one giant hockey stick of growth', as suggested by Metcalfe and illustrated in Figure 8.4. New ventures, visionary and innovative companies will take part at the beginning of each new 'S' curve, while the complacent companies feeling they have the right technology – such as some Web-based businesses designed for narrowband – will languish at the top of the older 'S' curve and be unable to survive the next wave of growth.

Gilder's Law

George Gilder, a graduate of Exeter Academy and Harvard University, where he studied under Henry Kissinger, helped found *Advance*, a journal of political thought, after his graduation in 1962. He is also a contributing editor of *Forbes* magazine. He is a frequent writer for *The Economist*, the *Harvard Business Review*, the *Wall Street Journal* and other publications. According to a recent study of speeches, Mr Gilder was President Reagan's most frequently quoted living author. In 1986, President Reagan gave George Gilder the White House Award for Entrepreneurial Excellence.[18] In

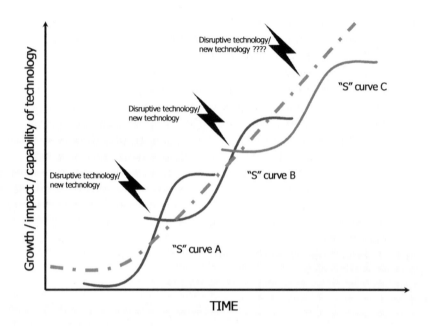

Figure 8.4 Metcalfe's Law and disruptive technology

1996 he was made a Fellow of the International Engineering Consortium. In his book *Microcosm* (1989), he explored the roots of the new electronic technologies and prophesied the future of computers and telecommunications in a restatement of Moore's Law. In his next book on the future of telecommunications, *Telecosm* (2000), he predicted a revolutionary new era of unlimited bandwidth, where the 'age of the microchip', which he calls the 'microcosm', is ending and being superseded by the 'telecosm', 'a world of infinite bandwidth, ultra high-speed networking, and communications power that liberates each desk from the limitations of the PC'.[19]

Gilder maintains that the bandwidth will come from low-flying satellites, from lasers and fibre optics, and from the evolution of other tools. For readers interested in this area, I recommend Gilder's book. However, some of the pertinent laws that have emerged include:

> The law of the telecosm states that as the total communications frequencies rise and wavelengths drop, digital performance improves exponentially. Bandwidth rises, power usage sinks, antenna size shrinks, interference collapses, and error rates plummet. This powerful new paradigm is just beginning to be felt. In short, bandwidth will increase at regular intervals, about every six months.[20]

Gilder's Law says that 'bandwidth grows at least three times faster than computing power costs . . . and will halve as speeds double for the next 25 years'. As an example, Gilder notes that backbone bandwidth on a single cable is now a thousand times greater than the entire average traffic on the global communications infrastructure was five years ago. In other words, in 2001 more information could be sent over a single cable in one second than all the information that was sent over the entire Internet in one month in 1997.[21]

Not only is bandwidth increasing but prices are also falling – Cisco's CEO John Chambers has predicted that voice calls will become just another class of data and therefore free. *Business Week* has suggested that the cash flow from AT&T long distance might go from US $17.5 billion in 2000 to US $9.5 billion or even zero by 2004.[22] New developments (for example, interactive games, music and full-motion video are starting to become available over the Web) seem to confirm that bandwidth availability will continue to expand at a rate that supports Gilder's Law, but physical implementation of this new technology might be a potential limiter to this law. Without the advances in the physics of lasers, optics, detection, and amplification, this could not be happening.

New laws of increasing returns and network externalities

A concept first described by Brian Arthur, a leading economist who graduated from the University of California, Berkeley, and progressed onto a career in academia, becoming Dean of Economics at Stanford University and a fellow of the Econometric Society, who was awarded the Schumpeter prize in Economics in 1990. This is related to Metcalfe's Law discussed above and encapsulates the idea of a network logic where each additional member of a network increases the network's value, which in turn attracts more members initiating a virtuous spiral of benefits. Brian Arthur described this effect thus: 'increasing returns are the tendency for that which is ahead to get farther ahead; for that which loses advantage to lose further advantage. They are mechanisms for positive feedback that operate within markets, business and industries to reinforce that which gains success or aggravate that which suffers loss.'[23] This positive feedback is created by network externalities[24] where a transaction between parties has had an impact on parties not involved in the transaction. For example, the total value of a telephone system lies outside the total internal value of the telephone companies and their assets. The value lies externally in the greater phone network itself.

> Mechanisms of increasing returns exist alongside those of diminishing returns in all industries. But roughly speaking, diminishing returns hold sway in the traditional part of the economy – the processing industries. Increasing returns reign in the newer part – the knowledge-based industries. The two worlds have different economics. They differ in behaviour, style and culture.

They call for different management techniques, different strategies, different codes of government regulation.'[25]

One of the major impacts of increasing returns and network externalities is that they can create monopolies largely because there is market instability with multiple potential outcomes and so there is unpredictability where the market may favour one or another of the products. However, once the product has gained market leadership, the market then favours the product further and the company creates lock-in and high switching costs, generating super-profits for the 'winner'.

One of the most famous examples of creating a monopoly through increasing returns and network externalities is Microsoft. By initially teaming up with IBM in 1980, their DOS system gained market leadership over Apple Macintosh (which was easier to use) and CP/M, which was first to the market in 1979. DOS/IBM's prevalence encouraged software developers such as Lotus to write software for DOS. This attracted more customers and complementary suppliers to use the DOS system. Once this lock-in had been achieved, switching costs were then too high to change to another operating system. So once the DOS system dominated the market, Microsoft was able to spread its costs of a very large base of users with highly competitive 'killer margins', despite the fact that computer professionals derided the operating system as not being the best product in the market. Often the cases of VHS and Betamax video machines, Apple Macintosh and Windows operating systems, and Dvorak and QWERTY keyboards are cited as examples of an inferior product being adopted as a result of the dynamics of increasing returns and network externalities. However, some argue that in fact Betamax format lost to VHS because it could not record for as long as VHS; Apple computers had an inferior price because of its monopolistic strategy; and the supposedly more ergonomic Dvorak keyboard lost out to QWERTY because in reality it was not any faster.[26]

Other laws

There have been a number of other laws that are relevant to the Network Economy. Some of those suggested by Alex Lightman, a venture capitalist and contributing editor of *Red Herring*, are worth mentioning very briefly here:

- *Ruettger's Law of Storage* states that companies double their digital storage requirements every 12 months. With the increased use of computing equipment and electronic means of communication this means there will be more digital data within an organisation that needs to be stored. However, Lightman estimates that still 70 per cent of information is in paper format.

- *Gene's Law* indicates that power requirements for semiconductors are decreasing exponentially, so as the infrastructure around processors is getting smaller, so batteries providing power will last longer.
- *Say's Law of Quality* states that quantity creates its own quality or supply creates demand, and is part of the reasoning for giving away products for free. For example, Netscape, Hotmail and on-line Internet services of recent years have all been free and have created entirely new markets and a whole range of complementary products and services that have added to the overall health of the world economy.

The majority of these 'laws' are based on observations of the physical elements of the infrastructure that is underpinning the 'new' economy. This technology includes electronic data and digitisation; computers and computing technology; telecommunications (broadband, satellite); and networks (Internet, intranet and extranets).

WHAT ARE 'WEBONOMICS'?

'Webonomics' is a term first coined by Edward Schwarz (author of *Webonomics: Nine Essential Principles for Growing Your Business on the World Wide Web*, published in the spring of 1997) to explain the new economy taking shape as a result of the growth of digital information, computing technology, the World Wide Web and the Internet.

'If you say "web economy" ten times fast, you get a new word – webonomics,' he explains. 'A lot of the old economic theories don't apply to the Web. A real economist probably couldn't have written this book because the web doesn't work that way. Most economics is ruled on the basis of scarcity, but nothing is scarce on the Web, except attention.'[27]

The so-called 'laws' that were observed and explained in the previous section underpin the whole body of webonomics.

Kevin Kelly's book, *New Rules for the New Economy*,[28] identifies the distinguishing factors of the new economy, which are very closely related to the technology that underpins it. For example: it is *global* – removing all geographical barriers; *favours intangibles* – where knowledge and data is valued because it is the lifeblood of networks and computing technology; *it is intensely connected* – a concept on which the World Wide Web was developed (hypertext) and which underpins networks.

Kelly's book identifies ten major effects of this 'new economy', all of which relate to the concepts and laws identified earlier in this chapter. Some of these major effects are:

- *Increasing returns* – where the number of connections between people and things improve the benefits for everybody directly and indirectly.
- *Plenitude not scarcity generates value* – again relating to Metcalfe and Moore's law where the more widely available a product or service, the more value it is.
- *'Free' services and products are the key to success* – because it takes advantage of the only true scarce resource in a network, which is human attention. Once this is achieved, then companies can create lock-in with high switching costs.
- *Companies must devalue and creatively destruct* – this relates back to the concept of disruptive technology – as innovation leads to success, then companies must destroy their existing product or service and create a new one to escape its eventual obsolescence and the company's being unable to compete in a market already dominated by players. So innovation becomes the normal way of operating the business.
- *Space is important not place* – this relates to the sense of 'anytime, anyplace, anywhere' where the physical and geographical is no longer important.
- *The concept of the 'prosumer'* – where there is no longer mass production but mass customisation and personalisation, where the customer is both the producer and the consumer of the product or service they are buying or using.

For a full exposition of the arguments and well-illustrated examples, read Kelly's book. This section on the impact of technology on the economy concludes with Graeme Philipson's[29] observations in October 2001:

> Lots of people have written lots of things about the information economy. Much of what has been said is absolute rubbish. But the fact remains that we have entered an important new era. . . . we have witnessed a massive paradigm shift.
>
> 'New rules for the new economy' four years after it was written . . . remains the best exposition . . . for the way the Internet is changing our society and our economy. Its lessons ring true even after the dot com crash and the turbulent events of recent months.[30]

WHAT ABOUT THE IMPACT OF 'E' ON MANAGEMENT THINKING?

The aim of this book has been to explain the impact of the Internet and new technology on business. New frameworks to address business issues such as security and business models have already been introduced in earlier chapters. This section will examine further the impact of the Internet and new technology on existing management thinking and theories.

STRATEGY

Strategy can be defined as an 'integrated set of actions aimed at increasing the long-term well being and strengths of an enterprise relative to its competitors'.[31] Figure 8.5 summarises the strategy formulation process, which does not in itself change as a result of new technology. There is still the need for the organisation to:

- Create a clear mission statement and set of organisational goals which underline the reason for the organisation's existence.
- Examine the industry and define how it works and how it is likely to evolve in the future.
- Develop the strategy, implement it and then continually assess and re-assess and feedback into the whole process to ensure that the key

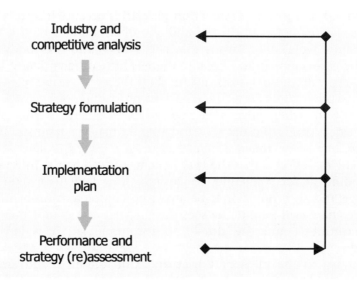

Figure 8.5   Strategic planning cycle

factors for success and the challenges the company faces are addressed regularly.

There is much disagreement and discussion about the impact of the Internet and technology on the economy and business, and the concept of the 'new economy' is disputed by many.

PORTER'S 'FIVE FORCES' AND THE 'NEW ECONOMY'

Michael Porter's 'Competitive Advantage' framework for analysing an industry's attractiveness and assessing the potential for competitive advantage has been one of the most influential since the 1980s. Porter's framework maintains that competitive advantage requires sustainable leverage over the five forces of new entrants, suppliers, buyers, substitutes and competitors within the industry sector. All these factors assess how attractive an industry is and the potential for obtaining a competitive advantage.

Porter brings his theory into the twenty-first century in a *Harvard Business Review* paper[32] where he discusses the impact of the Internet on his framework. He acknowledges the importance of new technology but feels there is a need to move away from the rhetoric and hype surrounding the Internet, e-business strategy and the idea of a 'new economy'. According to Porter, 'the Internet is not necessarily a blessing because it alters industry structures in ways that . . . dampen profitability . . . level business practices . . . reduce ability to sustain operational advantage'. Overall, he feels that the Internet has a negative impact on industries because it lowers barriers to entry; creates new substitutes; and the open systems of the Internet infrastructure technology means that it is available to everybody equally which increases competition because there is little differentiation between competitors. All these factors mean that there is greater pressure for destructive pricing and Porter even sees the probability of a 'zero-sum form of competition', where price is the sole variable. Demand is artificially high because prices are artificially low and this he believes is unsustainable – *'sooner or later some customers can be expected to return to more traditional modes'*. The net effect is that the very benefits offered by the Internet make it more difficult for companies to capture those benefits as competitive advantage and so profit. Porter believes the complete cannibalisation of the value chain will be rare; he sees the Internet as a complement rather than a cannibal, and the threat of disintermediation is lower than expected.

Contrary to the ideas of Bower and Christensen in nurturing disruptive technology, Porter believes that organisational separation undermines a company's ability to gain competitive advantage. By not integrating the Internet into an overall strategy, companies fail to capitalise on their traditional assets, reinforcing follower strategies and competitive convergence. He cites Barnes & Noble's decision to establish barnesand noble.com as a separate organisation as a vivid example of not capitalising on its physical assets to successfully compete against Amazon.

Porter believes however that his framework, which facilitates Industry analysis, is still crucial to illuminate attractiveness and determine profitability of the respective industry. He does acknowledge that each industry reacts to the Internet differently and gives the example of the car industry, when the Internet has had a negative impact on the car retailing sector. Because information is widely available, there are more options to purchase and more competition between dealers, which makes it more difficult to differentiate services on anything except price. On the other hand, for auctions the Internet has had a positive impact because there is no real substitute, the barriers to entry are modest and the likes of eBay do not compete on price. Overall, he feels that the Internet is very important as a facilitator where virtual activities do not eliminate the need for physical activities but amplify their importance and where strategy is more important and essential:

> The Internet is often not disruptive to existing industries or established companies. It rarely nullifies the most important sources of competitive advantage in an industry; in many cases it actually makes those sources more important. As companies come to embrace Internet technology, moreover, the Internet itself will be neutralised as a source of advantage. . . . The more robust competitive advantage will arise from traditional strengths such as unique products, proprietary content, distinctive physical activities, superior product knowledge, and strong personal service and relationships. . . .
>
> . . . the new economy appears less like a new economy than an old economy that has access to a new technology. Even the phrases new economy and old economy are rapidly losing their relevance, if they ever had any. The old economy of established companies and new economy of dot coms are merging and it will soon be difficult to distinguish them. . . . While a new means of conducting business has become available, the fundamentals of competition remain unchanged.

OTHER VIEWS

In his book *The Information E-conomy*,[33] Colin Turner echoes the observations that the world is in the midst of a major electronic transformation, where wealth creation is rapidly shifting from traditional manufacturing to the creation of goods and services based on digital bytes – this he calls the information e-conomy. He believes that in order for businesses to compete in this new digital age, they need to incorporate the rapid changes facilitated by IT, telecommunications and the Internet, and also to use information resources as a key competitive tool.

This new economy will create more rivalry amongst competitors mainly because of the lowering of barriers to entry and the convergence of previously distinct sectors. The organisation will be extended out over its external value system, where there will be new requirements to open up the enterprise to customers and suppliers – developing individual and personalised relationships with customers and working with suppliers to create mutually successful solutions. This will transform industries, where specialisations will be developed, and collaboration and infrastructure sharing with competitors will also happen. So companies will have to focus on customer requirements, exploit hybrid markets, and manage the network of alliances strategically in order to operate in this new environment. The technology to support this has already been developed and is discussed in Chapters 2 and 3.

Turner applies Porter's framework to identify three generic strategies for this new economy (as illustrated in Figure 8.6), which he sees as a means of achieving competitive advantage through using the Internet,

- To lower costs and achieve market share by being first to market.
- Offering greater differentiation through product innovation as a result of a highly skilled workforce.

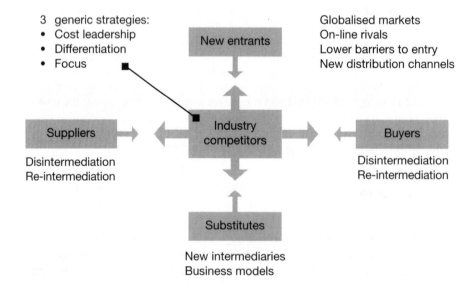

Figure 8.6 Turner's application of Porter's framework in the new economy

Source: Turner, C. *The Information E-conomy,* Kogan Page, 2000.

- Providing increased focus on customer relations by using information and the evolution of business models with increasingly networked business processes.

Turner believes that the process of disintermediation will take place but that re-intermediation will introduce new players entering the market to facilitate on-line transactions.

Both Porter and Turner agree that the value chain will become more integrated across sectors with suppliers, customers and channels working together. Turner takes this idea further and suggests that whole value chains will be competing against each other rather than single enterprises. Those achieving competitive advantage will be companies that have most successfully integrated their demand and supply chains to enable information of mutual benefit to flow freely along the value chain. This also means that the external four forces (suppliers, buyers, substitutes and new entrants) will integrate, forming a generic strategy, and so choice of strategy will increasingly become interdependent and integrated with value chain players. Competitive forces will also be influenced by the rules of cooperation and alliance management. The openness of the Internet infrastructure, which Porter sees as a source of levelling competitive advantage, Turner sees as a means of facilitating the creation and dissolution of alliances with different partners across value systems.

Turner sees the source of competitive advantage changing, with information being the key resource and the Internet as the key facilitator. He sees collaboration as a crucial factor to developing a strategy for competitive advantage. Porter on the other hand sees factors such as scale, the skills of personnel, product and process technology, and investments in physical assets as playing prominent roles: 'The Internet is transformational in some respects, but many traditional sources of competitive advantage remain intact.'

WHAT ABOUT UNLEASHING KILLER APPLICATIONS?

Larry Downes, co-author of the book *Unleashing the Killer App: Digital Strategies for Market Dominance*,[34] is a strong advocate of the idea that the world of commerce that Michael Porter describes is rapidly disappearing and that the time has come to move on from his methodology. Downes believes that digital technologies have 'thrown nearly every industry into a new era of competition in which none of the old rules are valid'.[35] Downes believes that Porter's style of planning assumes predictable or identifiable competitors, and business partners and customers where business environments stay the same – but these assumptions are no longer viable. He maintains there are three new forces that overwhelm Porter's five:

- *Digitalisation* is based on the observations of Metcalfe, Moore and Gilder that assume computing power and communications bandwidth will become cheap enough to treat as disposable. As a result of this, information and its availability will increase and explode, which will result in changed markets where competitors and partners change and 'mutate' before organisations can 'get comfortable with them'. Downes cites the example of shopping malls developers, where traditionally they developed competitive advantage through managing real estate. On the Web, electronic malls can offer a broader array of services and space, so, for example, a non-traditional competitor like Barclays Bank in the UK have set up their own on-line shopping mall – ShopSmart – with little investment in traditional 'real estate' infrastructure. Physical malls lose out on rent as well as location, which on the Web becomes irrelevant. Downes believes the rapid speed of digitalisation and the disruption it creates means that those using the traditional Five Forces Model will never see change coming in time to maintain advantage.
- *Globalisation* is again based on the concept of networks and their infrastructure and, as a consequence of digitalisation, this has resulted in improvements in distribution logistics and communications, allowing local business to become global once connected to this network. It is common for even small companies to draw on a global network of partners, suppliers and customers, and customers themselves are happy to engage in borderless transactions so long as their needs are served. This has resulted in increased competition that the traditional approach to strategy cannot handle.
- *Deregulation* is the removal of government control, regulations and tariffs within industries and between countries to enable open and international competition rather than protectionism. This has been an increasing trend across the USA and Europe in the last decade of the twentieth century, with the General Agreement on Tariffs and Trade (GATT), North American Free Trade Agreement (NAFTA) and the growth to prominence of the World Trade Organisation (WTO) agreements, as well as the growth of the European Union and the collapse of the highly regulated economies of the former Soviet Union. This is leading to an environment of open markets and 'frictionless' trading, which is facilitated by the new technology. Deregulation is contributing to the radical shrinking, outsourcing and restructuring of traditional enterprises.

Downes believes that these three forces feed off each other – for example, digital technology makes it easier to manage larger numbers of buyers and suppliers, thus speeding up globalisation. As economies become more global, so countries need to change regulations to ensure they can participate profitably in the global economy. As deregulation increases, so companies and industries that were previously protected have to improve their strategic use of digital technology, leading to a fundamental change in markets and business.

Downes believes that the main difference between strategy in the Porter world and in the new three forces world is the role of information technology. In the 'old' world, businesses dictated how they wanted the business to change. Today, Downes believes that technology, rather than being an enabler of new business strategies, is a disrupter of markets and business models. Downes and Mui suggest that the strategy for dealing with this disruption and maximising benefit from it is by developing a radical new approach to strategic planning, where an environment that values creativity and intuition encourages the creation of the 'killer application'.

The killer application is an innovative use of technology that has a direct impact in the short run but an even greater and far-reaching impact in the longer run. One of the oldest examples of a killer application is the stirrup, that was adopted from an Asian design by the Franks (Germanic tribes that ruled central Europe) in the Middle Ages. The stirrup ultimately changed civilisations because it was a catalyst to success in battle; the subsequent creation of cavalries; the change in war strategy as a result of mounted cavalries; the creation of a new social and political system, where landed gentry and knights funded and raised armies, partly by seizing Catholic Church holdings. 'Thus the lowly stirrup played a singular role in rearranging the political, social, and economic structure of medieval Europe. The Holy Roman Empire, in some form, lasted until World War I.'[36]

This story illustrates the direct impact of the killer application and the wider-reaching impact on a whole social, political and economic environment. The creation of the computer was also a killer application, as was the 0800 toll-free number – both changed not only the face of business but also society, politics and the economic environment; for example, resource-poor countries such as Ireland have created new industries around call centres and software development, changing the economic prospects of the nation.

THE KILLER APPLICATION

Downes and Mui propose 12 design principles that can guide an organisation into the development of a digital strategy for finding and shaping killer applications and achieving market dominance in the digital age. These 12 principles are divided up into three main areas:

- *Reshaping the landscape* by (i) Outsourcing to the customer – giving them the tools to navigate, customise and even develop their own products and services; (ii) cannibalising markets to make sure that the company itself is first in the new channels rather than new players or competitors; (iii) ensuring that each customer is treated as a market segment because of the ease and economy of capturing information about individuals and tailoring services or products to suit them; (iv) creating communities of value to enable collaboration and information sharing to improve products or service offerings.
- *Building new connections* by (i) replacing human interfaces with a more efficient automated interface that can collect information while giving the customer what they want; (ii) ensuring customer continuity by providing the customer with a service or product that solves a problem for them; (iii) having open systems and sharing information to ensure that value is added for all stakeholders; (iv) creating partnerships and joint ventures for business transactions.
- *Redefining the interior* by (i) recognising that physical assets become liabilities in the 'new economy' and so investment should be in digital capabilities such as information and knowledge; (ii) destroying processes within the value chain if they do not add value or improve processes within the organisation; (iii) recognising the high risk and uncertainty of certain projects and so managing them as a portfolio of projects rather than individual projects; (iv) hiring children who will not only be tomorrow's customers, competitors and business partners, but also have an implicit understanding of technology and so understand the needs of the next generation and can help build structures to take organisations forward.

The idea here is that the 'new' economy requires new paradigms for planning and developing strategies that are no longer based on traditional concepts and ideas; one such strategy development plan is that of Downes and Mui.

OTHER NEW TECHNOLOGY AND MANAGEMENT IDEAS

This chapter has explored the different ways in which the environment is changing and has also identified the need for a change in the strategic planning process to be able to maximise the benefits of the new technology for organisations. Other elements of the business that also need to change are the working practices of organisations. Prevalent and still current working practices have been based on the dominant business model created by Sloan in the early 1900s for General Motors. This highly structured model of command and control, where employees are viewed as overheads, is no longer relevant in the twenty-first century – employees are seen as assets rather than expenses. Because of the increasingly inter-connected nature of business where organisations belong to a network or web that extends far beyond itself and includes outsourced workers, suppliers and external customers, so employees work in a way that is more collaborative and meaningful and less structured and hierarchical. Herman and Gioia, strategic business futurists who concentrate on workforce and workplace trends, suggested that workers will increasingly become like independent intrapreneurs – a person within an organisation who takes direct responsibility for turning an idea into a profitable finished product through assertive risk taking and innovation. The way of working will mirror web and networking patterns, where people will come together, 'as needed, provide a particular function, disband and then merge into some other form to complete some other functions. We are seeing that now with outsourcing, contingency workers, people working at home part of the time. It's very fluid, very amoeba-like structure, where cells divide and come together again and again.'[37] They also see the role of managers changing to concentrate more on productivity, strategising and problem solving: 'Their roles will encompass . . . managing information flows, hiring and retaining qualified people as the competition for talent intensi-fies, monitoring intellectual property and keeping up with technological advances.'[38]

In his book *Business at the Speed of Thought*,[39] Bill Gates, the father of Microsoft and one of the most powerful players in the IT industry, believes that business will change more in the next ten years than it has in the past fifty. He says that the 1980s were about quality, the 1990s about re-engineering, and the 2000s will be about the speed of transactions and improvements in business processes. Gates identifies three fundamental business shifts that will occur as a result of the digital phenomenon:

- That most transactions will become direct digital transactions between the parties involved (i.e. business to business or business to consumer) without the need for intermediaries.
- Customer services will increasingly shift from the routine low value to the added value personal consultancy.
- Companies must adopt digital processes or perish.

These three 'Gatesian' revelations echo what the writers and thinkers have already said before.

However, Gates believes that companies are not using information well; he feels companies are only getting 20 per cent benefit of their investment in technology. Using an analogy of the digital nervous system (illustrated in Figure 8.7), Gates sees hardware and software infrastructure enabling a business to react to its environment, sense competitor chal-lenges and customers needs, and organise timely responses. A similar idea

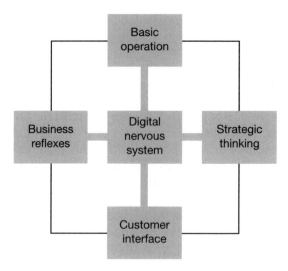

Figure 8.7 Bill Gates's business @ the speed of thought

was suggested by Moriarty and Moran[40] back in 1990. They felt that channel conflict and a hybrid marketing system could be overcome by establishing a centralised database. This would contain information about customers, prospects, products, marketing programs and methods, with all the marketing units passing their data through this system to ensure that all stages in the sales process were handled by the appropriate channel, optimising cost, coverage, customisation, conflict and control. Gates also sees the need for a business to develop an ideal picture of the information it needs to run the business. This type of information, then, must be available to the right people, in the right format, ready for immediate action, and this is what the systems must be developed to do. Like a digital nervous system, the system must distribute the right kind of information throughout the organisation's body at the speed of thought. The immediate availability of information can then change strategic thinking from a separate stand-alone activity to an ongoing process integrated with regular business activities and direct interaction with customers.

STRATEGIC IMPLICATIONS OF THE 'E' PHENOMENON

This chapter has highlighted many views of leading authors and practitioners in the field of business, management and technology. Some of these views oppose each other and the readers of this chapter may also have taken one view against the other. However, what is indisputable are the facts that surround the technology encapsulated in Moore's Law,

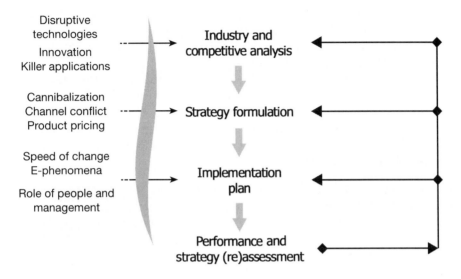

Figure 8.8 Strategic implications of the 'e' phenomena

Metcalfe's Law and Gilder's Law. These underpin the technology that drives business and, as such, business must adapt itself to these laws. The strategic and business planning cycles of the twenty-first century must incorporate many aspects of this new phenomenon. Figure 8.8 illustrates the implications of the 'e' phenomena which have been identified earlier at each stage of the strategic planning cycle. The strategic implications for organisations to be able to function successfully and at the leading edge is for each identified phenomenon to be integrated into the overall strategic plan of the organisation. Some of these would include:

- Disruptive technology – organisations must consider the implementation and development of new technology before the end of the old technology lifecycle to maintain competitiveness and remain/become industry leaders or cultivate new markets.
- Innovation is a catalyst that may change the face of the industry and is the premise behind the killer application. This is not a new phenomenon and is not unique to the 'e' revolution. Organisations must be aware of the importance of economic factors in their industry sector with each new innovation, and plan for potential changes.
- Cannibalisation, channel conflict, and pricing are all issues which have been heightened as a result of the 'e' phenomenon and must be considered in the strategy of the organisation. They are the inevitable consequences of fast moving, innovative environments.
- The 'Laws' try to explain and frame what is happening in the world of technical innovation. This is useful for forecasting and planning for

both the internal infrastructure of the organisation and the wider environment in which organisations are operating.

- The role of people and management is also part of the whole strategic process. With the lack of longevity of employees, the idea of serial intrapreneurs working for the organisation, and the increased importance and value placed on humans and knowledge, organisations must incorporate a procedure for protecting their knowledge. The organisation's main asset in the information age is its knowledge and this must be captured and protected for the long-term prosperity and survival of the organisation.

All these factors must be included at the relevant stages of the strategic planning process. Not only this, but the whole process itself must also reflect this new environment. Strategic planning cycles must mirror the technological change cycles – where technology is improving and costs are falling every 12–18 months. This means that strategic planning, any other business planning and feedback cycles must take no longer than 9–12 weeks to incorporate the changes taking place in the world of new technology and telecommunications.

SUMMARY

In the eighteenth century, when Adam Smith wrote *The Wealth of Nations*, the economy was framed in physical-world terms. A large part of the economic supply/demand equation was based upon how quickly *limited* raw materials could be found, used and replenished. Undoubtedly the world since then has changed – especially since the advent of the Internet and World Wide Web – but the debate is how fundamental has that change been. There are two main schools of thought on the impact of the Internet and new technology. One school of thought advocates that we 'rip up our economic text books' because these economic laws no longer apply. The other school of thought says 'technology changes, but economics laws do not'.

Innovation and technology as an economic and business catalyst is not a creation from the Internet, but rather it is as old as business and the economy itself. The disruptive technology theory identified the inevitable existence of technology as part of the ending of old technology and beginning of new technology. It also showed the importance of developing new markets to address unidentified customer needs and the necessity for disruptive technology development to be a small, flexible, decentralised unit that acted independently of larger organisations.

The impact of any kind of new technology and new channel creation results in disruption within the organisation, including cannibalisation.

This, however, should not be seen as a bad thing but as a good thing, a way of ensuring that the organisation can survive and grow, with new products and services being introduced rather than fall into decline.

A number of observations have been made by leading figures in academia and industry, which help frame the impact of digital technology on the economy. These include a prediction by Intel founder Gordon Moore that processing power and hence computing technology will get faster, cheaper and smaller in 12–18 monthly cycles. Metcalfe's Law values the utility of a network as the square of the number of its users and can be observed in the impact of telephones, fax machines, the Ethernet and internet protocols. Once a standard has achieved critical mass, its value to everyone multiplies exponentially.

These observations are based on the actual physical telecommunications infrastructure being used by business and society today, and are undoubtedly true and are still being borne out today. But will business (as Porter believes) still follow the old economic and business rules and patterns (as illustrated in his 'five forces model') they have always followed throughout the ages? Or has there (as Downes and Mui believe) been a fundamental change in the economic infrastructure (as explained in their 'killer application' concept) as a result of this revolutionary new technology, which means that business must re-think how they have traditionally done business in order to survive?

DISCUSSION QUESTIONS

1 Give an example of disruptive technology in an industry.
2 Prove Moore's Law by giving an example from your experience of computer usage.
3 Why is strategy important and what impact has the Internet and new technology had on strategic planning?
4 Explain why Porter's 'five forces analysis' of the impact of the Internet is negative.
5 Having examined the information presented here and read further on the subject, do you believe the impact of the Internet and technology means that we must 'rip up our economic text books' or 'technology changes, but economics laws do not'? Explain your decision.
6 Consider an organisation that you know well or have worked for. Review the strategy of that organisation, taking into consideration the factors relevant to the 'e' phenomena that have been identified.

REFERENCES

1 A. Smith [1776] *Wealth of Nations*, Glasgow Edition of the Works and Correspondence of Adam Smith, 7 volumes, edited by A.S. Skinner et al. (Oxford, Clarendon Press, 1976–1987).

2 N.D. Kondratieff [1926] 'The long waves in economic life', *Economic Review*, II, 4, Spring 1979, 519–62.

3 J. Schumpeter, *Theory of Economic Development*. Harvard University Press, 1961; J. Schumpeter, *Business Cycles*. McGraw and Hill, 1964.

4 P. Dicken, *Global Shift – The Internationalisation of Economic Activity*, 2nd edn. Paul Chapman, 1992.

5 G. Mensch, *Stalemate in Technology*. Ballinger, 1979.

6 M. Porter, *The Competitive Advantage of Nations*. Macmillan, 1990.

7 J.L. Bower and C.M. Christensen, 'Disruptive technologies: Catching the wave', *Harvard Business Review*, January–February, 1995.

8 P. Kotler, *Marketing Management, Analysis, Planning, Implementation and Control*, International Edition 8th edn. 1994, Prentice Hall, p. 441.

9 K.S. Moorthy and I. Png, 'Market segmentation, cannibalization, and the timing of product introduction', *Management Science*, 38, 345–359, March 1992.

10 T.K. Giap, 'The impact of information technology on banking and finance in Asia': www.worldbank.org/html/extdr/offrep/eap/eapprem/infogiap.pdf; L. Yerkes, 'Growing with technology: The benefits of internet banking', Bankinfo.com, 13/10/98: http://www.bankinfo.com/ecomm/growing.html (accessed January 2002).

11 G. Moore, Intel Corporation website: www.intel.com

12 B. Gain, 'Moore's Law exerts influence on fiber optic development', EBNews, 22/02/02: http://www.ebnews.com/story/OEG20010807S0021

13 R. Schaller, 'The origin, nature, and implications of "Moore's Law"', *The Benchmark of Progress in Semiconductor Electronics*, 26/9/1996: http://research.microsoft.com/ ~ Gray/Moore_Law.html

14 R. Schaller, 'The origin, nature, and implications of "Moore's Law"', *The Benchmark of Progress in Semiconductor Electronics*, 26/9/1996: http://research.microsoft.com/ ~ Gray/Moore_Law.html

15 R. Metcalfe, 'The Internet after the fad', Remarks of Dr. Robert Metcalfe at the University of Virginia May 30, 1996, Monticello Memoirs: http://americanhistory.si.edu/csr/comphist/montic/metcalfe.htm#me7

16 J.S. Rhodes, 'Less than Metcalfe's Law', Webword: http://www.webword.com/moving/metcalfe.html

17 W. Packard, 'The myth of Metcalfe's Law', *Redherring*, August 2000: http://www.redherring.com/mag/issue81/mag-ground–81.html

18 'About George', GilderTech Web page: http://www.gildertech.com/public/george.html

19 G. Gilder, *Telecosm – How Infinite Bandwidth Will Revolutionize Our World*. Free Press, 2000.

20 H.A. Lim, 'East–West High-Tech Networking for the e-Century', Annual Conference and Venture Capital Fair, Monte Jade Science & Technology Association, Greater Washington, DC Area (MJ-DC), 9/12/2000: http://www.d-trends.com/Album/MJ-DC/mj-dc_rep.doc

21 Gilder Technology Web page: www.gildertech.com

22 A. Lightman, 'The laws of exponential improvement', IntellectualCapital.com, 6/7/2000: http://www.charmed.com/html/corporate/people/alexlightman/07_06_2000_The_Laws_of_Exponential_Improvement.htm

23 B. Arthur, 'Increasing returns and the new world of business', *Harvard Business Review*, July–August 1996.

24 Externalities are the 'by product' of an exchange or transaction which impacts on those not involved in the exchange or transaction. There can be negative

externalities, for example pollution, where pollutants base their decision on marginal private costs to the company rather than the optimal cost to society and the environment. Education on the other hand is seen as having positive externalities – which means that the cost and benefit to the individual is considered lower than the benefit to society as a whole. Externalities are usually dealt with through intervention of government imposing taxation or subsidies to equate private and social costs and benefits.

25 B. Arthur, 'Increasing returns and the new world of business', *Harvard Business Review*, July–August 1996.
26 S.J. Liebowitz and S.E. Margolis, 'Winners, losers, and Microsoft: Competition and antitrust in high technology', Independent Institute, May 1999: http://www.utdallas.edu/ ~ liebowit/book/book.html
27 Union College website: http://www.union.edu/News/Publications/Magazine/Archive/v91n1/article20.htm (accessed January 2002).
28 K. Kelly, '*New Rules for the New Economy: 10 Ways the Network Economy is Changing Everything*', Fourth Estate, 1999.
29 Former editor of *Computerworld Australia* and contributor to research companies GartnerGroup, the Butler Group, IDC and the Yankee Group Australia.
30 G. Philipson, 'Forget Darwin, here's the IT industry's survival guide', *The Age*, 16/10/2001: http://www.it.mycareer.com.au/opinion/philipson/2001/10/16/FFXJUW36TSC.html
31 M. Ferguson, 'E-government strategies – the developing international scene', 2000: http://www.e.democracy.lcc.ufmg.br/e.democracy.nsf/palestras_furguson,html
32 M.E. Porter, 'Strategy and the Internet', *Harvard Business Review*, March 2001.
33 C. Turner, *The Information E-conomy, Business Strategies for Competing in the Digital Age*. Kogan Page, 2000.
34 L. Downes and C. Mui, *Unleashing the Killer App: Digital Strategies for Market Dominance*, Harvard Business School Press, Harvard, 2000.
35 L. Downes, 'Beyond Porter', *Context Magazine*: http://www.contextmag.com/setFrameRedirect.asp?src = /archives/199712/technosynthesis.asp (accessed January 2002).
36 L. Downes and C. Mui, *Unleashing the Killer App: Digital Strategies for Market Dominance*. Harvard Business School Press, 2000, pp. 17–18.
37 R. Herman and J. Gioia, *Lean and Meaningful*. Oak Hill Press, 1998.
38 R. Herman and J. Gioia, *Lean and Meaningful*. Oak Hill Press, 1998.
39 W. Gates and C. Hemingway (contributor), *Business @ the Speed of Thought: Succeeding in the Digital Economy*, 1st edn, Warner Books, 2000.
40 R.T. Moriarty and U. Moran, 'Marketing Hybrid Marketing Systems', *Harvard Business Review*, November–December 1990.

Conclusions

To the future and beyond

LEARNING OBJECTIVES

- To review the issues relevant to e-commerce and e-business.
- To evaluate the current state of e-commerce and e-business.
- To identify new technology trends and the impact on business.
- To have the knowledge to begin to answer the question 'what does the future hold'.

SO WHERE ARE WE NOW?

In an age dominated by technology, managers and decision-makers can no longer take a backseat or hand over decision-making when it comes to technology. Information and communications technology is no longer the province of the IT department. It is also a strategic, marketing, sales and business issue, and one which affects all parts of the organisation. As part of their job remit, business managers and decision-makers must understand the technology and its implications for the business in particular and their industry as a whole. This section will briefly draw together the different themes raised in the previous chapters of this book, reviewing and summarising the issues that are relevant to an understanding and management of e-commerce and e-business.

There is no one commonly agreed definition of e-commerce or e-business. Thus, there is a need to clarify terms that are being used and explain the context in which they are being applied. In this book we have taken e-commerce to mean the macro-environmental impact of electronic and digital technology, and e-business to mean the impact of that technology at the micro-level of the firm and individual businesses.

The technical infrastructure that underpins and enables e-commerce and e-business includes networking, computing, micro-processing and telecommunications technology. Gordon Moore of Intel accurately observed that processing power and, hence, computing technology gets faster, cheaper and smaller in 12–18 monthly cycles. It is crucial for business to understand these technical foundations – different types of technology and how each works; how it is implemented; the lifecycles; the business benefits and limitations; and the meaning of the technical jargon. Having explained the architecture of different networks, managers can now identify how each can be used to improve the performance of the organisation and add value to its stakeholders, while at the same time being able to identify all the necessary elements to ensure a secure, efficient, cost-effective infrastructure.

The major currency of this new technology infrastructure is information or data. Applications such as e-mail, Web browsers, hypertext mark-up language (HTML) and a host of others were developed to maximise the functionality of the telecommunications infrastructure. Fortunately they also achieve the major objectives of business which are information dissemination, communication, data capture, promotions and marketing, and transacting with stakeholders (customers, suppliers). By understanding both the infrastructure and the applications, managers can better understand and so deal with potential problems such as incompatibility between older legacy and newer systems; employee skills needed; security needed for data and transactions; privacy and other legal issues – all of which could be a potential barrier to the successful implementation and use of e-commerce and e-business.

There has been much hype and publicity covering the downside of the Internet and e-commerce – namely, security breaches and the dot com crash which left thousands of shareholders with negative equity. Security breaches and stock exchange crashes are not new and will never be eradicated no matter what medium is used. However, what is new is the speed, global impact and potential ease with which these can occur. Chapter 4 introduced a framework by which organisations can approach security holistically as a complete business system which affects and is the responsibility of all parts of the organisation, rather than being solely a technology issue and so the responsibility of the IT department.

Building on the knowledge and understanding of the 'new' technology, the events of the 'dot com crash' underline the importance of the lesson that the 'e' in e-commerce and e-business is not a reason for forgetting the basics of business modelling and planning, which is to achieve and sustain financial objectives. The impact of 'e' affects a business's value stream, revenue stream and logistic stream. Thus there is a need to re-engineer business processes and re-structure value chains for successful implementation of e-business for both the organisation itself and its stakeholders. Although there are frameworks for assessing the viability of business models, it is not and can never be an exact science. There are and have been different business models over the past few years, but because e-commerce is still in its relative infancy, 'the' business model suitable for Internet business has yet to be commercially and empirically proven over a sustained period of time.

Despite the enormous commercial potential and the benefits to consumers and businesses of e-commerce, there are political, legal and regulatory measures that contribute to the overall understanding and implementation of e-business. National and international governments are introducing new laws, and changing and modifying old laws, in order to keep up with the growth in development and use of the Internet and World Wide Web by a whole range of users – social, commercial, government, and so on. As with e-commerce itself, the legal infrastructure governing it is still in its infancy. Business must understand the legality of using e-mails, electronic documentation, digital signatures and website content. They must also be aware of the regulations that govern electronic privacy and data collection, as well as the liabilities they have for their own telecommunications infrastructures. Ethical issues relating to the monitoring of employees and the use of cookies to collect data must also be incorporated into an organisation's operating procedures.

There is a debate raging over whether there is now a new digital economy, one that follows the rules of the network and is dominated by technology and digitisation, where plenitude rather than scarcity creates value and the value of a network increases exponentially with each additional unit to that network (Metcalfe's Law). Or whether it is only technology that has changed and 'old' laws of economics remain the same. Although largely an academic debate, observations such as Metcalfe's Law and Moore's Law are based on the actual physical telecommunications infrastructure being used by business and society today, and are undoubtedly true and are still being borne out. What is important for the understanding of e-commerce and e-business is to be able to identify network effects and their impact on a business. For example, new channel creation, which brings about cannibalisation; volume creates value; lowering of industry entry barriers; increased competition; reduced lifecycles of products and services; the idea of developing a 'killer application' as a means of achieving competitive advantage. The degree to which these issues are acted upon depends on whether the organisation believes that business still follows the old economic and business rules and patterns they have always followed throughout the ages. Or whether there has been a fundamental change in the economic infrastructure as a result of this revolutionary new technology, which means that business must re-think how they have traditionally done business in order to survive.

AT WHAT STAGE IS E-BUSINESS AND WHERE CAN IT GO NEXT?

The development of Internet based e-business can be plotted as an evolutionary process, marked over time by a series of milestones based on the degree of implementation and development of technology and the integration of business processes (illustrated in Figure 9.1). Having understood the elements that are relevant to and enable e-business, the final element is to assess at exactly what stage an organisation's e-business is in the evolutionary cycle and whether it can evolve further. Professor Richard Nolan[1] of the London School of Economics introduced a six-stage model in 1979 describing the process in which IT and IT applications are introduced in organisations:

- *Initiation* – where the organisation has no IT system and a group of enthusiasts realise the benefits of IT for the organisation and introduce it to automate some processes.
- *Contagion* – following the initial deployment of IT, the 'me too' phenomenon comes into play where individuals have seen benefits and advantages of these systems. The technology begins to be widely applied on a piecemeal basis across the organisations, creating 'islands of automation'.
- *Control* – where there is an increase in IT spending and budgets are introduced to centralise purchasing and IT application standards. There is an increased demand for IT, and organisations begin to realise the potential problem of IT.
- *Integration* – the organisation then begins to understand the need for linking the 'islands of automation' developed at the contagion stage. There are problems of internal compatibility between different hardware and software applications throughout the organisation and also with external stakeholders and partners.
- *Data administration* – The next two phases focus more on ensuring organisations are networked together and systems are able to communicate together. This stage is where organisations realise that information is the key resource and so there needs to be a standard format understandable by all. This phase involves the building of the databases and networks (internal and external).
- *Data maturity* – this is the final stage where information is used as a key resource and for added value. Information is used in the battle for competitive advantage and information management and is a key strategy for the organisation.

Although this theory was developed more than twenty years ago, it is still applicable, and many authors discussing the different evolutionary stages of growth that e-business has experienced generally draw on the

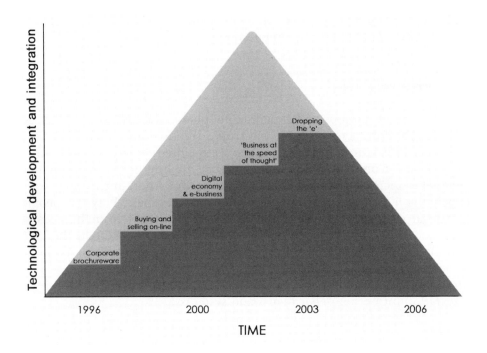

Figure 9.1 Stages in the evolution of e-business in Europe and the UK

tenets of these stages. Deise *et al.*[2] identify the different stages in achieving business value, moving from channel enhancement to value-chain integration, through industry transformation and finally to convergence and the full leverage of e-business, achieving maximum business value. Michael Earl[3] of London Business School identifies a number of similar stages for the evolutionary journey of e-business and concludes with lessons for businesses to follow to survive in the future. Figure 9.1 draws on these ideas, plotting the evolutionary stages of e-business and placing them within a very broad time frame, as they relate to the UK and the rest of Europe. The USA is some 12–18 months ahead of the identified milestones.

Phase one (1995+)

In the very earliest stages of the Internet's commercial use in Europe, organisations were using the Web as a means of establishing a presence in cyberspace, to show product and service information as an alternative channel for distributing and promoting the corporate brochure. By developing a presence on the Web, the organisation could also develop its image

and brand as being progressive, innovative and at the forefront of technological development and implementation.

Phase two (1998+)

After the initial cautious and experimental phase, organisations developed
facilities for conducting simple electronic transactions. There was very
little user interaction and transactions were closed largely off-line rather
than on-line. Companies were looking to use the Internet as an alternative
channel to increase revenue and sales. The main barriers at this stage were
largely the technology infrastructure and user awareness. Very few people
(potential customers) were 'connected' to the Internet from home and
there was still a novelty aspect and wariness about the Internet, the Web
and electronic transactions. Few (mainly larger organisations) had the
resources to invest in technology, skilled staff, training and awareness. On-
line buying and selling was largely a stand-alone process – with little
integration into other departments and systems.

Phase three (2000+)

This stage has begun for many companies and, for those few companies at
the forefront of innovative technological implementation, it is still developing. It involves the re-engineering of business processes to ensure there
is efficient integration between Internet-enabled capabilities and the back
office and legacy systems of organisations to provide high levels of service
to stakeholders. There is much talk of middleware in this phase of development, with organisations concentrating on achieving system compatibility
to support the changes to business processes and closer relationships with
customers, suppliers, manufacturers and other business stakeholders. The
progress of companies into this phase will boost the growth of an 'on-line
economy'. The legacy of the 'dot com bombs' has taught organisations
how they can exist and thrive in the virtual digital environment. The
growth in the 'on-line economy' not only involves commercial transactions, but is also a function of the increased confidence of consumers
and other business stakeholders to access on-line sources of information
and virtual communications. This is widened further by the increasing
accessibility (in terms of cost and connection) of telecommunications
infrastructures. Information, products and services are more personalised
and customised to individual consumers, ensuring a 'pull' by consumers
rather than 'push' by the businesses. Business has re-engineered its manufacturing and sales processes and re-ordered its value chain to ensure
customer requirements can be fulfilled. Information and services are

increasingly accessible from myriad multiple sites and on any device – for instance, mobile phones, personal digital assistants (PDA) and laptops. The goal is profit, where investment in the research and development stages should now yield commercial benefits that will ensure survival.

Phase four (2003+)

As with anything, predicting the future of e-commerce is difficult. A logical progression from the business process changes of phase 3, this phase will involve management process re-engineering. Integration of management and business processes means that newly designed business processes are not integrated and fully supported by the new technology and information systems. Organisational design and management will also have to develop and become integrated and synchronised. At this stage the organisation will have become so dynamic that it can continuously change and re-invent itself to adapt to the changing environment. Bill Gates calls this concept *'business @ the speed of thought'*,[4] where he suggests that for an organisation to work effectively in the twenty-first century, it will function as a nervous system where every part of the organisation will be linked to each other and be able to share and coordinate any task immediately. At this stage people will have highly developed information literacy skills and a knowledge-management infrastructure that ensures maximisation of information and data they collate. The goal here is continued growth and development.

Phase five (2006?)

At this stage, the business model will have developed to become dynamic as a matter of course and organisations will be so comfortable in the 'new' economy that it is no longer perceived as being new. Continuous learning and change will become the norm and the 'e' element will be dropped, as it becomes embedded in everyday processes and systems. Maybe it is at this stage a new phenomenon will emerge, starting a new wave of business activity.

WHAT WILL THE NEW TECHNOLOGY BE?

Without a crystal ball and a time machine it is impossible to predict the future accurately. Professor D.R. Hartree, in evidence to the Brunt Committee in 1949, predicted that 'a total of 4 computers would probably be sufficient to meet the computational needs of Britain.' It is useful to be aware of the environment and any potential changes by observing general trends in technology and telecommunications and more specifically any trends related to the particular industry sector in which organisations operate.

Research and development is continuing both within academia and industry itself. Some of the technology with potential for the future includes:

- *Smart cards* – This technology has been around for many years, initially with less sophisticated magnetic strips. Smart cards have advanced and are effectively a computer the size of a credit card with an embedded microprocessor chip. There are about 80–100 proprietary smart cards, each of which is used for storing different kinds of information such as health records and telephone cards. This means that an application and operating system is installed on the smart card and the issuer controls which application is required. Recent developments in the technology allows multi-application operating systems where several applications can be placed on a smart card at any time. Applications can be downloaded after the card has been issued to the cardholder, which reduces the cost of updates while adding functionality to the existing card. Use of smart cards is still in its embryonic stages and much piloting and research is continuing. IDC[5] predict that smart cards may one day supersede credit cards, although the timeframe is open to speculation. The advantages of smart cards are that they can have multiple uses and they provide an added layer of security, as they are difficult to forge. In early 1999, Microsoft announced its smart card for Windows operating system, where once loaded into the operating system any application could be downloaded.[6]
- *Biometrics* – This is the recording of unique personal characteristics. Systems are being developed to store, capture and recall people's unique biological characteristics.

CASE STUDY

One of the most graphic illustrations of biometric technology can be seen in futuristic films such as the James Bond series. Some examples of biometrics projects include:

- *Fingerprint recognition* at a standard workstation[7] or laptop avoids the necessity for providing documentation or remembering passwords. Fingerprint verification has been used in cash machines since 1997 in South Africa. In Spain the social security department is paying benefits using Identicator Technology's finger-imaging system with smart cards.
- *Dynamic signature verification* – where a touch-sensitive pad is used to capture the speed and style of a signature, not just its appearance. This was trialled in the UK for people claiming employment benefits and a canteen in Pentonville Prison.[8]

- *Face recognition systems* to identify troublemakers in a crowd, used by the majority of football clubs in the UK.
- *Iris recognition* – a unique personal identification method used by Iris Recognition Automated Teller Machine, being piloted in the USA (Bank United), Spain (Argentaria), Italy (Banco Ambrosiano Veneto), Norway (Den Norske), Turkey (Akbank)[9] and at check-in in airports.
- *Voice recognition* – where unique voice matching enables individual verification, used in telephone banking by Chase Manhattan Bank.

Although biometrics are increasingly more practical, viable and affordable for some organisations, plenty of organisations have taken a 'wait and see' attitude. Some technologies will remain in the province of James Bond films, but it is reasonable to predict that fingerprint readers and voice recognition tools will no longer seem exotic or unusual by mid-decade. The predominant thinking is that the least intrusive technologies – which do not involve exposing sensitive parts of the body, such as eyes, to the impact of scanning equipment – will be the most successful, and companies that approach biometric authentication as a productivity enhancement, instead of a security enhancement, will have the easiest time implementing this new technology.

There is also continuing development in telecommunications infrastructure. For example:

- *Internet II* – the new generation of the Internet is in development in the USA. It is funded by both private and public sectors, with investment from major corporations such as IBM, Cisco, AT&T and Ford, and involvement from over 100 universities and research centres in the USA. This network is some 1,000 times faster than the current Internet, with an ability to store terabytes (1,000 gigabytes) of data, using a combination of leading-edge fibre technology and routing technology, which will enable the most advanced applications,[10] such as improved video-streaming, videoconferencing and other applications not yet created. This is being designed primarily to offer high-speed communications between more than 100 university and research centres in the USA. Internet II is expected to become available to the public in the near future, but exact details are currently unavailable.
- *Photonics* – advanced network hardware based on optical technology, where switches and routers work with infrared transmission. The advantage over electrical transmissions is that infrared has a higher bandwidth because the frequency of infrared enables the transmission of millions of signals on an optical beam.
- *Internet Protocol Version (IPv6)* – the latest evolutionary level of the Internet Protocol (IPv4 being the current one) and is now included as

part of IP support in many products, including the major computer operating systems such as Linux and Windows XP. The most obvious improvement is that IP addresses are lengthened from 32 bits to 128 bits, to be able to cope with the anticipated future growth of the Internet and resolving (at least in the short to medium term) the potential problem of network address shortages. Changes to IP headers also improves efficiency, speed and overall reliability of message transmission. It also includes security features that allow a packet to specify a mechanism for authenticating its origin, for ensuring data integrity and for ensuring privacy.

This is just a tiny snapshot of the vast array of research and development projects that are under way around the world. What these trends suggest is that the Internet is here to stay for the longer term and that the infrastructure is continually improving in terms of speed, efficiency and security to maximise the use of the Internet's potential.

Another trend in telecommunications is *wireless technology*. Wireless is a term used to describe telecommunications in which electromagnetic or acoustic waves (rather than some form of wire) carry the signal over part or all of the communication path. Not a new technology, wireless was initially used in the early twentieth century for transmitting radiotelegraphy (Morse code) and later voices and music via 'radio'. It has been in practical existence in the use of remote controls, cordless telephones which have a limited signal range (not mobile phones), baby monitors and CB/two-way radios. However, wireless technology has been advancing and developing rapidly and is increasingly being adopted in both business and society.

There has been much development of *wireless LAN (local area networks)* for business. Wireless LANs (or WiFi networks) provide more efficiency and flexibility to business users. They enable users to physically move while using an appliance, such as a handheld PC or data collector. In a world where timing is crucial, increasingly more jobs require:

- Real-time access to information.
- To be aware of any changes to data immediately those changes happen.
- To be able to download and transmit data on demand.

This would be relevant to, for example, inventory and price control, healthcare and emergency workers, and police officers, amongst the many. Many retail stores use wireless networks to interconnect handheld barcode scanners and printers to databases having current price information. This enables the printing of the correct price on the items as they change. Another example of the use of wireless networking is in Formula 1 motor racing, where the cars have sophisticated data acquisition systems that monitor the various on-board systems in the car. When the cars come around the track and pass the respective teams in the pit, this information is downloaded to a central computer, thereby enabling real-time analysis of the performance of the racing car. Wireless LANs can also be more cost effective in the longer term than installing physical cabling or leasing lines such as T1.

> **CASE STUDY**
>
> However, a report by the BBC[11] highlighted some of the dangers of lax security of wireless network administrators. A trip around the square mile in London's financial centre found two-thirds of networks to be 'wide open'. The wireless networks were easy to locate and could be accessed using only a laptop, a wireless network card and a program written to detect these networks – a modified empty Pringles (potato crisp snack) tube was also found to be used by some hackers to improve the reception of the wireless network signal.[12] The software package commonly used by wireless networks to issue an IP address to any device it detects enables any device to join the network (behind any firewall), and access all the services available to any other organisation employee. This security breach was mainly because the in-built encryption system had not been activated when the network was set up. Without security, potential hackers could access the network and any of its services or data, launch an attack on other networks or distribute illegal material which might compromise the legal status of the company.
>
> > It is as easy as listening to the radio. What makes it easier is that everyone is broadcasting on the same frequency. Also attached to the laptop was a GPS handset that gave a more precise fix on where each network was detected from. Within the space of one kilometre we logged the existence of 12 networks. Only four of these had turned on the encryption system built into the wifi protocol. The other eight were wide open.[13]

But security remains a major issue for these networks. Security breaches can be overcome through greater awareness – for example, adding a firewall in front of the wireless networks, enabling the encryption and authentication procedures ensuring only trusted encrypted and authenticated traffic passes from the wireless to the wider network, and ensuring the set-up configuration is correct. The issues laid out in Chapter 4 are equally as applicable in this case.

> **CASE STUDY**
>
> One of the most recent phenomena to emerge which exploits wireless networks is warchalking, a cheap way of finding wireless Internet connections, which is fast growing into an international phenomenon. The idea is to use chalk marks on pavements and walls to indicate the existence of a wireless network that anyone with the right software and laptop can use for free to surf the Web. The basic symbol is illustrated in Figure 9.2.

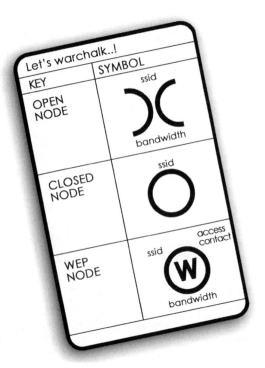

Figure 9.2 Warchalking – symbols indicating wireless network access points (www.warchalking.org)

A website (www.warchalking.org) has been set up to act as a community to support the growing numbers of warchalkers. Warchalking signs have been seen in the USA, Copenhagen and London. This is sparking off a new trend in wireless network access for 'legitimate' users. Many universities (such as London School of Economics and Bradford University School of Management) have set up a wireless network that students can use for Web access while near their buildings.

One of the more widely talked about applications of wireless communications is the mobile phone, and the business applications of mobile phones have been named '*m-commerce*'.

WHAT IS 'M-COMMERCE'?

M-commerce (mobile commerce) is a subject which could fill a whole book in itself. Very briefly, m-commerce is the buying and selling of goods and services through wireless handheld devices, such as the mobile telephone and personal digital assistants (PDAs – also known as handheld devices such as the PalmPilot or Palmtop). M-commerce is also known as the next generation e-commerce. It enables users to access the Internet using their handheld devices. The potential of m-commerce is linked to the massive growth in the worldwide use of mobile phones. In 2001, it was estimated that there were over 700 million phones in use and a ratio of two mobile phone users for every desktop Internet user (worldwide except in the USA). Mobile phone users are expected to grow to one billion by 2003.[14] These figures have drawn the attention of business to see how they can exploit this medium for financial benefit and competitive advantage. As content delivery over wireless devices becomes faster, more secure and scalable, there is wide speculation that m-commerce will surpass e-commerce as the method of choice for digital commerce transactions. The industries affected which could be most affected by m-commerce include:

● Financial services, which include mobile banking (when customers use their handheld devices to access their accounts and pay their bills) as well as brokerage services, in which stock quotes can be displayed and trading conducted from the same handheld device.
● Telecommunications, in which service changes, bill payment and account reviews can all be conducted from the same handheld device.
● Service/retail, as consumers are given the ability to place and pay for orders whenever and wherever they are.
● Sales and marketing for retailers and other service providers, where offers can be sent to shoppers' mobile phones or film clips can be viewed on mobile phones as potential customers are in the vicinity.
● Information services, which include the delivery of financial news, sports figures and traffic updates to a single mobile device.
● Automated point of sale payments, where payment for vending machines, parking metres and the like will be charged to their mobile phone bill. Pilot projects set up by Pepsi Cola and Coca-Cola in Japan and Scandinavia are currently testing this concept.
● IBM and other companies are experimenting with speech recognition software as a way to ensure security for m-commerce transactions.

The next section will look briefly at the technology behind m-commerce, and discuss whether there is real potential for m-commerce as a viable new way of doing business or as a fad that will disappear in the longer term.

HOW DOES THE TECHNOLOGY WORK?

Mobile phone networks operate through radio waves sent from communications towers or masts to the phone and back again. The networks are divided by service providers into 'cells'. The microwave radiation produced by these transmitters is considerable and has been the subject of some public health concerns. Mobile phones regularly transmit to networks their location (the disturbance you often hear when a mobile phone is near to any other electrical equipment) in order to avoid the inefficient expediency of trying to contact the phone in more than one cell.

Mobile phone technology has progressed fastest in Japan, followed closely by Europe, with the USA in this case being the followers rather than the leaders. The complex infrastructure of mobile telephone networks is succinctly illustrated by the Global System for Mobile (GSM) Association in a concept they call 'GSM The Wireless Evolution' (illustrated in Figure 9.3). They use a metaphor of the elevator to describe how the different platforms fit together. The idea is that network operators can begin with the GSM network (on the first floor) and then progress floor by floor through the other platforms or they can go directly to the latest platform (3rd Generation), offering a range of services provided by each platform according to the needs of their customers.

The GSM network is the world's leading non-proprietary system that is well established in Europe and offers international roaming capability and the same standardised number contactability in more than 170 countries. The GSM Association estimates that by the end of 2003 there will be more than one billion subscribers worldwide.[15] Also known as second generation wireless mobile networks, GSM deliver high-quality voice and data services, such as text messaging or SMS (Short Messaging Services).

Figure 9.3 GSM – the wireless evolution (GSM family images) GSM Association

Source: http://www.gsmworld.com/holden/page3.html

Another platform is *Global Packet Radio Service (GPRS)* – also known as $2\frac{1}{2}$G – where, similar to the Internet's TCP/IP, it involves 'packet switching' technology, where content is broken into individual packets sent to and from mobile telephones, without the need for the use of full bandwidth. This means that data can be sent via GSM mobile networks more than ten times faster at about 171 Kbps. GPSR involves software only, which means service providers do not have to buy or install new physical equipment. GPSR offers 'always on' capabilities, faster data rates and higher capacity (dependent on the handset technology), and users will be able to have access to colour Internet browsing, e-mail, multimedia messaging, visual communications and global positioning systems (GPS), where the location of the mobile phone can be detected and pinpointed geographically.

Further enhancement in data capability over the core GSM network will be provided by the introduction of *Enhanced Data rates for GSM Evolution (EDGE)*. This will achieve the delivery of advanced mobile services, such as the downloading of video and music clips, full multimedia messaging, high-speed colour Internet access and e-mail, three times faster than GPRS. EDGE is thought to be an efficient way of reaching complementary 3G coverage in the seamless network by re-using 2G investments.

Third Generation (3G), also known as Universal Mobile Tele-communications System (UMTS), is a new generation of wireless broadband, packet-based system based on GSM. It enables text, digitised voice, video and multimedia to be transmitted at high-quality and high-speed data rates of up to 2 Mbps (ten times faster than GPRS). Not only this, but 3G also offers a consistent set of services to mobile computer and phone users no matter where they are located in the world. 3G has already been introduced in Japan (autumn 2001), with Europe following closely behind. This will eventually replace GSM after a decade or so.

Fourth Generation (4G) is already in development in Japan and download speeds are expected to be ten times faster than 3G. These are expected to provide high-resolution films and TV programmes and feature personal identification applications.

There are a host of other applications and developments that can utilise and maximise wireless networks, such as:

- *'Bluetooth'*, a small radio chip that can be fitted into almost any type of electrical device and which works with wireless infrastructures. These chips will 'talk' to each other whenever they are close enough (10–100 metres). This will allow data devices such as mobile phones, palm tops, PCs and many more to 'speak' to each other without any connecting cables. A huge benefit will be industry-wide products that enable all data devices to communicate – for example, allowing desktops to be automatically updated with data from a laptop or other handheld device as soon as it is in the vicinity. It is thought these will also be fitted into more common household objects such as fridges, which will automatically re-order stocks of food when they are low, or any electrical appliance, which can be activated or de-activated without the need of a human being present. Some Bluetooth applications are being developed on the basis of voice recognition so that commands can be spoken.

● *Wireless Application Protocol (WAP)*, a set of communication protocols to standardise the way that wireless devices, such as cellular telephones and radio transceivers, can be used for Internet access. WAP was conceived by Ericsson, Motorola, Nokia and Unwired Planet (now Phone.com). The wireless device must contain a microbrowser (a small version of a Web browser to fit on the small screen of a handheld device) to access content and applications hosted on a server and in a format accessible by these devices. WAP has not yet taken off and some feel it will be superseded by newer and more reliable technology, largely because of reports that:

● It has been difficult to find phones with robust microbrowser software.
● It is difficult to find gateways that provide access to WAP sites.
● There is no inbuilt security.
● There are few websites written in special Wireless Markup Language (WML similar to HTML) to make it viewable on such a small device.
● Frozen connections.

This is yet to be seen.

● *i-Mode*, first introduced in 1999 in Japan, is a wireless data service which offers colour and video mobile computing services enabling users to do telephone banking, make airline reservations, conduct stock transactions, send and receive e-mail, and have access to the Internet. It does not use WAP but is developing its infrastructure to support it in the future.

Mobile technology is still in the very early formative, embryonic stages and only time will tell which technology will emerge as dominant. But we can see that technologically the potential for the kinds of services that can be possible over mobile and other handheld devices is enormous.

M-COMMERCE – IS IT COMING OR GOING?

There has been much speculation about m-commerce since the turn of the twenty-first century. Different reports published in 1999 and 2000 estimated the potential of m-commerce growing to US $24 billion by 2003, and valued at between US $250 million (pessimistic) and US $1.8 trillion (optimistic). In a recent survey based on interviews with 40 industry participants, including investment banks, involved in pilot mobile payment programmes, Frost and Company (January 2002) estimated that m-commerce would be worth US $26 billion by 2006. However, A.T. Kearney at Cambridge University,[16] conducting a time series survey (Mobinet) of 5,600 wireless phone users in the USA, Europe, and Asia, showed a steady decline and disinterest in most m-commerce offerings. They found that since June 2000 consumer interest in using mobile phones to make purchases has dropped from 32 per cent to only 1 per cent by January 2002. Although there was a 41 per cent increase of survey respondents' ownership of an Internet-enabled mobile phone, the number of owners using the handsets to check out Internet sites did not rise over the past six months. So which way will m-commerce go?

In order to explain the potential uptake of m-commerce, the framework introduced to identify and understand the drivers of e-commerce is equally as applicable. Figure 9.4 summarises the key drivers of m-commerce.

The *legal and political infrastructures* are similar to those for e-commerce because communications are largely based on electronic and digital data and signals. Development of these infrastructures will follow rather than precede m-commerce once it becomes more widely used.

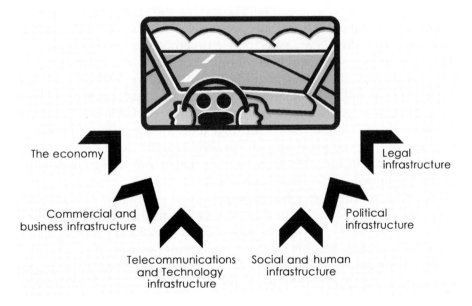

Figure 9.4 Key drivers of m-commerce

The *world economy* as it stands in 2002 is facing a mild recession – stock markets have experienced a sharp downturn, job losses and company closures are on the increase, corporate investment is falling and projections of annual growth of GDP for most developed countries for the next couple of years is barely above zero.

The *social and human infrastructure* in the case of m-commerce is more advanced than commercial and business infrastructures. The take-up of mobile phones in Europe has been great, with some Scandinavian and other countries, such as Finland, having a mobile phone penetration rate of nearly 98 per cent. In the UK, according to a recent report by the Office of Telecommunications (OFTEL),[17] some 75 per cent of UK adults claim to own or use a mobile phone, with 82 per cent of homes having at least one mobile phone. Younger consumers (15-34-year olds) and higher-income households are the most prominent owners of mobile phones (an average 90 per cent), but only 24 per cent penetration rate for those aged over 75, although this figure is rising. Ten per cent of all mobile phone owners have Internet-enabled phones – a figure which has grown from the previous quarter, indicating that there is an interest or at least a readiness for users to access the Internet via their mobile phones. This is bolstered by the fact that 93 per cent are satisfied with their mobile services and 85 per cent feel they are getting value for money. The Mobinet report found that 44 per cent of consumers would like to use their handsets for small purchases.

Another phenomenon and one of the key features provided by mobile networks are SMS or Short Messaging Services (text messaging), where virtually any mobile phone can send or receive 160-character messages for a nominal fee (about £0.10p per message). This trend has grown in popularity, with the GSM Association estimating that approximately 30 billion text messages are sent every month.[18] It is also estimated that 57.5 million text messages were sent on St Valentine's Day 2002 in the UK,[19] which has a population of around 60 million. There have even been reports that, as a result of texting, the physiology of new generations will change, with the thumb (the main digit used for tapping out messages) becoming more dextrous than past generations. This underlines the fact that the community of users is more than skilled and able to use mobile phones for purposes other than speaking.

Business and commerce has been quite slow to embrace m-commerce. One of the authors of the Mobinet report maintains that, although there is such a high ownership of mobile phones, business 'hasn't provided con-sumers with enough reasons to access the Internet with their phones'.[20]

The *telecommunications industry* has been slow to develop and imple-ment national and international infrastructures to support 3G mobile networks. The majority of the mobile telecommunications companies are also multinational global conglomerates with many interests in many countries and in complementary industries, such as fixed telecommunications, infrastructure technology and the media. The impact of the economic slowdown, overvaluation of market capitalisation and subsequent crash of stock markets (especially technology) have all had an effect on the lack of development of the infrastructures. But one of the main reasons is the spending on 3G licences. In Europe, a total of £75 billion (and £22.5 billion in the UK) was raised when governments auctioned licences for third-generation wireless services. In the UK, this amount was more than seven times the government's original estimate, and more than twice the amount the bidders themselves had predicted. Mobile phone operators have heavily over-borrowed. However, more spending is needed to finance the considerable costs of building the networks for 3G services – such as masts and switches – estimated at over £180 billion.

'The costs of the network are not the critical things for the operator,' said Mike Grant, head of the mobile communications division at consultants Analysys, one of the advisers to the British government on the sale of 3G licences. 'What is critical is the amount they will have to spend on developing the services – marketing them, subsidising the move to new handsets and so on. You have to look at what you think that will cost per customer per year to attract and keep them, and what you can generate from them.'

There are issues of how the industry will finance this investment and, even more importantly, how they will make a return on it. Interestingly, in Finland, a European country with one of the most advanced mobile network infrastructures in the world, the licences were free, enabling mobile phones to achieve mass market very quickly and giving mobile telecommunications companies positive cash flows and strong balance sheets.[21]

Considering all these issues – which at times are conflicting – it is obvious that mobile phones are a part of the social and business culture of the modern digital world. The proliferation of mobile phones in conjunction with Moore's Law, Metcalfe's Law and a few more of the other laws operating in the world of new technology means that mobile phones will increasingly get cheaper, more powerful and more valuable. Eventually, business will realise the importance of m-commerce and capitalise upon it by investing in the infrastructure that will enable it to deliver a variety of value added services to customers and other stakeholders alike.

M-commerce is the next trend, but it is complementary to and works closely with e-commerce rather than in opposition to it. The adoption of m-commerce will probably take the same kind of path as e-commerce; however, this time around, the dot com boom and bust phenomenon might have taught business a cautious lesson about how to implement and use m-commerce.

AND FINALLY . . .

The aims of this book have been to develop a framework that puts e-commerce in a context which business can understand and implement. This understanding has spanned many areas including:

- Technology infrastructure – how it works and how it impacts on the business as a complete organisation.
- Applications of technology to achieve business objectives.
- Limitations and potential problems of the technology and its applications.
- Business modelling and planning using the technology.
- The implications of not understanding e-business fundamentals, illustrated in the rise and fall of the dot coms.
- The legal infrastructure supporting e-business use of electronic contracts, e-mail content, use and download of material from the Web and a host of other issues for conducting business electronically.
- The strategic implications of operating in an environment dominated by new technology and the concepts of e-business.
- The future of e-commerce and e-business and the next wave of technology.

Having acquired an understanding of the concepts and frameworks for e-commerce and e-business, these can be broadly applied again to develop an understanding of any new wave of technology, such as mobile communications.

The question is often asked, is e-commerce and e-business just hype? Will it just wander into an elephants' graveyard and die a quiet death after the sound and fury of the past few years? Communication is the core of what human beings do whether in business or socially. The foundations of e-commerce and e-business enable global, faster, more efficient, more secure, instantaneous communication, which can only develop further.

Ask yourself this question: if the Internet and the Web were taken away today, what impact would this have on your business and everyday life?

DISCUSSION QUESTIONS

1 Analyse your business, or one that you know well. At what stage of the e-business evolutionary cycle is it? Explain why.
2 What new technology have you heard about and what impact do you think it will have on business.
3 Do you think e-business is here to stay? Explain why.

4 Explore the different ways in which m-commerce can be used by companies to create value and generate revenue.

5 What are the similarities between e-commerce and m-commerce?

6 Explain what you have learnt from this book.

REFERENCES

1 M. Corby, 'Strategic planning models, student accountant', ACCA website, 1/1/2002: http://www.accaglobal.com/publications/studentaccountant/256280
2 M.V. Deise, C. Nowikow, P. King and A. Wright, *Price Waterhouse Coopers Executive Guide to E-Business – From Tactics to Strategy*. John Wiley, 2000.
3 M.J. Earl, 'Evolving the E-Business', *Business Strategy Review*, Vol. 11, Issue 2, 2000, pp. 33–8.
4 Bill Gates, *Business @ the Speed of Thought*. Penguin Paperback, 2000.
5 G. Cole, 'Technology – smart cards', *Financial Times*, 22/2/99.
6 G. Cole, 'Technology – smart cards', *Financial Times*, 22/2/99.
7 www.government.ibm.com
8 J. Schofield, cover story, Guardian Online section, 20/5/1999.
9 K. Cottrill, 'Iris recognition', Guardian Online section, 6/11/97.
10 Internet II website: http://www.internet2.edu/html/faqs.html#
11 M. Ward, 'Welcome to the era of drive by hacking', BBC On-line, 6/11/2001: http://news.bbc.co.uk/low/english/sci/tech/newsid_1639000/1639661.stm
12 M. Ward, 'Hacking with a Pringles tube', BBC On-line, 8/3/2002: http://news.bbc.co.uk/low/english/sci/tech/newsid_1860000/1860241.stm
13 M. Ward, 'Welcome to the era of drive by hacking', BBC On-line, 6/11/2001: http://news.bbc.co.uk/low/english/sci/tech/newsid_1639000/1639661.stm
14 'GSM – the wireless evolution', website: http://www.gsmworld.com/holden/index.html (accessed March 2002).
15 'GSM – the wireless evolution', website: http://www.gsmworld.com/holden/index.html (accessed March 2002).
16 E. Sutherland, 'Is e-commerce coming soon or going soon?', 25/3/2002: http://www.mcommercetimes.com/Industry/227
17 'OFTEL – consumers' use of mobile telephony', summary of Oftel residential survey Q7, November 2001, 29/1/2002: www.oftel.gov.uk
18 'Mystery of missing text messages', BBC On-line, 25/3/2002: http://news.bbc.co.uk/hi/english/in_depth/sci_tech/2000/dot_life/newsid_1891000/1891818.stm
19 Phone4u Website: http://www.phones4u.co.uk/info/info_ultimate_ukmarket.asp (accessed March 2002).
20 Paul Collins, chief author of the Kearney study, 25/3/2002: http://www.mcommercetimes.com/Industry/227
21 V. Keegan, 'Second sight – Net news', Guardian Unlimited, 5/10/2000.

Index

Accenture 58
accessibility, of websites 13, 83
Actinic shopping cart software 103–5
added-value 157–8
Adobe Acrobat 161
Advanced Encryption Standard (AES)
   138
advertising
  business models 179–80
  via websites 91
affiliate programmes 91–2
Affuah, A. 194–5
AIM 210, 227n29
algorithms 137–9
allmybills.com.au 212
Alternative Gift Company 224
AltraNet 170–1
Amazon.com
  1-Click ordering 240
  affiliate programme 92, 158, 177
  disintermediation 175–6
  growth of 207
  re-intermediation 177
AOL
  instant messaging (IM) 189–90
  market share 196
  merger with Time Warner 218
  revenue stream 160
  virtual community 156–7
application level firewall 134–5
ARPAnet 115–16

Arthur, Brian 273
associate programmes 158
auctions 166–8
audit, organisation's security 127–31
authentification 144–5

Back Orifice programme 120
backbone, of the Internet 49–50
bandwidth, growth of 272–3
banner advertising 91
barnesandnoble.com 279
Barrett, Craig 204
BASF 38, 107
benefits, of e-commerce 12–14
Bensaou, M. 34
Berners-Lee, Tim 75, 80
Bezos, Jeff 175, 207, 208, 240
biometrics 302–3
Birbas, Nicholas 208
bit taxes 233–4
Blowfish 138
Bluetooth 309–10
Boo.com 211–16, 222
Bower, J.L. 261–2
brokerage business models 179
buffer overflow attacks 123
bulletin boards, electronic 108
bus network 41
business law, impact of e-commerce 12
business models 153–5
  classification of 179–81
  e-marketplaces 181–4